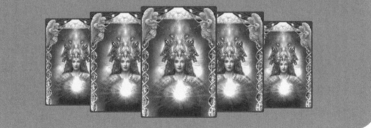

Free e-newsletters
from Hay House, the Ultimate
Resource for Inspiration

Be the first to know about Hay House's dollar deals, free downloads, special offers, affirmation cards, giveaways, contests, and more!

 Get exclusive excerpts from our latest releases and videos from *Hay House Present Moments*.

 Enjoy uplifting personal stories, how-to articles, and healing advice, along with videos and empowering quotes, within *Heal Your Life*.

 Have an inspirational story to tell and a passion for writing? Sharpen your writing skills with insider tips from *Your Writing Life*.

Sign Up Now!

Get inspired, educate yourself, get a complimentary gift, and share the wisdom!

http://www.hayhouse.com/newsletters.php

Visit www.hayhouse.com to sign up today!

 HAY HOUSE

 HAYHOUSE RADIO *radio for your soul*

HealYourLife.com

We hope you enjoyed this Hay House book. If you'd like to receive our online catalog featuring additional information on Hay House books and products, or if you'd like to find out more about the Hay Foundation, please contact:

Hay House, Inc., P.O. Box 5100, Carlsbad, CA 92018-5100
(760) 431-7695 or (800) 654-5126
(760) 431-6948 (fax) or (800) 650-5115 (fax)
www.hayhouse.com® • **www.hayfoundation.org**

◎ ◎ ◎

Published and distributed in Australia by:
Hay House Australia Pty. Ltd., 18/36 Ralph St., Alexandria NSW 2015 •
Phone: 612-9669-4299 • *Fax:* 612-9669-4144 • www.hayhouse.com.au

Published and distributed in the United Kingdom by:
Hay House UK, Ltd., Astley House, 33 Notting Hill Gate, London W11 3JQ
Phone: 44-20-3675-2450 • Fax: 44-20-3675-2451 • www.hayhouse.co.uk

Published and distributed in the Republic of South Africa by:
Hay House SA (Pty), Ltd., P.O. Box 990, Witkoppen 2068 •
info@hayhouse.co.za • www.hayhouse.co.za

Published in India by: Hay House Publishers India,
Muskaan Complex, Plot No. 3, B-2, Vasant Kunj, New Delhi 110 070 •
Phone: 91-11-4176-1620 • *Fax:* 91-11-4176-1630 • www.hayhouse.co.in

Distributed in Canada by:
Raincoast Books, 2440 Viking Way, Richmond, B.C. V6V 1N2
Phone: 1-800-663-5714 • *Fax:* 1-800-565-3770 • www.raincoast.com

◎ ◎ ◎

<u>Access New Knowledge.</u>
<u>Anytime. Anywhere.</u>

Learn and evolve at your own pace with the world's leading experts.

www.hayhouseU.com

The Tapping Solution *for*
MANIFESTING YOUR
Greatest Self

21 Days to Releasing Self-Doubt, Cultivating Inner Peace, and Creating a Life You Love

NICK ORTNER

HAY HOUSE, INC.
Carlsbad, California • New York City
London • Sydney • Johannesburg
Vancouver • New Delhi

Published and distributed in the United States by: Hay House, Inc.: www.hayhouse.com® • *Published and distributed in Australia by:* Hay House Australia Pty. Ltd.: www.hayhouse.com.au • *Published and distributed in the United Kingdom by:* Hay House UK, Ltd.: www.hayhouse.co.uk • *Published and distributed in the Republic of South Africa by:* Hay House SA (Pty), Ltd.: www.hayhouse.co.za • *Distributed in Canada by:* Raincoast Books: www.raincoast.com • *Published in India by:* Hay House Publishers India: www.hayhouse.co.in

Cover design: Julie Rosenberger • *Interior design:* Bryn Starr Best • *Indexer:* Shapiro Indexing Services

Library of Congress Cataloging-in-Publication Data

Names: Ortner, Nick, 1978- author.
Title: The tapping solution for manifesting your greatest self : a 21-day
   journey to creating your most fulfilling, rewarding life / Nick Ortner.
Description: 1st edition. | Carlsbad, California : Hay House, Inc., 2017.
Identifiers: LCCN 2017013535 | ISBN 9781401949884 (hardback)
Subjects: LCSH: Emotional Freedom Techniques. | Mind and body therapies. |
   Self-care, Health. | BISAC: SELF-HELP / Personal Growth / General. | BODY,
   MIND & SPIRIT / Healing / Energy (Chi Kung, Reiki, Polarity). | HEALTH &
   FITNESS / Alternative Therapies.
Classification: LCC RC489.E45 O7818 2017 | DDC 616.89/1--dc23 LC record available at https://
lccn.loc.gov/2017013535

Hardcover ISBN: 978-1-4019-4988-4

10 9 8 7 6 5 4 3 2 1
1st edition, October 2017

Printed in the United States of America

To the reader:
May you manifest all of your heart's desires

Note: A book will only reveal its deepest secrets if you finish it. To that end, I've made some special resources available to take your reading experience and results to the next level. You can access them for free at:
www.the tappingsolution.com/manifesting

(Take a moment to access this now—it'll be helpful from the first page on.)

CONTENTS

WEEK THREE: Creating a Life You Love by Manifesting Your Greatest Self

INTRODUCTION

This is my fourth book, and it's my most personal one to date.

It's not that this book is about me (although I do share some of my own story in it). It's more that the journey I take you on is similar to the one I went through to become my greatest self living my greatest life.

That journey inward is what has allowed me to wake up each morning in a home that I share with my amazing wife and our beautiful child, ready to do work that inspires me.

It's what has allowed me to enjoy vibrant health and an incredible group of friends within a community that I feel profoundly connected to.

It's why I regularly experience a deeper sense of joy and abundance than I imagined possible.

Who I am now is possible *because of* this journey.

I didn't know it at the time, but this journey, and hence this book, was born in my midtwenties. At that point in my life, I was living in an 800-square-foot apartment in Bethel, Connecticut. I was working in real estate back then, and my "office" was the kitchen counter I shared with my girlfriend.

I wanted *so* badly to enjoy the process of turning houses into beautiful homes. I wanted, *really* wanted, to run my business with kindness, gratitude, integrity—the same principles I was trying to live by.

But real estate is a cutthroat business, and there was no simple way out of the sizable debt I'd accumulated to get to the next big sale.

I loved my girlfriend, but there was no denying that our relationship wasn't meant to last. So while I wasn't often alone, I often felt incredibly lonely.

To add to my misery, my energy was constantly being drained by severe allergies and chronic insomnia.

In spite of these challenges, I tried every day to bring more ease, flow, love, and gratitude into my life. I really tried to focus on the "right" things.

But the fact was, my life wasn't working.

Have you ever had that experience?

When no matter how hard you push and direct or sit back and let go, the square pegs you're working with just won't fit into the round hole that is your life? When you start to lose confidence that you'll ever get it "right"?

Like I was, you're probably aware of your patterns. You probably know that you need to let go of the past, forgive that person, and show up to your life in new ways.

You know it's time to stop doubting yourself and finally feel the strength and confidence within you.

Yet somehow you can't quite do it.

In spite of all the "work" you've done to heal yourself and change your life, nothing seems to finish the job.

It's incredibly frustrating!

What if those roadblocks to deep, lasting transformation simply went away?

What if you could wake up as your greatest self, living your greatest life?

What would that look like? More important, what would that *feel* like?

Those are the questions I was obsessed with. To be honest, I still am.

Amusingly enough, when I look back, one of my greatest assets was my impatience. I simply couldn't accept the idea that personal development had to be *that* slow.

So I kept searching . . . and searching. I tried almost everything until finally, in 2003, I found Tapping.

That was when my life began to pivot toward fulfillment, love, abundance, community—all the visions, hopes, and dreams I'd held inside me.

If you'd told me back then that I'd now be spending my days helping people heal their lives and their bodies, I would have laughed.

Sure, I'd always loved personal development. I'd been devouring books and audios on personal empowerment, emotional healing, and more since high school. But pursuing personal development as a career? Me? The idea never crossed my mind.

But then I learned what I now know—Tapping can change everything.

I've never been a daredevil kind of guy, yet these days I select random volunteers from audiences of thousands—people I've never met and know nothing about—to come up onstage to heal themselves and their lives.

I don't do that because I've magically become fearless. I do that because I don't have to prove that Tapping works. The results it produces speak for themselves.

So now I'm that guy onstage who picks anyone from the audience and 20 minutes later half the audience is crying while the other half is gasping and applauding at the transformation they've witnessed.

There's science and research to back up those results, and of course I'll share that with you. Here's the great news, in a nutshell: Science has shown us that we're not the static beings we once thought we were. The brain that controls our thoughts, emotions, and behaviors is *neuroplastic*.

The human brain can and does *change*.

That means that lasting transformation and deep healing *are* possible.

And there's a growing understanding that the true gateway into the brain is through the body, which is exactly how Tapping works.

In fact, Tapping has been shown to relieve emotional, mental, and physical stress, even positively impacting gene expression in the body.

How cool is that?

Your DNA can work more effectively in your favor, thanks to Tapping.

So whether you want to heal your spirit and heart, your body and mind, your relationships, your finances, or something else, you can use this book.

As long as you do the tapping, you'll come out of this journey more firmly grounded in your greatest self, ready and able to step into your greatest life.

So tell me—when you begin waking up each morning feeling like your greatest self, what would you most like to experience?

More peace?

More abundance?

Greater physical well-being?

Deeper connection in your relationship?

Will there be more love, light, passion, and fulfillment in your daily life?

You can create your own happiness and then transform your outer world. Take it as far as you want to. Or farther.

Join me on this incredible journey toward manifesting your greatest self. Starting now the sky really *is* your limit.

GETTING THE MOST OUT OF THIS BOOK

In this book I share my journey within a 21-day timeline that will first allow you to clear the obstacles to manifesting your greatest self, and then support you in charting your personal path to a life of peace and purpose.

Each day guides you into the next step in the journey, inviting you to reflect on and, when you desire, transform your inner and outer worlds. Within each day you'll find a simple, easily doable daily challenge, as well as a Tapping Meditation script that I urge you to use to move forward in your journey.

To add as much ease and grace to the process as possible, here are some tips to keep in mind:

ABOUT THE 21-DAY TIMELINE

- This journey is presented within a 21-day time frame, but know that those days don't have to be consecutive. You can set aside two, three, or five days to digest and tap through each day's content.

- Take the time you need, but do commit to completing the journey in full.

- To help you move through it, you can sign up for my e-mail reminders and select the pace that works for you. If you select a three-day time delay between reminders, you'll receive an e-mail nudge from me every three days. If you select two or five, that's when you'll hear from me. If, as you move through the content, you want to change your pacing, simply return to that form and request a new time frame.
  To sign up for those e-mail reminders, go here:
  www.thetappingsolution.com/manifesting

A FEW OTHER THINGS TO KEEP IN MIND

- **Daily Challenge:** Since this book is intended to produce real-life re-sults, each day ends with a challenge. Often these challenges present new ways of thinking, different areas of focus, some kind of action to take.

Please *do* complete these challenges. They'll make a significant difference in the long run, allowing what you've learned to "stick" and positively impact you and your life.

- **Tapping Meditations**: Each day has its own Tapping Meditation script to guide you, with words and phrases you can use while you tap through the points. These scripts are in the Appendix so that you can easily find and return to them. By now hopefully it goes without saying that Tapping is essential to getting results from this journey. Do the tapping!

    Note: As you move through the tapping scripts in the book and the Appendix, feel free to tailor the words to reflect your experience. The goal with tapping is never to say "magic words," but to tap on your own experience.

- **Your 21-Day Journey Map**: At the end of this book, there's a journey map that summarizes each day of the journey. This is intended to provide you fast and easy access to content you want to revisit.

So glad you're here. Let's get started!

QUICK START:
LET'S GET TAPPING!

Imagine a day with fewer obstacles and irritations, a day where traffic isn't so bothersome, school mornings feel easier, money is less stressful, self-doubt fades away and confidence flows in, and everyday commitments create little, if any, pressure.

Can you feel that? Really see that as your life?

Ever since that day in high school when I discovered my mom's Tony Robbins audiotapes tucked away in a random pile, I've been doggedly focused on helping people live happier, healthier, more fulfilling lives.

The journey you'll soon embark on will guide you toward your greatest self, and from there, your greatest life. It all begins with shedding the stress and other negative emotional states and patterns that are keeping your greatest self just beyond your reach.

The first step is learning the only tool I've found that makes deep and lasting transformation possible in far less time than other methods—Tapping. Without it, you simply won't get the results you want and deserve. If you're well versed in how to tap, skip to Day 1 and dive in. If you're new to Tapping, or it's been a while, stay right here with me to learn how to tap.

YOUR MIND-BODY RESET BUTTONS

So how does this "tapping thing" relieve stress, and in so doing, give you faster, more complete access to your greatest self? As it turns out, the answer is in your biology.

In a double-blind study conducted by Dawson Church, Ph.D., participants were divided into two groups. One group was led through an hour of Tapping, while the other, which was the control group, was given an hour of conventional talk therapy.

The Tapping group showed an average of a 24 percent decrease in cortisol levels, with some experiencing as much as a 50 percent decrease in cortisol.

In contrast the control group, which received conventional talk therapy, showed only a 14 percent drop of cortisol.

Dawson recently published an additional study about the powerful effects of Emotional Freedom Techniques (EFT) on gene expression. This newer study was published in the journal *Energy Psychology*. Dawson summarized these new findings in this way:

> *Levels of gene expression are like the gradations of a light controlled by a dimmer switch; the expression of many genes can be dialed up or down. Stress, hunger, tiredness, mood and many other experiences affect gene expression levels.*
>
> *In this pilot study, investigator Beth Maharaj compared an hour of EFT to an hour of social interaction in 4 subjects. She found that 72 genes were significantly regulated after EFT.*
>
> *The functions of these genes are fascinating. Among them were: the suppression of cancer tumors, protection against the sun's ultraviolet radiation, type 2 diabetes insulin resistance, immunity from opportunistic infections, antiviral activity, synaptic connectivity between neurons, creation of both red and white blood cells, enhancement of male fertility, building white matter in the brain, metabolic regulation, neural plasticity, strengthening cell membranes, and reducing oxidative stress.*

This and other studies suggest that EFT is an epigenetic intervention, regulating the expression of many genes. Just an hour of EFT is doing your body a whole lot of good.[1]

Research has also shown that acupuncture increases endorphin levels in the body. Since tapping engages acupuncture points, tapping, like acupuncture, allows the body to release the endorphins that then reinforce positive feelings, as well as physical and emotional well-being.

The incredible results that tapping has on relieving stress may be explained, at least in part, by its ability to access what are called meridian channels.

Although awareness of these channels dates back to thousands of years of ancient Chinese medicine, it wasn't until the 1960s that these threadlike microscopic anatomical structures were first seen on stereomicroscope and electron microscope images.

Those scans showed tubular structures measuring 30 to 100 micrometers wide running up and down the body. Described in a published paper by a North Korean researcher named Kim Bonghan, they are also referred to as "Bonghan channels." As a reference point, one red blood cell is six to eight micrometers wide, so these structures are tiny!

You can think of meridian channels as a fiber-optic network in the body. They carry a large amount of information, often electrical and often beyond what the nervous system or chemical systems of the body can carry. By accessing these channels while processing emotions and thoughts, as well as physical conditions like pain, tapping gets to the root cause of stress more quickly than other stress-relief techniques can.

That is a very quick, cursory view on the science and research, but if you want to see some of the many papers published on its effectiveness, go here: research.EFTuniverse.com

So the science is in, the research is in, it's starting to make sense. But most important, what can it do for *you*?

Let's find out now!

WHAT'S BOTHERING YOU NOW

You'll find an interesting dichotomy in this book and the Tapping process, in that the main goal of this book is, as the title states, to help you manifest your greatest self.

That means we're going to work together to let your light shine brighter than ever before, to feel at peace in your body, to create the life experiences you most deserve and desire.

And while we will be focusing on these positive intentions and aspirations, the Tapping process itself, what I believe is the fastest process to manifesting your greatest self, starts someplace else, in the down and dirty of life! After all, it's our daily experience, the nitty-gritty of our day-to-day, that makes up the majority of life. By addressing (and when necessary, healing) the everyday, we become prepared to move forward in bigger, more powerful ways.

So let's start there as we explore Tapping, so you can really see and feel the transformation that can take place.

I find the easiest way to start is to focus on what's most pressing right now, on what's bothering you most, big or small.

So tell me—what is it? The weather? Not getting enough sleep? The e-mail you just got from your boss, or the text from your ex?

Really be honest here, because that's your most powerful starting point.

What's that annoying thing you just can't let go of?

What's taking up your mind space and energy right now?

What's got you doubting yourself and fearing the future?

What's in the way?

It's called your Most Pressing Issue (MPI), and you're about to learn to use Tapping to make that MPI shift in dramatic ways.

CLEARING SPACE

First, let me quickly share something about your MPI. People often worry that by focusing first on the negative, they're rooting themselves in it, somehow bringing it deeper into their lives.

On the contrary, by clearing out the stress, fear, and other negative emotions that we all naturally experience (more on that on Day 2), you can more quickly clear that mental and emotional "dirt" and create more space for authentic positivity to grow and thrive.

LET'S TAP!

Now that you've got your MPI, it's time to get started. Here's the basic outline of how to tap.

Step 1: Focus on Your MPI

As you focus your attention on what's bothering you most, your MPI, ask yourself questions like, *When I think about this issue, what do I feel in my body? Do I feel tension, pain, tingling, buzzing, heat, or cold? Emptiness, numbness, or nothingness?*

Pay attention to feedback from your body. There are no wrong answers here. Just try to be as specific as possible about your experience.

Step 2: Measure the Intensity

Next give your MPI a number of intensity on a 0-to-10 scale. This is called the SUDS, or Subjective Units of Distress Scale.

When you focus on your MPI, how intense does it feel at this moment? A 10 would be the most intense you can imagine; a 0 would mean you don't feel any intensity at all.

Don't worry about getting the SUDS level exact or "right"—just follow your gut instinct.

Step 3: Craft Your Setup Statement

With your SUDS level in mind, your next step is to craft what's called the "setup statement." This statement focuses your mind on your MPI.

The basic setup statement looks like this:

Even though I <describe your MPI>,
I deeply and completely love and accept myself.

So, for example, you might say, "Even though I'm so worried about my presentation, I deeply and completely love and accept myself."

Or "Even though my whole body tenses every time I think about my ex taking the kids this weekend, I deeply and completely love and accept myself."

Your setup statement should resonate with what you're experiencing when you begin tapping. There are no "magic words" that unlock the door to stress relief. Your goal is to say words that have meaning to you, so if the basic setup statement doesn't ring true or feel powerful, change it.

Here are a few (of many!) variations on the basic setup statement that you can use and change to fit your experience:

Even though I <describe your MPI>, I completely love, accept, and forgive myself and anyone else.

Even though I <describe your MPI>, I choose to forgive myself now.

Even though I <describe your MPI>, I accept and forgive myself.

Even though I <describe your MPI>, I allow myself to be the way I am.

Even though I <describe your MPI>, I'm willing to let go.

Even though I <describe your MPI>, I'm willing to hold a new perspective.

Even though I <describe your MPI>, it's over and I'm safe now.

Even though I <describe your MPI>, I choose to release this stress now.

Step 4: Choose a Reminder Phrase(s)

The reminder phrase is short—just a few words that describe your issue.

So, for example, if your setup statement is about your anxiety about a presentation, your reminder phrases might be: "This anxiety about my presentation."

You repeat your reminder phrase several times when you're tapping, so you can vary it, if you like, as long as you stay focused on your MPI. In this example, you might say, "All this anxiety about my presentation . . . so anxious about this presentation . . . so much anxiety about this presentation."

Step 5: Tap through the Points

Once you have created your setup statement and reminder phrase, you're ready to start tapping.

You'll start by saying your setup statement three times, all the while tapping on the Karate Chop point, which is on the side of your palm, just above the pinkie finger. You can tap with whichever hand feels most comfortable to you. Tap at a pace and force that feel right; you can't get it wrong!

After you've said the setup statement three times, you'll move on to tapping through the eight points in the Tapping sequence while saying the reminder phrase. These points are:

- Eyebrow
- Side of eye
- Under eye
- Under nose
- Top of head
- Chin
- Collarbone
- Under arm

You can tap on whichever side of the body feels best to you because the same meridian channels run down both sides of the body.

Tap five to seven times at each stop as you work through the sequence. This doesn't have to be an exact count. If it feels right to tap 20 times—or 100—on one point, then do it! The idea is to spend enough time at that point to speak your reminder phrase and let it sink in.

Don't worry about being perfect—just do what feels right and have the experience.

Here's a diagram of the tapping points for your reference:

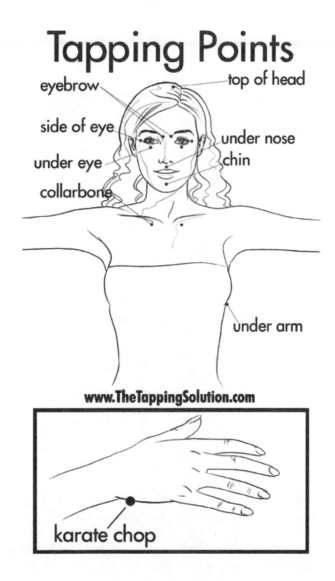

Step 6: Check In

You've now completed a round of Tapping!

First things first: take a few deep breaths.

Feel your body and notice what's happening. Did you experience a shift of any kind—in your emotions or in your body? How intense does your MPI feel on the 0-to-10 scale now?

If your MPI went from an 8 to a 7, that's huge! It means that tapping is beginning to relieve your stress. It means a shift happened in just a matter of minutes, so keep tapping. If there's no change, that's fine, too. It's common for people to need more than one round of tapping to experience relief, especially as they are new to the process.

As you check in with yourself to see if you experienced any shift, ask yourself a few questions:

- *What sensations did I experience in my body while tapping?*
- *What emotions came up while I was tapping?*
- *What "random" thoughts or memories came to mind as I was tapping?*

Yawning, Sighing, Burping, and More

People often ask if they're doing something wrong, since each time they tap, they begin yawning or experiencing other physical effects. These are all good signs! They're ways that your body is relaxing, moving and releasing energy, and letting go. When you tap, make a point of noticing all the ways your body responds.

Switching from the "Negative" to the "Positive"

Throughout the book, each tapping script begins with the "negative," or "truth," a statement that includes your MPI, and any related challenging emotions and beliefs. Most of the time, I'll end with at least one "positive" round of tapping, which presents a new way of moving forward.

For example, if you were tapping on anxiety around a presentation, you might end your tapping with phrases like, "I can release this anxiety now," "I can focus on practicing," "I'm safe being seen and heard by all those people," and so on.

As a general rule, it's best to get the intensity of the negative down to a 5 out of 10 before moving on to the positive, and then to keep tapping on the positive until the negative emotional charge has decreased to a 3 or lower.

Step 7: Test Your Progress

Once the intensity of your MPI has decreased, it's time to test your results. You can do this by refocusing your attention on your MPI.

If focusing on your MPI still feels emotionally charged, continue tapping through a few more rounds using the same language, and see if you can clear your MPI altogether.

Or you might find that, as you think about your MPI, your emotions change. Instead of feeling anxious, for instance, you now feel angry. That's great! That's an indication that you're getting to the root of your MPI. In that case, you can move on and tap on your anger. If, while tapping on that anger, you find that it's masking yet another emotion, like sadness, go ahead and tap on that sadness, as well.

Just keep tapping through the layers of your emotions until you experience the relief you're seeking.

AREN'T EMOTIONS A GOOD THING? WHY DO WE TAP ON RELEASING THEM?

People sometimes ask me why we focus on releasing emotions when we're tapping. Aren't emotions a good thing?

Yes, they absolutely are!

Our goal with tapping is never to stop feeling our emotions. Instead, tapping helps us acknowledge how we're feeling, and then feel that *more* fully. When we can do that, our emotions naturally progress. For instance,

---

if you tap on anger, that anger may then turn into sadness, which then becomes compassion.

As a result of this emotional processing and release, which often happens faster with tapping, we become more present in the moment. That presence then supports you in becoming your greatest self.

HOW-TO-TAP VIDEO

If you prefer video, you can watch this five-minute how-to-tap video online at: http://www.thetappingsolution.com/what-is-eft-tapping/.

Great! You're now ready for Day 1, which is also when we'll begin tapping.

WEEK ONE

Cultivating Peace

Day 1

Peace or Panic?

My morning didn't go quite as I'd planned.

Well, that's a bit of an understatement, but I won't start this book off too dramatically.

As I like to do, I'd set an intention the night before to get up at the crack of dawn, beating the frenetic rush that late mornings often bring, do some tapping, maybe a short meditation, play with my adorable one-year-old daughter, and then do some quiet reading before diving into my day.

Before falling asleep, I could *see* how great my day was going to be. I could *feel* how naturally my creative energy would flow. It was going to be amazing. A day for the ages!

What's that joke about making plans?

Somewhere around 3 A.M., my one-year-old woke up. And this wasn't a short awakening as often happens with toddlers; she decided that 3 A.M. was a fantastic time to be wide awake and play for an hour, so I had to join her middle-of-the-night tea party. (Actually a cup of tea would have been nice—this party just involved putting blocks in and out of a box for an hour.)

I then overslept. Those glorious morning hours as the sun rose were greeted by my profound snores. When I realized what time it was, I jumped out of bed and skipped my morning Tapping Meditation, as well as that peaceful reading I'd envisioned. In my groggy state, I defaulted to immediately checking my e-mail.

I did play with my daughter, but certainly wasn't fully present, and I received no answers to my kind questions as to why exactly she was up at 3 A.M. The fact that she doesn't speak yet certainly didn't help that dialogue.

Since I knew my in-box was bursting with urgent e-mails (again), I just waited impatiently for her wonderful mother and my wife, who was even more sleep deprived than I was, to wake up and take her. There were also several important calls I needed to make, as well as new employees to hire, mentor, and manage.

Plus, family was calling, I needed to schedule some renovations we were doing on the house, and I had to figure out my travel schedule for the next few months. And did I mention that I was sleep deprived, and like every new parent, had been on and off for months?

Oh, and I also had this book to write. Sorry to land you right in the middle of my messy morning . . .

Now, to back up so you don't think you've picked up the book of a complainer whose life is out of control.

Here's the reality: I feel enormously blessed in my life. I do work that I love. I'm in good health, and I have a beautiful and supportive family and friends. I live in a home and town I feel deeply connected to.

I am blessed. That is a given.

On any given day, though, I face the same choice we all face, even in the midst of everything that is wonderful about our lives.

Do I respond to these moments, these mornings, these daily challenges, from a place of peace or a place of panic?

Do I make lemonade out of the daily lemons, big or small, that life serves up? Or do I fight the lemons, plead to exchange them with some sweet oranges, question why there are so many sour lemons in my life . . . ?

Peace or panic?

Which do you choose?

The answer we all want to give, of course, is peace. When we're overwhelmed, exhausted, feeling dread at the sight of our in-boxes, overextended from caring for friends and family, home, work, and finances, choosing peace in a deep, authentic way is no small feat.

In many ways it's the biggest challenge we'll ever face.

Peace or panic?

It's also the one challenge we'll face billions of times (literally) in our lifetime.

Peace or panic?

Becoming your greatest self isn't about being faster than a speeding bullet or powerful enough to leap tall buildings in a single bound.

It's not even about realizing your biggest dreams and passions, changing the world, or being superhuman. Although those things—okay, *some* of those things—can and do happen, becoming your greatest self is more about the simple choices we each make every day, in our worst moments, our best moments, and the many others in between. It's those choices, the daily actions that then *allow* you to realize your biggest dreams and passions, *allow* you to change the world, *allow* you to be superhuman, and, heck, maybe even to leap a tall building in a single bound.

And within each of those moments is the reality of a simple choice: peace or panic.

THE MANY WAYS WE FREAK OUT

When we talk about feeling or experiencing *peace* or *panic*, we're not necessarily referring to a state of complete, uninterrupted monklike peace or absolute, frenzied manic panic. With both peace and panic, there are multiple levels we're likely to experience on a regular basis.

In Tapping, we use a 0–10 scale to rate the intensity of our emotions before we tap, and then measure the shift we experience as a result of tapping. That same idea applies to the concepts of peace and panic. If you pause in the midst of an especially busy day and do a few minutes of tapping, you may feel more peaceful, but not *completely* at peace. Similarly, there may be times when you experience low-grade panic. While you're not frantic, you don't feel a sense of ease, either. After tapping, you then feel *more* peaceful.

These shifts, however big or small, are *really* important! In fact, it's within the context of these small shifts (and sometimes you get a huge one thrown in for fun effect) that our lives are transformed.

Over a period of a few days or even a week, small shifts have a huge impact. Extend those small shifts out over years and decades, and *that* is how we manifest our greatest selves.

Noticing where you are on the "peace" or "panic" scale of experience will feel more natural as you continue through this 21-day process. You'll also begin to notice how each of these states tend to manifest in your experience, your physical body, and your life. For now, the simplest and most relevant definitions I can offer are the following:

When you're in an authentic place of peace, you're likely to feel more open, aware, even curious when faced with challenges. In the absence of certainty, you feel calmer than you might expect. Emotionally as well as physically, you may experience less tension, pain, resistance, and confusion.

When you're in a place of panic, you're likely to feel more closed off and shut down. This can also manifest physically as tension and pain, as well as an inability to make decisions, focus, and more. It can also manifest as a sense of overwhelm, even apathy toward people, places, or things you care about.

Which definition best describes you right now? Are you mostly in a place of peace or a place of panic?

THE TRUTH ABOUT POSITIVE PEOPLE

When I think about the authentically positive people I know, the people who live most often from a place of peace, there's one belief they all share.

Every single one of them views being positive as a daily practice. They never stop training their brains to see, feel, and experience the positive. They're never done being positive. It's a state of mind and a way of being that they constantly cultivate.

When they find themselves veering away from the positive, they pause, take a breath, and course correct.

POSITIVE GROWTH IS NEVER PERFECT

The process of first noticing if you're in a place of panic and then shifting toward peace sometimes takes a little time. Most often, though, it's an ongoing process that ebbs and flows along with your life.

Which brings me back to my morning.

So I'm in the thick of it, my energy is a bit off, not frantic, but not peaceful, either. Sure, I've gotten a bunch of things done, but the seamless creative flow I'd dreamed about hasn't happened (yet).

And I have a choice to make.

Am I going to take a few moments to notice and tap on what's going on—in my body as well as my mind (choosing peace)?

Or am I going to continue through my day, fueled largely by adrenaline and stress (choosing panic)?

Before I discovered tapping, let me be honest about the fact that I didn't always *want* to notice if I was living from a place of panic. At that point, awareness wasn't helpful. After all, if I notice that I'm living my day from a place of panic, but have no way to change that, awareness isn't useful. More often it's another reason to panic.

Think about that for a moment.

Have you ever been told to "chill out" or to "stop sweating the small stuff"? These messages are everywhere, and they're incredibly appealing.

Who *wouldn't* choose to "let it go"?

If it were that easy, we would all have chosen it long ago.

When we hear those messages, most of us respond, either out loud or internally, "Easier said than done . . ." That struggle to choose peace is the result of the brain's inherent negativity bias; there's a biological reason why it's easier said than done. We'll learn a lot more about that tomorrow, in Day 2, but for now, just know that you're not the only one who struggles to find a place of peace!

TAKING A BREATH

It wasn't until I began tapping that I began to really "get" the value of mindful awareness of my experiences. With tapping—this tool that can quickly transform my physiology, my state of mind, and my emotional experience—the simple act of noticing that my morning is (so far) coming from a place of panic is everything.

As with so many things, awareness is a skill, and to get good at it, we have to practice. Even now I don't always do that perfectly, which is why it wasn't until almost lunchtime that I realized I'd let a mild, adrenaline-fueled panic guide me through the early part of my day.

And let's be honest here. Even after recognizing that my morning had gone off course, it was easy to default to panic. Like most people, I know how to subtly beat up on myself for "losing" my morning. With Tapping, though, I have a

better option. I can accept this morning for what it was, stop, take a breath, and tap on transforming my experience.

And you can do that, as well.

Before we practice that and experience its power, let's first look at a core cultural belief that can have a profound impact on whether or not we stop and take that breath, or instead allow ourselves to be swept away in a familiar tidal wave of everyday panic.

LETTING GO OF THE CHICKEN AND THE EGG

Picture your perfect morning.

You can visualize it, right?

The sun is shining; you wake up feeling rested and rejuvenated.

You do a few yoga poses (how do they make it look so easy?); meditate (ommmmmm . . .); and begin your morning with some green juice (mmm . . . kale . . .) and perhaps tea or coffee (organic, fair trade, picked under the right moon of course!).

You shower, get dressed, have your perfect healthy breakfast (of whatever this year's "in" diet is), and dive into one of the most fulfilling and productive days you've had in a long time.

It's amazing and inspiring, and you end the day feeling so sure that the routine you began that morning is the one that will change your life. You tell yourself that if you repeat this morning every day, you and your life will be transformed.

There's only one problem.

Every morning won't unfold in exactly this same way. There will be mornings when you don't feel great. There will also be gloomy mornings when there's no coffee in the house and the dog is sick.

There will be a morning when, gosh darn it, you just don't want the green juice!

So what happens then?

There's a deeper challenge at play here, a belief that might just be keeping us stuck, and that's our cultural focus on the external world. When we envision a perfect morning, we focus first on the sunlight streaming in and on the simple but important things that we will *do*.

Yoga. Meditating. Green Juice.

Gotta be perfect. Gotta do it right. Gotta do what everyone else seems to be doing to be happy.

It's an understandable bias in a culture that emphasizes accomplishment and productivity, a culture that values *doing* over *being*. After all, for a lot longer than we've been told to "chill out," we've been told to get more done in less time.

Naturally, then, when we imagine a perfect morning, we begin by envisioning what we will *do* and how the world around us will *be*. We then credit those external factors for making us feel how we yearn to feel—peaceful, grateful, energized, fulfilled, happy, and so on.

My tendency is to focus on e-mail as the beast that has snagged me. When I have an off-kilter morning, I tend to blame my habit of checking e-mail as soon as I wake up for derailing my routine. Admittedly, e-mail is not the best way to wake up. Taking those 10 minutes for a Tapping Meditation, and then being fully present with my daughter before doing some quiet reading is a far more peaceful and enlightened way to start my day.

The reality is, though, there are days when I *do* need to get to my e-mail earlier than I'd like. There are also days when I'm overtired and less focused than I'd like.

The temptation here is to say that we need to stop pressuring ourselves and each other to do more, faster. And I do believe that's true, but I also know it's not

the answer. Doing less, or even just doing less of what doesn't fulfill us, doesn't guarantee a path to authentic peace.

Think about it.

Have you ever envisioned a day off after a long week as a relaxing, rejuvenating experience and then found, when it actually came, that you couldn't relax no matter what you tried? Although you did the activities you'd originally envisioned, the time didn't *feel* the way you had imagined it would.

That happens because peace is an entirely *internal* state of being. Peace happens when we're fully present in the moment. Nothing and no one and no place or circumstance outside ourselves can give us peace. Only we, ourselves, can choose to pursue it.

Which brings me back to the simple practice that turned my day around.

I stopped.

I noticed what was happening (living from a place of panic).

I took a breath, and I tapped.

When we take a few moments to take a breath and tap, we let go of stress (literally by lowering the levels of the stress hormone, cortisol, in the body) and redirect ourselves to a place of peace. From that place of peace, all sorts of magic and miracles manifest.

YOU'VE GOT THIS!

There's an incredible moment I've witnessed in hundreds of thousands of people in my years of tapping.

It's that moment when people connect with their power to transform their experience. It's like a huge lightbulb suddenly turns on, and they realize what I, too, realized when I first began tapping—that we can all use this incredible technique to shift our experience.

And that simple reality, that *you* are in control, that *you* can change your state, can change everything.

From one moment to the next, you can move toward peace and away from panic, toward health and away from pain and discomfort, toward love and away from conflict, turmoil, and even trauma.

Some people have this lightbulb moment quickly.

For others it takes time and repeated tapping. For now all I ask is your willingness to trust that you, too, have this power to shift your day, your night, and then your week.

One moment at a time, then one day at a time, you can tap away the varying levels of panic and discomfort and experience a deeper, longer-lasting sense of peace. And from there, from that place of peace, of openness, of willingness, your greatest self, and then your greatest life, will emerge without strain or struggle.

DAY 1 GREATEST SELF CHALLENGE: PRACTICING PEACE

Join me for our first challenge!

Every morning, notice if you're beginning your day from a place of peace or a place of panic. Whether it's in your first five minutes or your first hour, make a point of pausing to notice where you are mentally, and how you're feeling emotionally as well as physically.

Then take five minutes to tap on releasing any panic you're feeling.

As the days progress, see how this simple process changes your experience. Do you feel calmer? Do you feel more patient with your kids? More productive? Less anxious as you're sitting in morning traffic? Are you having creative ideas that might turn around your financial situation? Are you making healthier food choices? Notice these shifts in your daily experience.

Be sure to use the Tapping Meditation for today, *Day 1 Tapping Meditation: From Panic to Peace*, found on page 245 of the Appendix. Come back to it anytime it feels relevant.

◎ ◎ ◎

First, though, open your calendar and decide when you'll complete Day 2 of this journey. Will it be tomorrow, the day after, three days from now? Pick a day, commit, and add it to your calendar. Don't skip this step! Make this commitment to yourself now.

Day 2 is where you'll discover how your brain is hardwired, and use tapping to rebalance it in ways that support your highest vibration and greatest self. Don't miss it! It's a key concept we'll refer back to throughout this journey. You'll be amazed (and possibly relieved, too) to discover what your brain's been up to . . .

Day 2

Negativity, Hardwired:
A Look at the Primitive Brain

Grog and Thor sit perched at the edge of their cave.

You know Grog, your great-great-great-great-great-great-great-ancestor. You'd recognize him; you both have the same nose. He's waiting patiently but alertly with his friend Thor. They've been hearing some saber-toothed tiger sounds, not too far from their lovely abode.

Grog says, "Ughr all ogg ogg ralf woomr." Oh, you don't speak caveman? I'll translate for you the rest of the way.

"I'm pretty nervous about that tiger. It sounds like a big one, and it's coming our way."

Thor, twiddling his thumbs, half meditating in a lotus position, says, "Brother man, there is nothing to worry about! The sun is shining, we've discovered fire and some basic tools, and this cave is luxurious. Bask in gratitude and the joy of life!"

Grog looks around nervously. It sounds like the tiger is getting closer, and quickly.

"Thor, I'm going to higher ground. We're tiger meat in this spot, and I don't think the two of us are going to be able to handle this guy."

"Grog, you are *so* negative! Always talking about what could go wrong, always 'moving to higher ground' or worrying about this or that. You know, you're just not going to attract what you want in your life with that attitude!"

Sensing the tiger's approach, Grog scampers away at a full sprint toward higher ground, where the tiger can't climb. He makes one last desperate call to Thor, "Please! Run!"

Thor continues his peaceful meditation.

And is swallowed almost whole by one of the largest saber-toothed tigers to roam the ancient world.

Well, at least Thor seemed happy until his untimely death.

Grog lives, and with him, his DNA. And partly because of his negative, pessimistic, cautious attitude, he survives.

Thor has vanished, along with his "happy" genes.

And so it goes, again and again and again and again . . .

And thus, the human brain evolved, literally clinging for dear life to something we call the "negativity bias."

YOUR BRAIN'S PRIMITIVE PANIC BUTTON

Yesterday we looked at peace and panic, and we began using tapping to have a new experience.

Ever wondered why we even *need* to do that? Why there always seems to be *something*—or several things—standing between us and happiness, us and peace, us and fulfillment, and so on.

Why is it so much easier to choose panic over peace?

Sometimes it seems like our "default" setting is to be negative and fearful . . . and that's because in large part it is.

For our own protection—cue Grog and the "negativity bias" that saved his life—the brain evolved to assume the worst. It's biased toward negativity. In his book *Hardwiring Happiness*, Rick Hanson, Ph.D., explains this concept in more detail:

> *Our ancestors could make two kinds of mistakes:*
> *(1) thinking there was a tiger in the bushes when there wasn't one, and*
> *(2) thinking there was no tiger in the bushes when there actually was one.*
> *The cost of the first mistake was needless anxiety, while the cost of the second one was death.*
> *Consequently, we evolved to make the first mistake a thousand times to avoid making the second mistake even once. . . .*
>
> *In general, the default setting of the brain is to overestimate threats, underestimate opportunities, and underestimate resources both for coping with threats and for fulfilling opportunities. Then we update these beliefs with information that confirms them, while ignoring or rejecting information that doesn't. There are even regions in the amygdala [which is an almond-shaped part of the midbrain that's intricately connected to the body's "stress response"] specifically designed to prevent the unlearning of fear, especially from childhood experiences. As a result, we end up preoccupied by threats that are actually smaller or more manageable than we'd feared, while overlooking opportunities that are actually greater than we'd hoped for. In effect, we've got a brain that's prone to "paper tiger paranoia."*[1]

Most of us can recognize this experience in our daily lives. We get an e-mail or text that feels unclear, whether in meaning or tone. Immediately, we go to

the negative. Or we get a call, and someone says something vague like, "Hey, do you have a minute? We need to talk."

For most of us, it takes only a second or two to assume the worst. Without thinking, our brains translate "we need to talk" into "something's wrong." Similarly, rather than noticing that the text message we just received is unclear, we default to the negative—deciding, for instance, that it's hurtful or insulting.

We then feel fearful, angry, sad—any number of negative emotions that reinforce our need to defend ourselves from (yet another) attack. Before we've even considered that the person may have been in a rush and carelessly worded the text message, we're ready to retreat and/or attack him in return.

And because of how our brains have evolved, this process is so automatic that we often don't even recognize when it's happening.

When you really think about that, it's pretty extreme. It's also the reality of the human brain, which defaults to a negative lens so powerful that it easily and quickly taints our entire experience.

TRICKY, SNEAKY, AND SUBVERSIVE, TOO

Sometimes the "negativity bias" is even subtler and harder to notice. For example, in the off-kilter morning I shared in Day 1, my negativity bias might look like me deciding that I can't control my mornings, even if I don't love how they feel.

Oftentimes we brush off these decisions casually.

"What are you gonna do?" we ask.

"It's just life," we say as we return to our to-do lists.

While it's true that we often have limited control of the external world around us, these reactions can, at times, support us in lowering our expectations. In tiny ways we don't consciously recognize, we then give the brain's negativity bias room to thrive.

Best-selling author Brené Brown sums it up this way: "We think if we can beat vulnerability to the punch by imagining loss, we'll suffer less."[2]

We see this tendency to focus on negative experiences more than positive ones in research studies, as well. The psychologist Daniel Kahneman received the Nobel Prize in economics for showing that most people will do more to avoid loss than to benefit from an equivalent gain. In intimate relationships we typically need at least five positive interactions to counterbalance every negative one. And for people to begin to thrive in life, they usually need positive moments to outweigh negative ones by at least a three-to-one ratio.

I would argue that these numbers might be even larger than the research suggests. I know that one negative review of my books on Amazon can easily overwhelm 100 positive reviews—if I don't tap on it, that is!

. . . .

*For people to begin to thrive in life, they usually need
positive moments to outweigh negative ones by at least
a three-to-one ratio.*

. . . .

So how can we reverse this "negativity bias" in the simple everyday ways that allow our greatest selves, and then our greatest lives, to emerge?

It starts with cultivating simple awareness about how those three pounds of gray matter that you're carrying around (aka your brain) actually work. Just being aware of your brain's negativity bias is a huge first step in overcoming it. That basic understanding encourages us to view positivity as a practice rather than an attribute or personality trait.

Being positive then becomes a skill we can consciously choose to hone every day.

DAY 2 GREATEST SELF CHALLENGE: REDIRECTING YOUR BRAIN

So how do we actually bring positivity practice into our lives?

On a day-to-day, week-to-week basis, how can we reprogram our brains to recognize and accept positivity without becoming so detached from our surroundings that, like Thor, we're prematurely devoured?

Start by simply *noticing* when you default to the negative.

Start with the little things, like that e-mail or text that feels unclear. Your brain's natural bias will lead you to assume the worst. Your brain's innate negativity bias will *support* you in feeling judged, accused, and so on.

Starting today, make a point of simply noticing when your brain's "negativity bias" is being activated.

Remember, it's a hardwired response that we *all* experience, so there's no need to blame or shame yourself for it. Don't stress or worry about it. Just notice it.

And once you see your brain's negativity bias at work, pause and ask yourself:

Could this be my brain's negativity bias talking?

That's it—just notice it for now, say hello, maybe introduce yourself, and we'll use that awareness to build from in the coming days.

Make sure to take time to use the *Day 2 Tapping Meditation: Turning toward the Positive* to begin reorienting your primitive brain to notice and value the positive. You'll find it on page 248 of the Appendix.

You're beginning to create an important foundation for choosing peace!

◎ ◎ ◎

When will you complete Day 3 of this journey? Open your calendar, commit to a day, and add it now.

Day 3 is when you look at the role of community and how to transform your experience within it. Even people who are often surrounded by friends, family, and colleagues are surprised by the impact this day has on them.

Day 3

The Upsides of Us:
Harnessing the Power of Community

Eight hugs per day.

That's the prescription from Dr. Love, aka Paul Zak, Ph.D., to increase our levels of oxytocin, also known as the "cuddle hormone."

Oxytocin occurs naturally in the brain and bloodstream, and it supports those good feelings we all crave: connection, love, affection. Oxytocin is also associated with childbirth and nurturing, since it's involved in breastfeeding, as well as maternal and paternal bonding with newborns.

Not surprisingly, people with higher oxytocin levels tend to be happier. There is a catch, though. Oxytocin only increases as a result of stimuli. Left to their own devices, our oxytocin levels naturally hover at a baseline that's around zero.

So while we're wired to release oxytocin and enjoy the positive feelings it creates, we have to *do* something to initiate that process. Hence the eight hugs

per day! Whether you initiate or receive them, hugs are known to stimulate oxytocin in the body. That's also one of the reasons that hugs feel so good. They don't need to come from a significant other. Anyone you care to hug counts!

While most of us are generally aware of the positive power of connection, as we run through our days, going from one task to the next, we often forget how hardwired we are to benefit from a simple hug.

And if hugs are in short supply these days, you can boost oxytocin by watching an emotionally compelling movie, exercising with a friend, singing, or dancing. All are "feel good" alternatives that work just as well as hugs. I know the idea of *eight* hugs can seem overwhelming.

That same principle applies to our innate need for community. Although we know on some level that we're wired to connect with people, we don't always make meaningful connection an everyday priority.

Today we look at ways to bring more everyday connection and community—as well as oxytocin—into your journey. We begin by first looking at the effects of their polar opposite—loneliness.

STICKY, ICKY LONELINESS

Have you ever noticed how loneliness grows like a vine, quickly overtaking your entire experience?

Guy Winch had that experience on his birthday one year. It was during his first year of graduate school in New York City, thousands of miles and an entire ocean away from his twin brother. It was the first time they'd been separated, and the distance proved painful for them both.

Since Guy and his brother were both on tight budgets and international phone calls were expensive at the time (there were no cell phones yet and definitely no free Skype video calls!), they typically spoke for only five minutes per week. On their birthday, to celebrate, they agreed to talk for ten minutes.

On the morning of their birthday, Guy paced and paced around his tiny apartment, waiting for the phone to ring. Minutes passed, then hours, but his

phone never rang. Overwhelmed with sadness, Guy assumed that his brother was out having fun, surrounded by friends and family, not missing him at all.

When Guy awoke the next morning, he looked over and noticed that his phone was off the hook. He'd accidentally kicked it while pacing his apartment the day before. Seconds after he put the phone back on the hook, it rang. It was his brother, furious that he hadn't been able to get through for the past 24 hours.

Guy explained what had happened, but his brother couldn't understand. If he'd wanted to talk, why hadn't he picked up the phone and called?

In that moment, Guy couldn't answer his brother's question. The truth is, it had never occurred to him to do the one thing that would have quickly alleviated his loneliness—pick up the phone and make the call he was waiting to receive.

As he shares in his TED Talk, "Why We All Need to Practice Emotional First Aid," it wasn't until much later that Guy realized what had happened that day. He was in the grips of loneliness, but he hadn't realized it, since he was surrounded by people all day, every day.

I love this story because it's such a poignant depiction of how loneliness makes us feel. Once it sets in, loneliness acts like a cracked lens that distorts our view of everything and everyone around us.

Can you recall a time when you felt so overwhelmed by loneliness that everything and everyone around you only magnified the feeling?

"Loneliness" often conjures up the idea of being physically alone, but think of it also as being emotionally alone or disconnected. We can be surrounded by friends and family and still feel emotionally isolated.

Once loneliness takes over, we're often unable to take positive action. We get so stuck in loneliness that we begin working against ourselves. We decide that people don't care when they really do. We convince ourselves that we're not welcome when we definitely are. We feel sure that we don't belong when we're surrounded by people who love us.

For Guy on his birthday, he was so overwhelmed by his loneliness that the simple solution that was at his fingertips—calling his brother—never even crossed his mind.

That's pretty amazing when you think of him, alone all day in a tiny studio apartment. When you visualize that scene, it's hard to imagine how he *didn't* notice that the phone was off the hook.

Yet most of us have had some version of that experience—where we feel so lonely that we literally *can't think*. Stuck in our own loneliness, we become absent from our surroundings and our lives. We stop seeing what's right in front of us, and lose the ability to recognize the simple, accessible opportunities at our fingertips.

FROM DISCONNECTION TO RECONNECTION

One of the reasons we struggle with loneliness so acutely is because we're hardwired for social connection. Feeling connected to community is so important, in fact, that persistent loneliness has been shown to decrease our life span by a whopping 14 percent.[1]

Chimpanzees, who are closest to humans among primates, follow daily hygiene rituals that are structured in part to ensure sufficient connection with other chimpanzees. We humans, on the other hand, are increasingly isolating ourselves in front of our computers, in office cubicles, and by staying "stuck" to digital devices and TVs that increase our feelings of loneliness. (Hugging a cell phone doesn't quite feel the same!)

As we embark on this 21-day journey, it's incredibly important to incorporate community and social connection into your daily experience. When we feel connected, it's easier to take positive action, including overcoming old patterns that have limited us.

I've been reminded of that recently, thanks to an ongoing family challenge we began a few months ago. Determined to overcome seasonal bouts of (relative) inactivity, we created an online leaderboard to track how many steps we're each taking daily, all automated through our nifty new pedometers.

The results have been amazing!

Beyond competing to "win"—there's no prize, so winning is more theoretical than anything—it's been really entertaining for us all. In addition to tracking our steps, we've continually traded group texts about it, joked, and had a good time cheering one another on.

Since the competing has been so good-natured, the experience has been far more about giving us an additional way to connect than any one of us needing to "win." Not surprisingly, we've all been more physically active, as well.

One of my favorite stories from our group challenge happened one day when my brother, Alex, updated his steps after several days of leaving his numbers blank in the weekly challenge. Once his numbers updated into our shared leaderboard, he had taken so many more steps than my sister, Jessica, that she promptly hopped on the treadmill and ran for 45 minutes longer than usual! That, of course, then spurred on Alex to take more steps.

It was fun, it was entertaining, it was connection. They joked and laughed about it, and the healthy competition got them moving.

What's interesting about the challenge is how it changed our attitudes first, and behavior second.

Because we created this little community around taking more steps, we all feel more motivated to exercise, even on cold, rainy days. Ultimately, that's the real magic of making changes within a supportive community—it boosts your energy and helps you feel more motivated to make the changes you know you need to make.

HARDWIRED TO INTERACT

So other than hugging everyone we see, which may feel a little awkward in some circumstances, how else can we benefit most from community-inspired oxytocin boosts?

Obviously the answer to that question varies from one person to the next, but one clue may lie in an informal experiment Dr. Love conducted with a fel-

low researcher. After taking a blood sample from his friend, he put his colleague in a room with his smartphone for 10 minutes. His friend was instructed to engage on social media for the entire time. Dr. Love took a second blood sample once the 10 minutes were over.

During those 10 minutes of social media interactions, which were largely with people he'd never met, Zak's colleague's oxytocin levels increased by 13.2 percent. Meanwhile, his cortisol, or "stress hormone," levels decreased by 10.8 percent.

Interestingly, during those 10 minutes, his colleague reported experiencing an average set of social media interactions and being left feeling mildly entertained. His body, though, had a significant positive reaction. As Dr. Love put it, "E-connection is processed in the brain like an in-person connection."[2]

In other words, connecting with people online may be interpreted by the brain in similar ways to in-person connection, like hugging. It makes a lot of sense when you consider that Facebook has more than 400 million users, and a healthy percentage of those people check their feeds multiple times per day. Without realizing it, they may be logging in to experience an oxytocin boost.

Other studies show similar findings. For example, one study found that people with established friendships get sick less often, even when those friends live far away. Another study in Australia found that people with a sizable network of friends tended to live longer, even when those friends didn't live near them.

Of course, when it comes to creating community, as well as boosting oxytocin and well-being, not all social media is created equal. There are times when social media can have negative effects, causing us to compare ourselves unfavorably with others, or to be triggered by negative attitudes or news. Filtering your social media news feeds as much as possible away from negativity can help maximize the positive effects.

In-person contact is also very important. Increasingly, though, our packed schedules prevent that from happening as often as it once did. In its absence, it seems better to maximize social media than to have less overall social contact.

Over the years I've noticed how powerful some social media communities can be. In our years of hosting private Facebook groups around our online programs,

I've been amazed by how positive and supportive these communities quickly become. I think a lot of that magic lies in the fact that the members of these groups are on the same journey. They then naturally construct supportive, cohesive communities that create positive momentum around shared goals and intentions.

It's incredibly inspiring to watch!

Take a moment to think: if you felt connected to and supported by a like-minded community, what positive action might you be able to take?

Would you tap more often?

Procrastinate less?

Have more energy, or feel generally more positive?

GIVING *IS* GETTING

Beyond social media, there are, of course, any number of other powerful ways to benefit from community. According to research, in fact, our need for social connection isn't just hardwired; it's specific. The longest and largest longevity study in recent history, known as The Longevity Project, showed that helping others, in particular, boosts our longevity even more than having great relationships does.

Begun in 1990 by psychology professors Howard S. Friedman and Leslie R. Martin, The Longevity Project resulted from data that had been collected by psychologist Dr. Lewis Terman and his research team over a period of nearly 70 years.

In an attempt to study the social predictors of intellectual leadership, in 1921 Dr. Terman selected 1,528 San Francisco–based 11-year-olds to participate in a long-term study. He and his team interviewed the children's parents and studied their play habits, lifestyle, defining personality traits, and more, on an ongoing basis every 5 to 10 years. After Dr. Terman passed away in 1965, the work continued, thanks to his successors, who, as the study participants aged, continued to ask the group the same questions Dr. Terman had originally asked.

When Friedman and Martin began exploring the nearly seven decades of data that were available to them in 1990, they realized that Terman's data also told an important story around longevity. In combing through it all, they found that the longest-living participants had, among other things, consistently dedicated themselves to helping others. More than any other social habit, helping others appeared to contribute to longevity.

When you think about it, that finding makes sense.

Have you ever noticed how amazing it feels to help others, not just in the moment but also when you think back on the experience?

It's an incredible feeling, and it's also why I enjoy my work so much. I wake up every day and get to help thousands of people. It's amazing! As I've shared, it's also hugely motivating knowing that by making positive changes to my own habits, including my mornings, I'll be better equipped to help more people.

So now that we've seen how important community is to our long-term health and well-being, let's look at how to harness that energy as we move forward in this journey.

DAY 3 GREATEST SELF CHALLENGE: COME JOIN US!

Ready to feel more supported and connected? It's time to take action! For today, and in the days to come, begin noticing little ways that you can meaningfully connect with people.

Since relationships (which we'll get into later in this journey) can feel like "work," start with easy, everyday ways of connecting. For example:

- Notice simple ways of helping people, and then notice how helping them makes you feel.
- Call, e-mail, or text friends who make you feel good.
- Gather a group of like-minded people who all want to read this book and go through this journey together.
- And last but not least, join the greatest self online readers group!

Inspired by Dr. Love's work, I decided to conduct my own little experiment. For the first time, I'm offering a free, private Facebook group exclusively for my readers. It's a private place online where you can connect with and support like-minded people who are also committed to manifesting their greatest selves. So come, join, and see how much more momentum you can gain by connecting with the group!

It's free and completely private, so you can share your thoughts, ideas, and challenges without any of your other online friends seeing it, and it might be just what you need!

To join: go to www.thetappingsolution.com/manifesting

Make sure to use the *Day 3 Tapping Meditation: Letting Go of Loneliness* before moving on. You'll find it on page 251 of the Appendix.

◉ ◉ ◉

When will you complete the next day of our journey, Day 4? Pick a day and add it to your calendar now. *Important note*: Some people find that certain days bring up a lot of stuff for them, especially when doing the tapping. If you notice that for yourself, feel free to schedule the next day a little further away. There's no rush to get all this done in 21 consecutive days, but it *is* important to get through the whole book.

So be patient and aware of your experience, and schedule accordingly. But no matter what, make sure to schedule it!

Day 4 is a big one, the day when we look at what's true for you right now and use Tapping to see, accept, and transform it.

A Brief Interruption . . .

Why are you on this journey?

I have news for you . . .

If you didn't already believe in the potential of your
greatest self, you wouldn't be here.

You can do this.

You are doing this.

Keep up the great progress!

I've worked with people around the world whose lives have
transformed in incredible ways thanks to Tapping.

So yes, do the tapping.

You may enjoy the journey without tapping, but you won't get
the same powerful results . . . unless you do the tapping.

Keep tapping and keep reading. We've got
some powerful clearing to do.

You're doing great!

Day 4

Tell the Truth: Accepting What Is

"If you're going to clean a house, you have to see the dirt."

The answer floored me.

So simple yet so profound.

It was Louise Hay's answer to one of the first interview questions I ever asked her.

I was in sunny San Diego in the fall of 2013, and it was my first time on camera with Louise, best-selling author of *You Can Heal Your Life* and founder of the publishing company Hay House. I was excited, and a bit nervous, about interviewing her.

As usual, she was gracious and welcoming and, of course, as inspiring as ever.

The question she was answering was about an experience I've had repeatedly over the years. Oftentimes when I talk to people about tapping on what's happening, aka the truth, they tell me that they don't want to look at what's

happening, at these "negative" experiences. They say that they'd rather move to the positive and do affirmations instead.

When I asked Louise, who is known as one of the pioneers of positive thinking and affirmations, why we need to look at the truth first, her complete answer was the following:

> If you're going to clean a house, you have to see the dirt. If you're going to clean a turkey pan, if you're going to do the dishes, you have to see the dirt that you're cleaning. And then when you do that, then you can do lots of good affirmations.

I've shared this simple but profound piece of wisdom with countless audiences since.

I can't tell you how many times I've heard audience members gasp when I read Louise's words, shocked by their simplicity and truth and by the awareness that they've been ignoring the "dirt" in their lives.

Like most of us, those audience members have been conditioned to avoid the emotional and spiritual "dirt" they've been carrying around. They've been told to "tough it out" and "fake it until you make it"; to "get over it" and "move on"; to "be positive" and "ignore the negative."

After decades of positive intentions and considerable effort, they eventually find themselves surrounded by more, rather than less, of that emotional and spiritual "dirt." Over time, in fact, it begins to overtake their lives. They then look around and notice that their finances aren't working, their relationships aren't working, they're miserable in their jobs, and they're waging a daily war with their bodies.

Call it the truth. Call it what's happening. Whatever you call it, at some point, you realize that denying and pushing away the emotional and spiritual "dirt" that is your truth is a *lot* of work. It's exhausting and counterproductive.

With Tapping, you can change the game. Tapping *is* the cleaning process Louise was referring to, and also one that Louise herself, who at the time of that interview was 86 years old, used.

By tapping on the emotional and spiritual "dirt" we've been carrying around, we can see it and then clear it. That's when we become our greatest selves, willing and able to create our greatest lives from a place of peace.

Today, we take a big and important step forward. We use Tapping to begin telling the truth. Starting today, you begin seeing your own "dirt," so that you, too, can clear it out.

IS YOUR CUP OVERFLOWING?

Zen master Nan-in was visited by a foreign scholar of Eastern religions who'd come to inquire about Zen. Instead of listening to the master, he began talking about his ideas and everything he knew to be true.

After a while, Nan-in served tea. He began by pouring tea into the visitor's cup until it was full, and then he continued pouring. Soon the tea spilled over the cup saucer and onto the man's pants. Finally, the visitor asked, "Don't you see that it is full? You can't get any more in!"

"Just so," Nan-in replied. "And like this cup, you are filled with your own ideas. How can you expect me to give you Zen unless you offer me an empty cup?"

As you consider telling your truth, what is filling your cup?

Do you feel sure that looking at your truth won't do any good?

Does your truth feel too negative, intense, or complex to look at?

If, for instance, you try to be positive all day, and then beat yourself up for "failing" at it, it may be time to notice that you're filling your cup with the belief that you either can't face or can't change your truth.

The fact is, force-feeding yourself positive emotions and positive beliefs is inauthentic. It doesn't work. Over time it adds to the emotional and spiritual "dirt" you're carrying around.

Before you begin seeing the "dirt" of your own truth, it's important to notice what's in your cup—the emotions and beliefs preventing you from speaking

your truth. We often resist the clearing process that's required to get to that place of peace where we can enjoy a cleaner slate.

Why is that?

LOOK, I GET IT—YOU DON'T WANT TO

What happens if you admit to hating the job you depend on to support your family?

What happens if you admit to feeling lonely in your relationship?

What happens if you admit to feeling betrayed by your body for not looking, feeling, or reacting the way it "should"?

What's most challenging about looking at the truth is not the process itself but how vulnerable it makes us feel.

When we look at our present-moment experience—the truth of what's happening—we can get overwhelmed by unsettling emotions like anger, shame, fear, and sadness. They're big emotions that most of us were taught to control and tamp down.

Were you ever punished for expressing anger, or labeled as "sensitive" when you were sad? At young ages many of us learned to avoid our big, dark emotions, and when we do feel them, to push them away.

Unfortunately, like denying the truth of what's happening, pushing away intense emotions doesn't make them go away. They stay with us and contribute to the emotional and spiritual "dirt" that, over time, discolors our entire experience.

With Tapping, we can finally empty our cup. We can peel off that dark lens and clear out that "dirt." We can feel the full scope of our emotions, and then release them. We can let them go and begin anew with a cleaner, clearer slate.

That process begins with allowing yourself, even just a little bit, to be vulnerable.

THAT GUY CRYING ONSTAGE? YEAH, THAT'S ME

Let me first be honest and say that whenever it happens, I feel a little embarrassed.

The truth is, though, I occasionally cry onstage.

Especially when I'm talking about my hometown of Newtown, Connecticut (site of the Sandy Hook school shootings), and The Tapping Solution Foundation's work supporting trauma survivors, I sometimes get teary.

I cry in front of thousands of people and on camera. I don't feel 100 percent comfortable, but I do it. I can't help it because it's authentically who I am and how I feel.

As tempting as it is to run offstage and hide, when it happens, people walk up to me and thank me for being vulnerable. After I share that side of myself, they feel validated. It's amazing to feel that support, and to know that it's okay to be vulnerable, even when I'm standing in front of thousands I've never met.

Still, though, I don't love it!

Even surrounded by caring, supportive people, I don't want to dwell on how I just cried onstage. It's a little bit uncomfortable. (I'm sure part of the programming is the whole "boys don't cry" thing.) Yet once it's over, the experience of being vulnerable has helped me and others. (And I know I need to do more tapping on letting myself be that authentic onstage! Haha!)

I share this so you know that feeling vulnerable as you look at your truth is normal and okay, even when it doesn't feel that way.

After being told for many years, even decades, that vulnerability is weakness, we understandably resist the vulnerability inherent in looking at our truth. We prefer to gloss over the truth and resist our own vulnerability. We try to move on, but we do it so quickly that we never give ourselves the chance to see the dirt, much less clean it.

If you feel uncomfortable looking at your own truth, know that that discomfort can be a kind of North Star, telling you that you're heading in the

right direction. Instead of resisting it, move into that discomfort, and trust that Tapping will support you in feeling calmer and more supported as you move forward and release it.

OPENING THE DOOR

To begin the process, let's do a calming Tapping exercise on feeling more comfortable looking at your truth. We're going to do this now, as opposed to at the end of the chapter, because it will help you explore the rest of this chapter.

To start, notice how you feel, both emotionally and in your body, when you focus on looking at your present-moment truth.

Your present-moment truth may be that you feel angry, sad, lonely, or unloved. Your truth may mean facing money challenges or breakdowns in your relationships, career, or health. Whatever your truth is, notice what it's bringing up for you when you focus your attention on it.

When you think about telling the truth about what's happening in your life right now, do you feel any physical tension, pain, tightness?

Do you feel anxious or fearful?

Rate how intense your resistance to looking at the truth feels on a scale of 0 to 10 with 10 being extremely resistant.

Take three deep breaths.

We'll begin by tapping three times on the Karate Chop point.

KC *(repeat three times)*: Even though it's so uncomfortable looking at my truth, I deeply and completely love and accept myself.

Eyebrow: All this resistance

Side of Eye: I don't want to look at what's happening right now

Under Eye: I'd rather skip this part of the process

Under Nose: I want to move to the good stuff

Under Mouth: I don't want to look at what's happening

Collarbone: I want to leap into a new and greater truth

Under Arm: I don't want to look at my present-moment truth

Top of Head: It's too uncomfortable

Eyebrow: My present-moment truth feels too raw

Side of Eye: I don't want to look at it

Under Eye: I want to avoid it

Under Nose: I want to push it away

Under Mouth: This present-moment truth

Collarbone: I want to resist it

Under Arm: That's okay

Top of Head: I can let myself feel that resistance

Eyebrow: I can feel how much I want to avoid my present-moment truth

Side of Eye: And I can let that resistance go

Under Eye: I can relax when I think about facing my truth

Under Nose: I can feel calm in my body and mind

Under Mouth: It's safe to look at what's happening now

Collarbone: I can relax about it

Under Arm: Trusting that it's safe to look at my truth

Top of Head: Choosing to relax when I focus on my truth

Take a deep breath, and notice again how intense your resistance to looking at the truth feels now. Give that resistance a number on a scale of 0 to 10. Keep tapping until you get the desired relief.

You can either keep using the language above, again and again, or add your own language. These scripts are meant as guideposts to get you started—the key is to focus on your specific emotions, feelings, and ideas.

TELLING YOUR TRUTH

It's time to practice telling your truth.

This exercise serves two purposes. First, it helps you see your truth, which is your emotional and spiritual "dirt." Second, it helps you see which areas of yourself and your life most need your attention.

Now read the following prompts aloud, making sure to complete each sentence before moving on to the following one.

Note: If, at any point, you experience resistance around telling your truth, including feeling blank or numb, begin tapping through the points while focusing on that resistance. For example, if a statement like "I don't know what my truth even is" rings true, tap through the points while saying that. Tapping will help you relax and begin releasing your resistance so that you can have more clarity around your truth.

The truth about my work/career is . . .

The truth about my relationships is . . .

The truth about my finances is . . .

The truth about my health/wellness is . . .

The truth about my body is . . .

The truth about my life right now is . . .

The truth about how I feel about myself is . . .

As you read through your completed sentences, notice which one creates the most intense negative reaction. Since we're focusing on clearing, begin with the area of your life that feels the "dirtiest."

As you read through that sentence aloud, notice what comes up for you. How does your body feel? What emotions do you experience?

Rate the intensity of your overall reaction to reading that sentence on a scale of 0 to 10, with 10 being intensely negative.

Take three deep breaths. We'll begin by tapping three times on the Karate Chop point.

KC *(repeat three times)*: Even though <part of my life here, such as "my finances," or "my health"> feels so challenging right now, I love myself and accept how I feel.

Eyebrow: <State the area of life, such as "my finances" or "my relation-ships">

Side of Eye: It feels so challenging

Under Eye: It's overwhelming to think about

Under Nose: I'm still not sure I want to look at this mess

Under Mouth: It's too much

Collarbone: It's uncomfortable

Under Arm: That's okay

Top of Head: I can let myself see the truth of <this area of my life> now

Eyebrow: I can let myself see what's happening in this part of my life

Side of Eye: I can acknowledge and notice how that truth feels

Under Eye: It's safe to feel these feelings

Under Nose: It's safe to see and feel this truth

Under Mouth: I can feel these feelings now

Collarbone: I can let them come up when they need to

Under Arm: I don't have to push them away

Top of Head: I can see the truth of <state area of life here such as "my body" or "my work">

Eyebrow: I can notice what's really happening in this part of my life

Side of Eye: And feel the feelings that come up

Under Eye: And then I can let them go

Under Nose: I can release these emotions

Under Mouth: And trust that by seeing this truth

Collarbone: I can create new truths

Under Arm: Relaxing into this truth now

Top of Head: Feeling safe looking at this truth now

Take a deep breath, and notice how resistant you feel now when you think about the truth of this one area of your life. Give your resistance a number on a scale of 0 to 10. Keep tapping until you get the desired relief.

People sometimes worry that by accepting what's currently happening, they're rooting themselves in negativity. I get it, but remember that by tapping on relaxing when we look at the truth of our lives, we're giving ourselves a chance to clean it out. Once you can see and accept your own truth, which is your emotional and spiritual "dirt," you begin clearing space for a new, greater truth to emerge.

DAY 4 GREATEST SELF CHALLENGE: TELLING YOUR TRUTH

Congratulations on beginning to tell your truth! Let's keep that momentum going.

Starting today, select *just one part* of your life where you'd like to make progress. You can include the one area of your life you just tapped on, or not, as long as you're focusing on *just one area* of your life.

Once per day, practice telling yourself the truth about that area of your life. It can be as simple as saying, "I feel discouraged about my health and don't think it will ever improve," or "My finances are a mess, and I'm ready to give up on them."

Keep in mind that it's normal to fear and/or resist your truth(s). Our truths can get buried over time, and excavating them may take time and patience. If this process feels overwhelming at any point, pause to tap on those feelings of overwhelm. If there are bigger truths that feel like too much, put them aside or seek out a certified EFT practitioner to guide you.

You may also want to turn to the *All Is Well Tapping Meditation* script, which is at the end of the Appendix on page 308. Tap through it at any time to regain a sense of safety and calm.

Remember, there's no need to pressure yourself to "fix" anything. Your goal here is to get comfortable with telling the truth.

Just see your truth, tell it and accept it, and then watch, over time, as it transforms.

Complete the *Day 4 Tapping Meditation: Accepting Your Truth* before moving forward. You'll find it on page 254 of the Appendix.

On Day 5 we move deeper into practicing peace by bringing a new and energizing element into our daily experience—joy.

When will you complete Day 5? Pick a day and add it to your calendar. Your joy is waiting!

Day 5

Practicing Peace, Welcoming Joy

At 29,029 feet, Mount Everest has the highest mountain peak above sea level on earth.

The trek to the summit is notoriously perilous, posing intense physical, mental, and emotional challenges to all who attempt it. Nearly everyone who reaches the summit has a long story to tell about the journey up and back. For today I'll focus on just three of them.

Each of these three climbers successfully reached the summit.

Each had a unique experience once at the peak.

One climber explained that she'd anticipated reaching the summit for the previous two years. Countless times she'd imagined standing at the highest peak, feeling like the luckiest person on earth.

When the moment actually came, she felt a brief but enormous wave of relief, followed by an immediate, urgent desire to begin descending down the mountain.

The temperature and weather conditions on Mount Everest are extremely unpredictable. Getting down while the weather permits can be a matter of life or death. After a few brief moments at the summit, she and her team promptly began their descent.

The second climber had nearly summited Mount Everest twice but didn't make it to the actual summit until his third attempt.

As he stood at last, gazing down from the highest perch on the planet, he felt elated but also distracted.

He needed to record a video, or at least take a photo, for the employer who had funded his climb. Since the cold had frozen the team's video camera, he and his team had to wait three long hours in subfreezing conditions before someone arrived with a camera. After taking a photo of his team at the summit, they then began the long trek down the mountain.

The third climber stood at the peak of the planet's highest mountain in a state of awe and wonder. It was a moment like none he'd ever experienced. Amazed by where he was, he stood in absolute silence, savoring the view and the many victories, big and small, that had allowed him to make it to this place at this moment.

Think about those three experiences for a moment. The first and second climbers made different decisions but were both equally focused on surviving. Only the third climber stopped to celebrate the moment.

These climbers accomplished the same feat, yet each one had a very different experience once at the summit.

What do you do when you experience some sort of "win"?

How do you feel when you complete a task or get through a challenging day or week?

Do you celebrate, or do you immediately focus on the next task?

THE MOUNT EVEREST IN OUR MINDS

Granted, few of us even *want* to climb Mount Everest.

The stress of preparing for it is deterrent enough!

At the same time, we sometimes *feel* like we need to climb the equivalent of Mount Everest. Between life, finances, family, work—whatever is on our to-do list—we may *feel* like we have to undergo an extreme endurance test to get through the day or week.

Today we're going to look at a simple, powerful way to disrupt that feeling. Using tapping in a specific way, we're going to develop the mental muscle to do something our brains are not inherently wired to do—celebrate victories, big and small, monumental and (seemingly) mundane.

On Day 2 we learned about the brain's negativity bias. We saw how the human brain evolved to protect us by focusing more on threats than on opportunities. We also learned that the primitive brain is trained to default to a state of high alert, encouraging us to be like cautious Grog, instead of peace-loving Thor, who ignored danger and was promptly eaten by the tiger.

Put differently, our brains have evolved to see everyday challenges as the mental, emotional equivalent of climbing Mount Everest.

The problem is, the constant dangers we were once faced with—that saber-toothed tiger, for example—are no longer relevant.

We're faced instead with relationship challenges, financial pressure, traffic jams, 24-7 media cycles, never-ending e-mails, texts, and more. While these things are important, they're rarely life threatening. Unfortunately, the primitive brain doesn't understand that. The primitive brain is still mentally and physically preparing us to fend off a tiger when in fact, we're running late for a meeting.

This tendency to overreact to stressors is so ingrained that it quickly impacts the body. Our hearts pound; we may sweat. Our mental abilities—to think clearly and problem solve—are sidelined. We then anxiously count each second spent stuck in traffic, and then on the elevator, to get to that meeting.

By this point, the primitive brain has taken over. It is busy reinforcing feelings of panic, and preventing us from remembering that being late to a meeting isn't actually life threatening.

So how can we reprogram the primitive brain to quiet the panic response when it isn't necessary, and instead enjoy more peaceful, positive moments when they're available?

STUCK IN OVERDRIVE

It typically takes 40 days to climb Mount Everest.

In poor weather conditions, the journey can take longer. Along the way, the body must withstand extreme temperatures, as well as oxygen deprivation that cause any number of challenging, potentially lethal physical symptoms.

The ascent is so physically, mentally, and emotionally taxing that before reaching the summit, climbers have to stop and acclimatize at a series of different base camps. Often during these stays climbers report experiencing intense anxiety and physical distress, as well as extreme cold and biting winds.

Stop now to imagine your week as a climb up Mount Everest.

Imagine that by week's end you need to be at the summit.

As you ascend, you're required to stop at several base camps.

What do you do when you reach the first base camp?

Do you take a moment to pump your arms in the air, and declare, "Woohoo, we made it!" or do you immediately focus on the many challenges ahead?

THE HIGH PRICE OF SKIMPING ON JOY

When we don't intentionally train the brain to notice and celebrate each and every base camp we get to, we can't appreciate that moment when we arrive at the summit, either.

Translated into daily life terms, it goes something like this:

When we don't take a moment to celebrate simple, everyday victories, we get too stuck in stress overdrive and panic to enjoy our big victories.

In other words, when we don't celebrate the little wins, we feel less joy across the board.

We see that pattern play out in the three climbers' stories. After years of anticipating reaching the summit, once there, the first climber we met was too panicked about surviving the remainder of her journey to enjoy a moment she'd long dreamed of celebrating.

The second climber was equally distracted, although his panic was around proving himself to his employer, which was how he would survive after his descent.

Both of these climbers essentially reacted to their incredible accomplishment—summiting the highest mountain on earth—from a place of panic.

To be clear, their reactions aren't wrong or bad. In fact, they're completely understandable. Before reaching the summit, they underwent enormous physical, mental, and emotional strain. In literal terms, and for many good reasons, they were stuck in survival mode.

Their inability to savor that moment at the summit makes total sense.

As we saw with Grog, even when we're not literally climbing Mount Everest, we do need to be aware of dangers, and at times react to them. However, it's also important to remind ourselves that the brain's default is to assume the worst. The primitive brain will, by default, convince you to skimp on joy and overindulge on worry, fear, and stress. We then spend so much of our mental and emotional resources on surviving that we don't notice opportunities to thrive.

It's a critical point, so I'll say it again.

. . . .

By depriving ourselves of brief, everyday bursts of joy,
we end up depriving ourselves of joy across the board.

. . . .

CHANGING CHANNELS

So how do we train the brain to be more like the third climber, who was overwhelmed with joy and gratitude as he stood at the highest point on earth, reveling in his surroundings, his journey, the incredible feat of making it to this place?

It sounds simple, but when the brain and body are stuck in panic mode, trying to force yourself to a place of peace and joy can seem impossible.

Feeling more peace and joy is a practice that begins with training your brain and body to notice and appreciate the smaller wins. It's about seeing and celebrating your versions of reaching the different "base camps" along your journey.

And let's be clear, the journey to that base camp might be tough. It's likely a slog, it's likely challenging, it might include a little frostbite or some other unforeseen challenge, which to me, is even *more* reason to celebrate every win you can along the way.

Your life is going to have problems.

It's easy to say, "I can't celebrate until *all* my problems go away," but what would happen if we started to celebrate our progress, big or small?

Next we look at how to use Tapping to do that.

SAVORING THE SMALLER WINS

When you think back on recent days, what everyday "wins" have you had?

For starters you're on Day 5 of this book.

That's a win unto itself! (Please accept my virtual congratulations and big hug for making it this far.)

You're also probably not climbing Mount Everest, which means you're far less likely to suffer frostbite.

Win number two!

Really think about what good has happened in your life.

Have you tapped today? That's a win.

Did you go to bed earlier and wake up feeling more rested? Great!

Were you calmer than usual when you got stuck in traffic? Well done.

Were you more patient with your children, spouse, or co-worker? Impressive.

Think back on the past few days or week, and notice any and all victories.

Either on paper or in your mind, list three of those wins now:

My first win is _____

My second win is _____

My third win is _____

With your list in mind, we're going to do some positive tapping.

Positive tapping is a powerful way to train your brain and body to notice those everyday wins in your life, and feel the positive emotion they can generate.

To start, focus on your list of wins, and notice how much positive emotion you feel.

Give that positive emotion a number on a scale of 0 to 10, with 10 being the most positive—joyful or grateful, excited, and so on—that you can imagine feeling.

With positive tapping, instead of lowering stress, the goal is to elevate positive emotion. That means that your goal is to *increase* your SUDS number, which is the number of intensity scale.

For example, if your joy begins at a 3 out of 10, your goal with positive tapping is to make the number go up, perhaps to a 5 out of 10, or an 8 out of 10.

So let's get started!

Take three deep breaths.

We'll begin by tapping three times on the Karate Chop point.

KC *(repeat three times)*: Even though I forget to notice the good in my life, I can see it now and let myself feel joy and gratitude.

Eyebrow: I <first win here>

Side of Eye: It feels good to notice!

Under Eye: I also <second win here>

Under Nose: It feels good to notice this, too!

Under Mouth: I also <third win here>

Collarbone: It feels great to notice all this!

Under Arm: It's safe to feel good about this

Top of Head: But it also feels weird to celebrate these little wins

Eyebrow: I forget to notice them most of the time

Side of Eye: I can see them now

Under Eye: They came from positive choices

Under Nose: I can start noticing my everyday wins more often

Under Mouth: And let myself celebrate each one

Collarbone: I can feel more joy more often

Under Arm: I can stop and feel gratitude for these everyday victories

Top of Head: Even though they seem small and meaningless sometimes

Eyebrow: I can stop and notice them

Side of Eye: I can feel joy about them

Under Eye: I can give them the meaning they deserve

Under Nose: It's safe to feel this joy more often

Under Mouth: It's safe to notice these little things

Collarbone: It's safe to value these everyday wins

Under Arm: Letting myself feel joy now

Top of Head: Feeling joy and gratitude now

Take a deep breath. Give your positive emotion a number on a scale of 0 to 10. Keep tapping until you get the desired effect.

TAPPING TIP

If at any point, you struggle to feel genuine positive emotion from positive tapping, you may need to release something negative first, before positive tapping can feel authentic.

If that happens, pause your positive tapping and do a few rounds of tapping while asking yourself questions like:

Why can't I feel good about these everyday wins?

What is holding me back from feeling more joy about them?

Once you have a clearer sense of why positive tapping isn't resonating, tap on releasing the negative emotion, limiting belief, and/or event that's distracting you. Then, when that negative charge has gone down and you are ready, return to positive tapping.

DAY 5 GREATEST SELF CHALLENGE: CELEBRATING YOUR WINS

Have you noticed that I've congratulated you each day for completing the chapter?

That's the kind of simple, everyday celebrating I want you to do at least twice per day from now forward.

Stop and notice—did you recently have a breakthrough while tapping?

Did you notice your brain's negativity bias taking over at any point during your day?

Did you feel more relaxed in situations that usually stress you out?

Those all count as wins! They mean you're making progress, and each step forward counts. When possible, give yourself the gift of one minute of positive tapping for each win you notice.

Over time that simple daily habit will retrain your brain to see and feel more authentically positive.

You're making great progress! To wrap up, complete the *Day 5 Tapping Meditation: Positive Tapping* to practice instilling joy and seeing more "light." You'll find it on page 257 of the Appendix.

◉ ◉ ◉

And remember to open your calendar and pick a day to complete Day 6! It just takes a few seconds. You can write, "Read Day 6 today! Time to find out what feeling peace in my body really feels like!"

Day 6

What's It Saying?
Listening to the Body

What's your itty-bitty left pinkie toe saying to you right now? Seriously, tune in and listen.

Which suppressed emotion is stuck in your knees? Go ahead—feel it.

What memory has gotten lodged in your stomach, refusing to let go? Can you sense it?

Really, I'm honestly asking.

In case you're wondering, no, I haven't completely lost it as I ask these seemingly strange questions.

And that's because I know that the body has things to say, stories to share, messages it wants you to hear.

If your stomach is upset, stop and notice. What's it upset about? And what other emotion is beneath that upset—fear, sadness, anxiety?

Take a moment to breathe. Yeah, right now, take one deep inhale and exhale and . . .

Listen to your body.

How is your back feeling? Is it angry? Since when, and at what or whom?

And your shoulders, with the many burdens they've carried over the years. Let them speak to you. Be their audience.

Your body is talking to you right now. Are you listening?

Is your neck stiff? Can you roll it in a full circle without pain or discomfort? Why not? What emotions does it need you to release before it will move with greater ease?

And your head. It has led you to so many places, guided you in so many ways. Does it throb after repeating thoughts that begin with "I can't _____" or "I'll never _____"?

If so, why?

Again and again over the years, I've asked questions like these of audiences around the world. Over and over, people surprise themselves by not hesitating before explaining the event that's stuck in their stomach, the unresolved anger in their back, the sadness that's in their knees.

The body is speaking to each of us at all times. Today, using Tapping, we're going to begin listening to what it's trying to tell us.

MOVING BEYOND BETRAYAL

Have you ever had a friend that you just kind of tolerate? If you're honest, you don't especially like that person. Sometimes you actually dislike them. You tolerate them for one simple reason—they're always around.

That's how a lot of us relate to our bodies—as that annoying friend who's always there. That friend who slows us down, weighs us down, makes us feel limited, stuck, maybe even sick and in pain. Why would we listen to that friend?

We're tired of that friend! We want a *new* friend, which in this case may mean wanting a healthier, happier, maybe better-looking, or slimmer body.

You may have heard it before, but it's such an important part of becoming your greatest self that I'm going to say it here and now.

Your body and mind are interconnected. Your experiences, emotions, and beliefs affect your body. Your body also shapes your experiences, emotions, and beliefs. One feeds the other, which in response feeds the other back. The mind-body and body-mind are on an endless loop, always influencing each other.

On Day 4 we began telling the truth about our feelings, our lives, ourselves. It's time to bring the body into that process. Your body is, after all, the one "friend" who's with you for every second of your entire life. Your body is also your most powerful and potent truth teller. It absorbs everything, and if you don't give it a chance to "speak" to you, it will get your attention through chronic pain, fatigue, sleep disturbances, digestive distress, and more.

To be your greatest self, you need to befriend your body, rather than just tolerate it.

The first step in creating a more trusting relationship with your body is telling the truth about how you feel about it.

Maybe you feel like your body betrayed you by becoming sick or disabled. Maybe you blame it for not looking the way you want it to, or the way it used to. Maybe you dread the allergy symptoms it causes you.

Whatever the truth of your relationship with your body is, it's time to tell it.

Note: Every chapter has a Tapping Meditation that you can find in the Appendix, but some chapters included Tapping within the body of the chapter, because that Tapping is necessary to move the conversation forward. So whenever you find it in the chapter, try to tap right then and there, and if you can't tap in that moment, at least think through the discussion.

DISCOVERING LIMITING BODY BELIEFS

Without thinking too much about it, complete these three sentences.

Body Belief #1:

My body can't _____

Body Belief #2:

My body is always so _____

Body Belief #3:

My body will never _____

Read through your list. Pick the one limiting belief that feels most true right now.

Say that belief to yourself, either silently or out loud. How true does that belief feel on a scale of 0 to 10? Give it a number now.

When tapping on limiting beliefs, you'll likely want to decrease your number. For instance, if the belief "my body is weak and tired" feels true at a 9 out of 10, your goal with tapping is to lower that number.

Take three deep breaths.

We'll begin by tapping three times on the Karate Chop point.

KC *(repeat three times)*: Even though I have this belief that <state belief>, I love myself and accept how I feel.

Eyebrow: <State belief>
Side of Eye: This limiting belief
Under Eye: It feels so true
Under Nose: <State belief>

Under Mouth: It feels like the truth

Collarbone: It feels like my reality

Under Arm: It's what's happened in my body

Top of Head: <State belief>

Eyebrow: This belief

Side of Eye: It feels so true

Under Eye: And it makes me feel stuck

Under Nose: This isn't a belief—it's the truth!

Under Mouth: No, it's not . . .

Collarbone: Yes, it is!

Under Arm: What if I could change this belief?

Top of Head: What if I could start to let it go?

Eyebrow: What if it doesn't have to be completely true?

Side of Eye: What if it's only partially true?

Under Eye: And then maybe I can release it completely

Under Nose: And start to form a new, empowering belief

Under Mouth: Letting this old belief go

Collarbone: From every cell of my body

Under Arm: Right now

Top of Head: Letting this old belief go now

Take a deep breath. Check back in on how true your belief feels now. Give it a number on the 0–10 scale. Keep tapping until you get the desired result.

Beliefs tend to run deep, so releasing and transforming them often takes more than a few rounds of tapping. The tapping you just did can help you create a healthy distance from your belief. By beginning to see your belief *as a* belief rather than the truth, you can begin to notice that it's not always true.

That's when you can begin to release it and replace it with a more empowering body belief.

THE POWER OF THE PLACEBO

We've looked at limiting body beliefs, so now let's consider the flip side—how positive, empowering body beliefs impact us.

In his book *The Biology of Belief*, developmental biologist Bruce Lipton, Ph.D., demonstrates how beliefs impact the body at a cellular level. He shares stories of sick children who, on the way to the doctor, suddenly get well. Over and over again, their high fevers suddenly disappear, horrible coughs and colds almost instantaneously go away, stomach troubles vanish—and all these "miracle" cures happen before the children even reach the doctors' offices.

Those cases are just some of the many examples of how beliefs impact the physical body. Once those children are on the way to the doctor, they believe that healing is on the way. That belief is so firm that the body gets to work and quickly heals itself.

Similar to the placebo effect in research studies, where patients are "miraculously" cured by a sugar pill, these children's bodies are benefiting from positive, empowering beliefs around the body and healing.

What might your body be capable of if it were infused with positive beliefs?

OH, WHAT A PINKIE TOE

Think of one positive thing you believe about your body.

It can be your perfectly shaped pinkie toe. It can be your bright smile, your laugh, the sound of your voice, the color of your hair, or the strength of your legs. It doesn't matter what it is, as long as you focus on it right now.

Note: Your positive body belief doesn't have to be related to the limiting body beliefs you discovered in the last exercise. Your goal here is simply to bring more positive energy into your relationship with your body.

Really let yourself feel appreciation for that pinkie toe, your nose, your singing voice—whatever it is, really let yourself love it now.

On a scale of 0 to 10, rate the intensity of your positive emotion about this body part or physical attribute now—here again, we're going for a higher number being positive.

Take three deep breaths.

Begin by tapping three times on the Karate Chop point.

KC *(repeat three times):* I <positive body belief>, I really love this about my body, and I'm letting myself appreciate and feel grateful for it now.

Eyebrow: My <positive body belief>

Side of Eye: My <positive body belief>

Under Eye: I really love it

Under Nose: I'm truly grateful for it

Under Mouth: Letting myself feel this love

Collarbone: Letting myself feel this gratitude

Under Arm: I love it!

Top of Head: I feel so grateful for my <positive body belief>

Eyebrow: It's a bright spot!

Side of Eye: Something I love about my body

Under Eye: My <positive body belief>

Under Nose: I really love it

Under Mouth: It's safe to love my <positive body belief>

Collarbone: It's safe to feel really good about my <positive body belief>

Under Arm: I love this about myself!

Top of Head: I feel grateful for my <positive body belief>

Eyebrow: All this love

Side of Eye: All this gratitude

Under Eye: My <positive body belief>

Under Nose: I really love it

Under Mouth: I deeply appreciate it

Collarbone: Letting myself feel really good about my <positive body belief>

Under Arm: I can feel this feeling

Top of Head: And let it grow and grow

Take a deep breath. Check in with your positive emotion again, and give it a number of intensity on a scale of 0 to 10. Keep tapping until you feel as positive as you desire.

REBALANCING THROUGH ATTUNEMENT

Now that we've looked at negative and positive ways of relating to the body, how can we get better at listening to what the body is trying to tell us?

The answer lies in a concept that best-selling author Gabor Maté, M.D., calls *attunement*. Although he discusses attunement in relation to parenting, it's a concept I think also plays a huge role in our relationships with the body.

Here's how Maté defines it:

Attunement is, literally, being "in tune" with someone else's emotional states. It's not a question of parental love but of the parent's ability to be present emotionally in such a way that the infant or child feels understood, accepted, and mirrored. Attunement is the real language of love, the conduit by which a preverbal child can realize that she *is* loved.[1]

Imagine that your mind is the "parent," and your body is the "child." In that case, we'd define attunement as something like this:

Attunement is, literally, being "in tune" with the body's responses. It's a question of your mind's ability to be present in such a way that your body's signals and responses to your experiences, emotions, and beliefs can be understood, accepted, and fully released. Attunement is the conduit by which the body can realize its full potential to feel loved, and in turn, to support its own, and your greatest self's thriving.

Using that definition as our basis, how do we then become more attuned to the body? Maté explains that there is no perfect way to practice or demonstrate attunement. He calls attunement a "subtle process . . . deeply instinctive . . . easily subverted when the parent is stressed, depressed, or distracted."[2]

If the mind is the "parent," it's easy to see how we become mis-attuned to the body. We're often so stressed and distracted by what we need to do and be that we may not take quiet time to be still and listen to what the body is trying to say.

With tapping, we can let go of stress, quiet the mind, and slowly tune in to what the body is saying. Keep in mind, there's no need for your tapping to feel laborious or serious. By all means, keep it light and fun!

Whenever possible, be playful with your tapping. Tap while talking to your left pinkie toe or asking your belly button how it's feeling today. Over time, as you release emotional and physical stress, it will be easier to hear what the body is saying.

TAPPING FOR CHRONIC PAIN RELIEF

I've seen such incredible results with tapping for relief of chronic physical pain that I wrote an entire book on it! If you suffer from chronic pain, check out *The Tapping Solution for Pain Relief*.

DAY 6 GREATEST SELF CHALLENGE: TUNING IN TO THE BODY

Your challenge for today and the days to come is to bring your body into this journey. From today onward, open to the possibility of attuning to your body. Whenever possible, listen and notice what your body is saying.

Of course, Rome was not built in a day. Similarly with tapping, you may need to practice "talking to" your body and listening to what it's saying.

I'm not asking you to use tapping to release your every limiting body belief right now, or to become best friends with your body this week. For now I'm just asking you to notice what your body is saying, to be a little more willing to hear its messages.

In the morning or at bedtime, before you begin tapping, check in with your body. Mentally scan your body and simply notice what you feel.

Check out the *Day 6 Tapping Meditation: Body Attunement* in the Appendix on page 260.

◉ ◉ ◉

Make sure to schedule Day 7 into your calendar now, too.

Day 7 is where you learn two key practices that will help you get the most out of this journey. You'll experience a greater sense of ease and flow with these two add-ons in your spiritual toolbox.

You're nearing the end of Week One, kudos!

Hey, can I let you in on a little secret?

This journey isn't actually about becoming your greatest self.

*This journey will guide you in ways that allow you to shed
the layers of "stuff" that have kept you from accessing your greatest self.*

*Because the truth is, you already **are** your greatest self.*

*Through this journey, you'll manifest your greatest self by **clearing**
and **releasing** those layers of "stuff" that are keeping your greatest
self stuck deep down inside.*

And you're making great progress, so keep it up!

Day 7

Ritual and Repetition: Making Transformation Stick

Throughout his record-breaking NBA career, basketball superstar Michael Jordan wore his North Carolina (college basketball) shorts under his team shorts for every game.

Benjamin Franklin, one of the Founding Fathers of the United States, also the face of the U.S. $50 bill, was a leading author, printer, political theorist, politician, Freemason, postmaster, scientist, inventor, civic activist, statesman, and diplomat. Although his work covered multiple areas, Franklin followed the exact same schedule every single day.

Wade Boggs, former third baseman for the Boston Red Sox, woke up at the same time each day. He also ate chicken before each game, took exactly 117 ground balls in practice, took batting practice at 5:17, and ran sprints at 7:17.

Ritual is a powerful tool that has been shown to lower stress. One study in Brazil even found that formulaic rituals improved people's chances of solving specific problems, including quitting smoking and curing asthma.[1]

Like many prolific authors, Dr. Maya Angelou also clung to ritual. She regularly rented a plain, undecorated hotel room, free of distractions, where she did her writing.

Throughout history, people have relied on ritual to make consistent progress in ways that create a sense of ease and peace of mind.

By definition, *ritual* is a routine that's repeated in the same way, often at the same time and in the same place, over and over again.

Both ritual and its necessary companion, frequent repetition, are powerful tools you can use to make positive steps forward on a consistent basis.

As we wrap up the first week of this journey, we'll take a step back, look at the progress made, and see how ritual and repetition—the two R's—can help us move forward.

MANY RECIPES, SAME DELICIOUS APPLE PIE

The great thing about ritual is how easy it is to personalize. While some may appreciate the relative complexity of rituals like Wade Boggs's and Maya Angelou's, others may yield equally positive results from much simpler rituals.

Just like you can make delicious apple pie using any number of different recipes, each of us can discover the ritual that works best for us.

A ritual as simple as waking up and setting a daily intention while tapping for a few minutes can transform an entire day, then a week, month, and so on.

What rituals do you use in your life?

Is there a past or current ritual that you can resurrect or reinvent, adding tapping to maximize its impact?

Is there a new ritual that you can create around tapping before bed to support more restful sleep?

How can you use the power of ritual to soothe some of the "pain points" in your life, and in the process, support you in becoming your greatest self?

RINSE & REPEAT, RINSE & REPEAT, RINSE & REPEAT

On Day 1 I shared my struggles to follow the morning ritual that works best for me—taking quiet time to read something inspiring before beginning my workday.

Being more consistent with my morning ritual is something I need to focus on. With that said, I often still find myself pushing back on the idea of adopting rituals. Even while tapping, I'll catch myself thinking, *I don't like constraints. I like to go with the flow. I like to be free.*

The truth is, rituals actually free you to live your best life! So if part of you thinks, *Routines drive me mad!*, remember that you are the one making the choice and are always in control. By making your best habits routine, you free up your life for creativity and joy.

The other "R"—repetition—is a tool that I have used regularly for years. In fact, I credit the power of frequent repetition for enabling me to become more of my greatest self over the years.

For me repetition has been most powerful with reading (and rereading) and listening (and relistening) to books by some of my favorite authors.

When Wayne Dyer, whom I had the privilege of getting to know personally over some years, passed away in August 2015, I once again returned to repetition to begin processing my grief.

Over a period of days, I listened again to his audiobooks, and once again, his words inspired new insights and ideas. I took comfort in celebrating his message of love and peace by immersing myself in his work. I noticed how years of listening to the same material over and over again had changed me in incredible ways. I was so moved by that experience that I wrote a poem about him, his life, and the impact his work has had on me.

Days later I read that poem at a live tribute event in front of thousands and then shared it online. That process—listening to his work again, then writing, reading, and sharing the poem it inspired me to write—was incredibly healing. (If you want to see the video of that poem, you can find it here: https://www .facebook.com/nortner/videos/426226317567415/.)

With the power of repetition in mind, think back on the first week of this journey. What day(s) from this week would you like to repeat? Circle below:

Day 1: Peace or Panic?

To kick off the journey, we look at how we feel on any given day. Are we going through our days from a place of peace or a place of panic?

In that process we also examine the subtler ways that we "panic" and what peace looks and feels like. We also look at the effort and daily practice that positive people put into choosing peace, and use tapping to experience more of it.

Day 1 Greatest Self Challenge: Practicing Peace (page 12)

Day 1 Tapping Meditation: From Panic to Peace (page 245)

Day 2: Negativity, Hardwired: A Look at the Primitive Brain

Remember Grog and Thor? They sit perched at the edge of a cave, and only one of them gets eaten by the tiger. Who is it, and why?

Through that story, we learn about the brain's negativity bias. This is also where we learn a bit more about the science of tapping, and how it communicates with the body and "primitive brain" to balance our negativity bias.

Day 2 Greatest Self Challenge: Redirecting Your Brain (page 18)

Day 2 Tapping Meditation: Turning toward the Positive (page 248)

Day 3: The Upsides of Us: Harnessing the Power of Community

Can you be surrounded by people, yet still feel lonely?

On this day we look at how loneliness impacts us, and how community can support us in taking this journey and feeling more fulfilled in our daily lives.

We also learn about Dr. Zak, aka Dr. Love, and his surprising prescriptions for overcoming feelings of isolation.

Day 3 Greatest Self Challenge: Come Join Us! (page 27)

Day 3 Tapping Meditation: Letting Go of Loneliness (page 251)

Day 4: Tell the Truth: Accepting What Is

On this day we get inspired to take an honest look at our lives, to see the "dirt" we need to see in order to clean it and begin moving into our greatest selves.

For many this day is a powerful eye-opener, and important day for establishing a foundation for the journey ahead.

Day 4 Greatest Self Challenge: Telling Your Truth (page 39)

Day 4 Tapping Meditation: Accepting Your Truth (page 254)

Day 5: Practicing Peace, Welcoming Joy

Three climbers summited Mount Everest, yet each had a very different experience. Which climber resonates most with you?

On this day we begin to pay more attention to how much joy we let into our lives, and use Tapping to see more opportunities to celebrate the little everyday victories we all experience.

Day 5 Greatest Self Challenge: Celebrating Your Wins (page 50)

Day 5 Tapping Meditation: Positive Tapping (page 257)

Day 6: What's It Saying? Listening to the Body

Is your lower back trying to tell you something? (Not to worry—I haven't gone off the deep end!)

On this day we look at how the body communicates with us, and use Tapping to begin tuning in to what it's saying.

We also look at limiting beliefs about the body, and begin to practice cultivating positive beliefs and emotions about the body.

Day 6 Greatest Self Challenge: Tuning In to the Body (page 60)

Day 6 Tapping Meditation: Body Attunement (page 260)

DAY 7 GREATEST SELF CHALLENGE: ADDING NEW TOOLS

Your challenge, starting today, is to add the two R's to your toolbox.

Have you already, or can you now, create a daily ritual around Tapping?

Experiment and figure out what works for you. Your ritual can take 60 seconds, 5 minutes, or much longer.

Whatever your ritual looks like, commit to doing it every day.

As for the second R, repetition, pick one day that you circled in the previous list and give yourself the gift of repetition. Do that day over, and notice what new or deeper insights and/or relief you experience.

Ritual.

Repetition.

Incorporate these powerful tools into your journey and let them steer you toward your greatest self.

Congratulations! You've completed Week One of this journey. You're moving closer to peace with each new day.

Make sure to complete the *Day 7 Tapping Meditation: Peace & Patience*. You can find it in the Appendix on page 263.

◎ ◎ ◎

If you need extra time to wrap up Week One, go ahead and take it. There's no rush here; the key is you stick with it and get through the book in the perfect time. Just be sure to add Day 8 to your calendar now. Think about how great you will feel when you get all the way through the book. The sense of accomplishment, the sense of pride that you stuck with it! You've got this.

Day 8 is when you set your sights beyond the immediate horizon, and prepare to dive into a process of deep release and healing.

Releasing the Emotions and Experiences Keeping You Stuck

Day 8

Planting the First Seed: A New Vision

Imagine yourself nestled in bed on a beautiful morning. You awaken briefly before dipping effortlessly back into a deep sleep. Just as you're waking up for good, your spiritual guide, be it God, the Universe, an angel, or other, whispers these words in your ear:

You are light.

You are love.

A blessed creature whom I will join with to co-create your most fulfilling life.

Your mission, if you choose to accept it, is to spread love and magic to all whom you meet today.

Should you consent to this mission, you will be tasked with revealing beauty and wonder where others haven't yet seen it, with sharing love when others can't yet do so.

Go forth and do as your heart guides you.

Seconds later, your eyes open.

The words reverberate in your mind.

I have a mission. I have been tasked with spreading wonder, magic, beauty, and love, creativity, joy, and knowledge.

You get out of bed feeling better than you have in ages, rested and peaceful, yet energized for the day ahead. It's been years since you started a day feeling this sure of your purpose.

You have a mission. You are love. You are light. You are joy. And you are ready to share it.

From that moment onward, what does your day feel like? You still have a schedule to keep, maybe there's also time that you need to fill. There is still traffic to contend with, bills to pay, and obligations you must meet. You don't have the free time you'd like to bask unburdened in this mission. And yet this mission is yours to accept, and your heart is saying yes.

How do you feel now that you've been freshly equipped with this mission? Does your normal routine feel the same, or does it feel somehow new?

We've spent the past seven days shedding stress and practicing ways of choosing peace over panic. Today we step back and look at the larger journey to create a vision of you as your greatest self.

THE LOOKING GLASS

Now that your passion and sense of purpose have been ignited through your divinely appointed mission, tell me—what does your greatest self look and act like?

Rest assured; there's no need to define or envision every last detail of your greatest self. No one can do that. At this point in the journey, the most we can do is indulge in fantasies and desires—and that's the whole point!

It's time to imagine what's possible.

Let's look at what it might feel like to go through a day as our greatest selves, and see what bubbles up.

To do that we'll first shift our focus to how you, as your greatest self, would like to feel.

For example, do you want to feel more seen and understood in your relationships?

Do you want to feel safer with money?

More at ease in your body?

More inspired by your work?

More fulfilled on a spiritual level?

As you begin creating a vision of your greatest self, focus on how you would like to feel, rather than what you hope to accomplish.

If you also have specific goals in mind, that's fine. They can be useful guideposts, but only when you can work toward those goals from a place of peace, rather than panic.

You can be your greatest self at any income level, age, weight, or relationship status. In fact, any specific outcomes you desire will likely result from you becoming your greatest self, rather than the other way around.

The focus of this journey is on *being* your greatest self first and foremost, and from there you will be able to transition peacefully into doing what you aspire to do.

Let me say that again.

This journey is first and foremost about how you're *being*. It's about how you're showing up. Once you begin showing up as your greatest self, you can then create and achieve any goals that align with your greatest self.

Did you get that?

Being first, before doing.

And look, I know that prioritizing how you're being—how you're showing up in your life—can feel awkward, vague, and slow. It's especially frustrating when you're panicked to reach the finish line you have in mind, whether it's that bigger paycheck, physical transformation, relationship, or other. However, it's through being your greatest self that you will create your greatest life.

Being before doing. It's a concept we've all heard, yet rarely are we taught how to practice it. We begin that now by looking at how emotions affect how we're being.

FROM FEELING TO BEING

How we're being—how we show up in our lives—is closely linked to how we're feeling at any given moment.

If, for example, you walk into a meeting feeling stressed out (coming from a place of panic), you'll be more likely to have a negative experience. Because you're feeling panicked, you're more likely to find your co-workers annoying. You may also feel impatient, counting the seconds until the meeting is over. You're also less likely to have creative ideas to contribute to the discussion.

While that meeting may never qualify as exciting no matter what you do, you'll experience it differently if you arrive feeling relaxed and present (coming from a place of peace). Instead of noticing everything you don't like, you'll be more likely to engage with co-workers and contribute to the discussion. Things that might have annoyed won't seem as bothersome, and you'll be better able to absorb and integrate new information.

In other words, you'll show up differently because you're *feeling* better. By changing your mental and emotional state, which you can accomplish faster and more easily with Tapping, you're better able to show up as your greatest self.

It boils down to this:

. . . .

Changing how you're feeling transforms how you're being.

. . . .

To begin transforming how you're being, we'll look at the difference between how you want to feel and how you actually feel.

I WANT TO FEEL _____

Over the past couple of days, we've focused on telling the truth. That's our starting point once again.

Without overthinking it, complete these sentences, using *specific emotions* (angry, frustrated, afraid, excited, loving, etc.) and *avoiding* general, nonspecific words like *fine*, *okay*, and *good*:

Most often, I feel _____ in my body.

Most often, I feel _____ in my relationship(s).

Most often, I feel _____ about my family.

Most often, I feel _____ about my friends.

Most often, I feel _____ about my finances.

Most often, I feel _____ about my work/career.

Most often, I feel _____ about/in my life.

Take a deep breath, and focus next on how you would like to feel as a result of this journey. Again, without thinking too much and making sure to use specific feeling words, complete as many of these sentences as you can:

I intend to feel _____ in my body.

I intend to feel _____ in my relationship(s).

I intend to feel _____ about my family.

I intend to feel _____ about my friends.

I intend to feel _____ about my finances.

I intend to feel _____ about my work/career.

I intend to feel _____ about/in my life.

If you feel stuck around filling in some or all these blanks, pick one and begin tapping through the points while asking yourself relevant questions. For instance, if you're unsure how you'd like to feel about your family, tap through the points while asking, *How would I like to feel about my family?* Keep tapping until you get more clarity.

If, even after tapping, you can't yet complete all these sentences, don't worry. There's plenty of time. Keep moving forward, and know that the answers will come.

MOVING YOUR BODY

In addition to tapping, one of the most powerful ways to get unstuck is to get up and move your body. Do jumping jacks, take a brisk walk around the neighborhood, try a little yoga, go to the gym, or head out for a run.

Moving your body has been shown to elevate mood, improve memory, boost creativity and problem solving, increase energy, and support more restful sleep, as well as slow down aging in the brain and body. So whether you're doubting your vision of your greatest self, or just feeling the blahs, get up and move!

NOT ANOTHER VISION BOARD

As we're telling the truth about how you feel now and envisioning how you'd like to feel as your greatest self, I can hear you secretly thinking—*another* vision?

Another journey inward?

As amazing as it is to see people committed to healing themselves, their lives, relationships, finances, and health, the truth is, a lot of us are tired, and maybe bored, as well.

We want results.

We don't want more techniques to improve ourselves. We don't want to get attached to another vision, only to watch it get swept away by competing priorities and overcrowded schedules.

Have you read other books and taken other courses, but still find yourself feeling unfulfilled?

Or maybe you've experienced gradual, incremental success, but feel frustrated that you haven't yet made that huge leap forward. Or maybe you're just sick and tired of trying to improve your life, period.

Look, I get it.

When you're not getting the results you hoped for, all the effort and time you dedicate to improving yourself and your life gets exhausting! The frustration we feel also turns into another reason to beat up on ourselves. We skip meditating or tapping, and we scold ourselves.

Or maybe it's taken a month to get to Day 8, and instead of congratulating yourself for returning to the journey, you silently berate yourself for being less committed than you'd hoped.

It's time to let this journey and Tapping be a source of peace—*without* the side serving of guilt, blame, and shame about how you're showing up. Whatever resistance you're feeling about this journey, before we move forward with creating your vision, let's do some tapping on clearing your emotional "slate" around personal development now.

CLEARING THE SLATE

Take a moment to be honest with yourself about how you feel about going on this journey. Do you believe you'll actually become your greatest self? Are you secretly wondering if Tapping is for you? Is it scary to dream and hope because you're afraid of being disappointed—again? Are you bored with books and courses that don't produce the results you hope for?

If it helps, write down your thoughts, and also notice the primary emotion you're feeling, whether it's boredom around personal development, fear of failing to become your greatest self, regret about not putting enough effort into previous programs, or something else altogether.

Once you're clear on the emotion, give it a number of intensity on a scale of 0 to 10.

Take three deep breaths.

We'll begin by tapping three times on the Karate Chop point.

KC *(repeat three times)*: Even though I feel so much <emotion> about personal development, I choose peace now.

Eyebrow: So much <emotion>

Side of Eye: Not another journey inward

Under Eye: Not more work to do on myself

Under Nose: I'm tired of trying to improve myself

Under Mouth: Bored with trying to up-level my life

Collarbone: All this <emotion>

Under Arm: I'm not sure I have the energy for this journey

Top of Head: I'm not sure I'll ever be my greatest self

Eyebrow: I'm not even sure what my greatest self is

Side of Eye: I'm not sure what my greatest self even means

Under Eye: I want to feel different

Under Nose: I want my life to feel different

Under Mouth: I don't know if it'll ever happen, though

Collarbone: I can let myself feel this <emotion> now

Under Arm: I can feel it fully

Top of Head: And I can let it go

Eyebrow: Letting go of this <emotion> now

Side of Eye: Releasing it from my body now

Under Eye: Releasing it from my mind now

Under Nose: I can feel at peace in my body now

Under Mouth: I don't need all the answers

Collarbone: I can feel present in this moment

Under Arm: Wherever I am in this journey, I can trust that I'm safe

Top of Head: Feeling at peace now

Take a deep breath, and check back in on how intensely you feel your primary emotion now. Rate it on a scale of 0 to 10. Keep tapping until you get the relief you desire.

ALIGNING WITH YOUR VISION

Now that we've cleared some of the resistance around taking this journey and crafting a vision of your greatest self, let's get back to your vision!

Read aloud the statements you wrote down about how you intend to feel as your greatest self. Notice which one emotion is most appealing, the one that's really calling to you right now.

For instance, maybe you're really craving a sense of safety around money, or more comfort in your body, or feeling more nurtured in your relationship.

(When you look at the flip side of this emotion, you'll also find the pain point in yourself and your life that you most want to heal.)

As you read and reread that one positive feeling statement, notice any resistance that comes up. When you imagine feeling this way you desire to feel, do you experience tension or clenching in your body? What emotions come up? Really notice how this being/feeling intention resonates with you physically and emotionally.

As fun as it can be to envision positive future outcomes and ways of being, most of us experience some opposition as well—emotions like fear, anxiety, and more. In order for your vision to be your anchor, it's important to take note of these different forms of resistance, and then use Tapping to release it. Once you do that, you can be more fully aligned with your intention.

That's what we'll do next.

FEELING AT PEACE WITH YOUR INTENTIONS

Focus on the resistance you experience around your intention. If it's a physical experience like tension, put your attention on that. If it's an emotion like fear of failing, focus on that.

Give your resistance a number of intensity on a scale of 0 to 10.

Take three deep breaths.

We'll begin by tapping three times on the Karate Chop point.

KC *(repeat three times)*: Even though I experience this resistance around my intention to <feeling intention>, I accept how I feel and choose to feel peace now.

Eyebrow: This <describe resistance>

Side of Eye: I can feel it

Under Eye: I feel it when I think about how I want to feel <feeling intention>

Under Nose: All this resistance

Under Mouth: I can feel <describe resistance>

Collarbone: It's in my mind

Under Arm: And I can feel it in my body

Top of Head: This <describe resistance>

Eyebrow: I feel it when I think about how I want to feel <feeling intention>

Side of Eye: Not sure if I can do this

Under Eye: Not sure if I'll really feel the way I want to feel

Under Nose: I want to feel <feeling intention>

Under Mouth: But I'm not sure it will happen

Collarbone: It's okay to feel unsure

Under Arm: I still really want to feel <feeling intention>

Top of Head: I can let go of this <describe resistance>

Eyebrow: Releasing this <describe resistance> now

Side of Eye: I can feel peaceful when I think of feeling <feeling intention>

Under Eye: I can choose peace when I think of feeling this way

Under Nose: It's safe to trust in this intention

Under Mouth: It's safe to feel safe when I think of feeling <feeling intention>

Collarbone: I choose peace when I think of feeling <feeling intention>

Under Arm: Feeling peace in my body now

Top of Head: Feeling peace in my mind now

Take a deep breath. Check back in on the intensity of your resistance, and give it a number on a scale of 0 to 10. Keep tapping until you feel the peace you desire.

For each feeling intention that really calls to you, use this process to release any resistance you experience along the way. If you need to tap through resistance multiple times during this process, don't worry! That's completely normal.

DAY 8 GREATEST SELF CHALLENGE: BEING INTENTIONAL

Remember how the Universe or God or your angels whispered in your ear that you are light, you are love?

Remember imagining beginning your day with that mission, that sense of deeply rooted purpose and passion?

Starting today, your challenge is to create and re-create that experience.

The feeling intentions you created in this chapter *are* your divine guidance. They are your sacred messages from your inner angels, your inner spirit guide, the divine spirit within you, whatever form it may take.

Your challenge, beginning today, is to stay true to that mission—to remind yourself each morning of your intention to feel this certain way. You can focus on one feeling intention, or pick no more than three to support you in moving forward throughout the remainder of this journey.

Each morning, as you wake up, read your feeling intention(s). Speak them to yourself in the shower. Write a note with these intentions and put it in your pocket or your wallet. Repeat these intentions to yourself throughout each day, noticing when you feel out of alignment with them, and when you feel more closely aligned with them.

Over and over and over again, return to these intentions. Let them anchor you. They are the very core of your new mission, should you choose to accept it.

You'll find the *Day 8 Tapping Meditation: Aligning with Your Intentions* on page 266 of the Appendix.

Make sure also to take those few seconds right now to add Day 9 to your schedule. If tomorrow feels too soon, acknowledge and accept that. Pick a different day that works better.

We're heading into an important leg of our journey, so write into your calendar: "Read Day 9! Major relief starting today!"

Day 9

Where Are Your Energy Leaks?

Let's imagine that you wake up every morning with a full "tank" of energy inside you. That tank contains the exact amount of energy you have at your disposal for the day. Once your tank is at zero, you're forced to surrender until the next day or borrow from future energy reserves.

Think about that for a minute.

Knowing that you have that same fixed amount of energy available to you each day, how would you use it? How are you using it today? Are you spending it mindfully or accidentally letting it leak out?

These are questions we tend to brush aside until it's too late. Usually it's when we feel mentally, physically, and emotionally depleted that we stop and wonder, *Where did my energy go?* By then, though, our mental, emotional, and physical energy is sapped.

We're empty, cooked, toast.

On other days that may look similar on a calendar, we have a different experience. Instead of feeling spent, we feel ready and able to take on the rest of the day.

Why is that? Why, on some days, do we feel depleted before the day is done, and on other days, do we feel ready to move through the remainder of the day?

Where is our energy going?

During the first week of this journey, we began looking at ways to go from a place of panic to a place of peace. Starting today, we begin looking at the past, including patterns we've developed over the years and how they impact the ways we show up in our daily lives.

FINDING THE LEAKS

We've all lived through "those days" hundreds of times. Even if we wake up feeling fine, the day somehow gets away from us, and we inevitably end up feeling pulled in too many directions. We're worn out, tired to the bone.

Why is that?

Where are we leaking energy, and how can we repair those leaks?

Oftentimes the biggest and most pervasive leaks happen when we hold on to the past.

Because it's often difficult to pinpoint which emotions or issues from the past are the leakiest, the easiest starting point is often with our current daily patterns. Let's take a quick look at how one leaky pattern might play out on a given day:

You wake up feeling pretty good, set on having a pleasant, productive day.
　　Soon afterward you get a text message or e-mail from your mother, your boss, your ex, or your client—someone who triggers you often and easily. After reading it, you feel stressed and upset. Without thinking about it, you begin to mentally write and rewrite the "perfect" reply.
　　By the time your day is in full swing, you've lost sight of your goals and intentions for the day, and instead begin reacting to what's happening around you.

You soon fall behind in your to-do list, arrive late to meetings or appointments, and then have to skip your midday workout to make up what you didn't get done in the morning.

You then spend most of the day rushing from one task to the next, which causes you to forget to tap. And in spite of your considerable effort to get caught up, you get a lot less done than you'd intended, which creates more stress, which causes even more energy to leak out.

By the time your day is done, you're exhausted. You have little patience left for loved ones, and no interest in cooking, so you eat out in spite of your vow to eat out less often in order to save more money.

By bedtime the day feels like a total flop, and all you can do is hope tomorrow will be better. It's been "one of those days."

What's most frustrating about a day like this is that most of us are aware of the pattern that derailed it.

We *know* that the text message or e-mail started the day off on the "wrong foot." We *know* we need to change the pattern in that particular relationship. We *know* we need to stop letting this person treat us in certain ways, and so on. We *know* that this same pattern has been playing out for months, years, even decades. Whatever the issue is, we're fully aware of it—yet it keeps happening!

We may even be vaguely aware of the domino effect this pattern creates in our lives. Because of this pattern, we suffer emotionally and get less done (because we're distracted by our emotions).

We also push aside our physical well-being (by skipping exercise), our mental/emotional wellness (by forgetting to tap), our relationships (by being irritable, impatient, and so on), and sometimes our finances (by making choices from a place of panic and exhaustion).

In my first book, *The Tapping Solution: A Revolutionary System for Stress-Free Living*, I discuss these patterns in detail:

I don't have to be a psychic to know that you have been running the same patterns, sometimes with little change, for your whole life. I don't have to even meet you to guess that you are frustrated with doing the same things

over and over again—and, as can be expected, getting the same results.

You've probably said to yourself countless times, "Oh, I can't believe I did that again!"

"Why did I say that to him . . . again?"

"Why did I eat that food . . . again?"

"Why did I skip exercising . . . again?"

"Why am I short on money . . . again?"

"Why am I frustrated [or angry, lost, overwhelmed, anxious, tired, or whatever your 'thing' is] . . . again?"

And I'm being easy on the language here. It's likely you're not as kind to yourself. Most of us add in a $*@%# or two!

On top of your negative thinking and behavior, there's the fact that you are trying to improve. And yet . . . you're still not getting the results you want. It adds insult to injury!

It would be one thing if you were unaware of your patterns and behaviors. But you are!

And yet they keep running. As we'll explore, much of your current behavior actually started before you were several years old! And it was learned from parents, teachers, society, and friends.[1]

The longer these patterns run, the more energy they tend to take from us. After repeating themselves many, many times, these patterns also create a convincing illusion that we're unable to control how and when they play out.

Fortunately with Tapping, we can take back that power, first by noticing our patterns and then by transforming them. Tapping is so powerful in helping us overcome old leaky patterns because it involves the *real* captain of the ship—the unconscious mind, also known as the *primitive brain.*

Bringing the *primitive brain* into the process is critical because even when your conscious mind wants to change, your unconscious mind is programmed to resist it.

And as we've seen, your unconscious mind will resist change *even when that change is desirable* and *even when that change is good for you.*

With Tapping, you can quiet the unconscious mind's resistance to change. You're then free to create positive change, transforming past patterns that are probably robbing you of more energy than you realize.

ON BEING HUMAN

Before we look at your leaky patterns and how to use Tapping to transform them, let me take a minute to confess something. It's a basic truth we all have in common, but it's also one we too often fault ourselves for. You ready?

Here goes . . .

I'm human.

Flawed.

Imperfect.

I work hard and mean well, but I make mistakes sometimes. I occasionally make choices I regret. I still have some patterns I'd like to change but haven't taken the time to tap on.

Did you get that last part?

I spend my days tapping with people, writing books on tapping, but I don't always tap on my own patterns when I know I need to.

Like I said, I'm human. Flawed. Imperfect.

As confessions go, this one may not seem groundbreaking.

In fact, if you're rolling your eyes, saying, "Duh, Nick," that's understandable! Nonetheless, this whole being human "thing" is something we're taught to feel ashamed of. We fall back into our old leaky patterns and then make matters worse by shaming and blaming ourselves for not "fixing" them yet.

Sadly, that guilt, blame, and shame—whichever negative emotions you tend to inflict on yourself—then make the pattern leak even *more* energy. By getting

down on ourselves for having these patterns, we're literally draining ourselves of energy we need to overcome the patterns themselves!

The fact is, we *all* have messy, imperfect patterns. We all mishandle these patterns sometimes, pushing them away or ignoring them when we'd be better served by healing them.

That's okay.

We're all spiritual beings having a human experience. Nothing's perfect. Nor are we.

Even as I write this book, I have messy patterns, like my mornings, that I need to heal. I'm working on it, but it's a process, and the first step of that process is choosing self-acceptance and self-love—even when you catch yourself diving headfirst, yet again, into that same old leaky pattern.

So before we begin identifying some of the leaky patterns you may be running, let's do a few rounds of positive tapping on feeling more at peace with yourself.

CHOOSING SELF-ACCEPTANCE AND SELF-LOVE

To begin, take three deep breaths.

Start by tapping three times on the Karate Chop point.

KC *(repeat three times)*: Even though I have these old leaky patterns, I love myself and accept myself as I am.

Eyebrow: These patterns

Side of Eye: They're ingrained in me

Under Eye: I should be over them by now

Under Nose: I shouldn't still be falling into them

Under Mouth: But I do

Collarbone: I still stumble into these old, familiar, leaky patterns

Under Arm: I don't like that it happens

Top of Head: But it happens

Eyebrow: And that's okay

Side of Eye: I accept myself with these patterns

Under Eye: I love myself with these patterns

Under Nose: It's safe to notice the emotions buried in these patterns

Under Mouth: I can begin to hear the limiting beliefs that fuel these patterns

Collarbone: And I can love myself throughout it all

Under Arm: There's no shame in having these patterns

Top of Head: They're part of my human experience

Eyebrow: I can look at them with new awareness

Side of Eye: Without guilt or shame or self-criticism

Under Eye: I can see these patterns with new eyes

Under Nose: And I can love myself throughout the entire process

Under Mouth: I can accept myself throughout my entire experience

Collarbone: It's safe to love and accept myself now

Under Arm: Letting myself relax

Top of Head: Choosing to feel peace now

Take a deep breath, and keep tapping until you get the desired relief. Use your own words or repeat the same rounds.

WHERE ARE YOUR PRESSURE POINTS?

When we talk about noticing leaky patterns, we're basically looking at the parts of your life where you consistently feel emotional heaviness and pressure.

Keep in mind that pressure isn't always a bad thing. For example, if you're working hard to meet a deadline for a project that you're excited about, you may feel pressure. That pressure might be exhausting at times, but it also motivates you to do your best.

That pressure is also self-contained, since once your deadline is met, you get to take a big sigh of relief. That's one example of how pressure can be positive, helping you be your greatest self.

In other areas of your life, however, you may feel a persistent pressure that depletes your energy tank more than it fills it. Those are the pressure points we'll be identifying and tapping on next.

Note: This is a great exercise to do on paper or record digitally, so grab a device or pen and paper before you begin.

Take three deep breaths, and envision the start of an average day. Imagine your tank filled to the top with energy.

Ask yourself, *What's the first thing that drains my energy?*

For example, do you get up feeling overtired from poor sleep?

Do you feel frustrated trying to get your children out of bed in time for school?

Do you feel depleted by physical symptoms, like chronic pain, digestive distress, or something else?

Are you stressed about a work deadline, what mood your boss will be in today, or an argument you had with your partner or a family member?

Do you feel overwhelmed by how much time you have to fill and stressed about how to use that time?

Are you grieving the loss of a loved one, marriage, or other elements of your past?

Note what drains you first, and guesstimate how much energy it takes from you. Does it take 5 percent of your energy? Ten percent? Or more?

Write it down.

Go through the entire day, continuing to take note what drains you of energy and how much energy each one takes. (If it helps, you can assume that your full tank contains 100 units of energy and then subtract units for each leak you notice while navigating your day.)

Also consider what thoughts and memories rob you of energy.

For instance, do you often feel guilty about not exercising or meditating?

Do you have unresolved emotions around your marriage, partnership, or lack thereof?

Does a certain friend or family member drain your energy more than most?

Do you worry about money most days?

With these questions in mind, go through the day, noting each person, place, and event (past and present) that drains you, and how much energy each one takes.

When you get to the end of that day, how much energy do you have left? Are you looking at a negative number?

> **Remember This!** There are no right or wrong, good or bad answers here. Ending your day with a negative number doesn't mean you're "broken." This exercise is creating a deeper awareness of the patterns that are causing your energy to leak out.
>
> The point is to notice your patterns while trying *not* to drain your energy further by adding shame, blame, guilt, and other negative emotions onto your list.
>
> In other words, try not to stress about your stress!

As you look through your list, notice which two items drain the most energy.

Add the two energy numbers together. That's the amount of additional energy you'll have at your disposal *every single day* once you relieve these pressure points!

SEEING THE STORY

When we look at our leakiest patterns, those pressure points that eventually turn into energy leaks, there's one thing we all have in common. We have a *lot* to say about them!

For example, if one of your biggest leaky patterns is hating your job, I can almost guarantee that as soon as I mention it, you'll have a story to tell about why you hate it, how your boss plays into that hatred, how your job makes you feel, what you believe to be true about it, and on and on.

You may also talk about feeling trapped because you need the income, and believe that you can't do anything else. That feeling of being trapped makes you feel resentful, which makes doing the actual job you hate even more painful.

And then there's that client you have to work with, and also that co-worker who always criticizes you when the boss is around . . .

Like I said, we all have big stories to tell around our leakiest patterns!

These patterns, or pressure points, often have a long history. Some of them may be tied to childhood, repressed emotions, and limiting beliefs we took on at a young age.

While there's no need to map out every element right now—we'll do that gradually during this journey—keep in mind that these patterns, and the larger stories they're connected to, often run deep.

In this exercise you'll use Tapping to tell the story around your leakiest pressure point.

Look back at your list of energy leaks for the day, and focus on the number one biggest energy leak.

When you think about that pressure point in your life, notice the emotions that come up.

Also notice any events or memories that come to mind.

Finally, take note of any limiting beliefs that may be associated with this energy drain.

For example, let's say communicating with your ex about your children is taking 20 percent (or 20 units) of your energy most days.

When you think about communicating with your ex, what emotion comes up most intensely?

Do you feel angry, afraid, sad, ashamed?

Are there specific events around communicating with your ex that stand out?

Are there limiting beliefs related to this pattern?

For instance, do you believe she or he will always get under your skin, or that you'll always clash with him or her, and so on?

These are all elements of your story around this pattern. Next you'll tap while telling this story.

RELEASING THE STORY

Now that you're aware of this story bubbling inside you, let's give it what it wants—airtime!

You can begin telling your story from the beginning or from your present experience around it. Keep in mind—your story doesn't need to make sense to anyone but you. Your goal is to tell it as you tap through the points.

For instance, if your story around communicating with your ex begins with the text message he or she sent you this morning, start your story with that text. Tell the story of what the text said, how it makes you feel, what other events it reminds you of, and so on. As you tell it, you may rewind to past events, which is great. Roll with it.

Here are general guidelines for tapping through a story:

- Make a point of adding in as many sensory experiences—sights, sounds, feelings—as you remember.

- Tap on the emotions that this event made you feel at the time (if you remember), as well as the emotion(s) it evokes in you now.

- Don't worry about how you tell the story; just tap as the event(s) comes back to you, making your story as detailed as you can. There's no "right" or "wrong" way to tell your story, so don't worry about story chronology, structure, and so on.

Before you begin tapping, first notice how emotionally charged your story around this leaky pattern feels, and then give it a number of intensity on a scale of 0 to 10.

Take three deep breaths.

Starting with the Karate Chop point, be as honest as you can, telling the complete story of what happened as you begin tapping through the points.

Karate Chop . . . Eyebrow . . . Side of Eye . . . Under Eye . . . Under Nose . . . Under Mouth . . . Collarbone . . . Under Arm . . . Top of Head . . .

Karate Chop . . . Eyebrow . . . Side of Eye . . . Under Eye . . . Under Nose . . . Under Mouth . . . Collarbone . . . Under Arm . . . Top of Head . . .

Karate Chop . . . Eyebrow . . . Side of Eye . . . Under Eye . . . Under Nose . . . Under Mouth . . . Collarbone . . . Under Arm . . . Top of Head . . .

Continue telling your story around this leaky pressure point as you tap:

Karate Chop . . . Eyebrow . . . Side of Eye . . . Under Eye . . . Under Nose . . . Under Mouth . . . Collarbone . . . Under Arm . . . Top of Head . . .

Karate Chop . . . Eyebrow . . . Side of Eye . . . Under Eye . . . Under Nose . . . Under Mouth . . . Collarbone . . . Under Arm . . . Top of Head . . .

Karate Chop . . . Eyebrow . . . Side of Eye . . . Under Eye . . . Under Nose . . . Under Mouth . . . Collarbone . . . Under Arm . . . Top of Head . . .

Continue tapping through the story for as long as you need to in order to lower the emotional charge you feel around it.

When you're ready, retell your story from beginning to end. Has the emotional charge gone down?

Rate the emotional intensity again on a scale of 0 to 10.

Once you can tell and retell the story around this leaky pattern without experiencing the original emotional intensity that story caused, you know you've released it.

Don't worry about how long this process takes. You may be able to release some of the stories around your leaky patterns in five minutes, while other stories may take repeated tapping over a period of days or weeks to release fully. The length of time doesn't matter, as long as you continue tapping until the story is fully released.

DAY 9 GREATEST SELF CHALLENGE: NOTICING KEY PATTERNS

You know that moment when you sit down after giving a presentation, walk offstage after a speech, successfully meet a deadline, or pass some other important milestone?

It's that amazing moment when all the pressure you felt leading up to it suddenly dissipates. You did it, and at long last your brain is telling your body to relax. *Ahhhhh!*

That's the experience you'll likely have as I guide you through the next several days. To get there, you're going to need to see and feel the pressure. You're going to have to tap through it. And you're going to feel an *incredible* sense of relief as you do.

To kick it off, your challenge, starting today, is to focus on the one pattern you identified as your biggest energy leak. Every time you notice this pattern playing out in your day, stop and tap.

Even if you can only tap for two minutes, carve out that time and tap on the story you need to tell around this pattern. Continue tapping on it as often as you need to.

This simple habit of noticing your pattern and tapping on releasing your story around it is freeing up energy, bringing you closer to peace, and creating more space and time for your greatest self to emerge.

Just think about the enormous relief and relaxation you'll feel once that "extra" energy is liberated from your old leaky pattern!

Take a few minutes now to complete the *Day 9 Tapping Meditation: Letting Go.* You can find it on page 269 of the Appendix.

◉ ◉ ◉

Keep up with the great progress! You're shedding and releasing what no longer serves your greatest self. There's more relief on the way, so make sure also to take 60 seconds right now to add Day 10 to your calendar.

Yep, we're still looking at the past, but you may surprise yourself and appreciate how amazing it feels to *finally* have that emotional weight off your back.

I know looking at the past may not be your favorite pastime.

Totally get that.

Here's the thing, though . . . as long as you do the tapping, clearing the mental and emotional "gunk" from the past is the quickest, most direct path toward your greatest self and your greatest life.

And here's the amazing part—you're doing it!

Give yourself a sincere, heartfelt pat on the back. You've earned it.

Keep tapping and know that you can do it.

And one other thought . . . while this book is laid out in a linear way, this won't necessarily be a linear process for you. You might have to go back to one day, or skip a day when it doesn't feel right, or do one day three times. Listen to your gut and intuition, and know you're doing great!

Day 10

Letting Go of the Past

Dr. Vincent Felitti was shocked.

After years of hard work, it was suddenly obvious that the research study he and his team had conducted was, by conventional standards, a flop. After a promising start, the study had taken an abrupt turn. In the end it would fail to meet its original objective.

But, then, amazing things often happen in surprising ways. And it was clear to Dr. Felitti that this failure was leading toward a much bigger, more important discovery.

As the founder of the Department of Preventive Medicine at Kaiser Permanente, Felitti had dedicated his career to helping patients lower their health risk. Through that work, he had become interested in solving obesity, which would prevent a long list of health complications and help people live longer, healthier lives.

The research study that he and his team conducted, which was originally intended to address obesity, had initially seemed like a huge success. When pa-

tients followed Felitti's weight-loss regimen, some lost as many as 300 pounds within a year.

The results seemed incredibly promising—until something unexpected happened. Many of the patients with the most significant weight loss regained all the weight within short periods of time.

Curious why this was happening, Dr. Felitti began asking questions.

Among the study participants was a 28-year-old woman who had come to Felitti's clinic a year earlier. She'd weighed 408 pounds at the time. Following Felitti's weight-loss regimen, she successfully lost 276 pounds in just 51 weeks. After maintaining that weight loss for several weeks, she rapidly regained all the weight.

When he asked her what had caused her to regain the weight, she hesitated before explaining that she'd been propositioned by an older man at work. He then asked why that event prompted weight gain. She shared that her grandfather had molested her from age 10 through age 21.

Felitti soon learned that 55 percent of the participants in his team's major obesity study had suffered sexual abuse in childhood. Many had also suffered other adverse experiences, including what he called heavy-duty physical abuse, as well as emotional abuse, neglect, loss of a parent/divorce, having a parent who suffered from addiction or was incarcerated, and more.

Stunned by the prevalence of these events, Felitti partnered with the Centers for Disease Control and Prevention to conduct a massive study of 17,421 predominantly middle-class adults. That study, known as the adverse childhood experiences (ACEs) study, shed new light on the connections between childhood experiences and adult health and wellness.

The study focused on 10 common categories of ACEs, and found that one in every six adults had suffered at least four of them.

A whopping 1 in every 11 adults experienced six or more of them. Adults with an ACE score of six or higher were also 4,600 percent more likely to become IV drug users and had a more than 3,000 percent increased risk for at-

tempting suicide. An ACE score of six or more also decreased the life span by more than 20 years.

How do these childhood experiences show up in our health and wellness decades later? The study points to two main factors.

First, adults with high ACE scores are more likely to turn to substances, food, and other behaviors to distract from the deep emotional pain they've felt for decades.

Second, the chronic major unrelieved stress caused by these experiences leads to increased levels of pro-inflammatory chemicals in the body that may contribute to disease, partly by suppressing the immune system.

Felitti summed it up:

What we found in the ACE study involving 17 and a half thousand middle-class adults was that life experiences in childhood that are lost in time, and then further protected by shame and by secrecy, and by social taboos against inquiry into certain realms of human experience, that those life experiences play out powerfully and proportionately a half century later in terms of emotional state, in terms of biomedical disease, in terms of life expectancy.[1]

In other words, the ACE study proved that time alone does *not* heal deep emotional wounds from childhood.

ACEs, all which qualify as trauma, take over the brain, controlling which neural connections are formed and not formed. These neural pathways then support destructive emotional patterns and behaviors.

As time goes by, the brain then becomes *more* deeply wired around childhood trauma, rather than less.

The longer I do the work that I do, tapping with clients, tapping with audiences, on radio shows, online, and beyond, the more convinced I am that the fundamental discovery of the study—that ACEs have a huge impact on our adult health and wellness—applies to everyone.

Regardless of your ACE score, and whether or not you had a "happy" childhood, in my experience nearly everyone has some, if not several, events from childhood that we need to clear before we're ready to step wholeheartedly into our greatest selves.

Today we rewind to those early years to heal old wounds and clear emotional stress we may have been carrying for decades.

Ready to experience deep and lasting relief?

UGH! ICK! ANYTHING *BUT* THE PAST!

Before we go any further, let me first acknowledge how normal and understandable it is to feel resistance, such as anxiety, panic, physical symptoms (pain, headache, fatigue, and so on), avoidance, and so forth, at the idea of looking at the past.

I mean, it's over, right?

Can't we just stuff it down?

Run it over with a dump truck?

Tempting, I know, but the enormous relief that awaits you is simply too amazing and too important to overlook.

So if you're feeling any form of resistance around looking at your own history, stick with me.

Give that resistance a number of intensity on a scale of 0 to 10.

Take three deep breaths. We'll begin tapping on the Karate Chop point.

KC *(repeat three times)*: Even though I don't want to look at the past, it's too much and I'm sick of it, I choose to feel safe now.

Eyebrow: All this stuff from the past
Side of Eye: Why won't it go away?

Under Eye: I'm sick of dwelling in the past

Under Nose: But it's still with me

Under Mouth: I can feel it in my mind and body

Collarbone: All these emotions from the past

Under Arm: These past events I can't seem to get rid of

Top of Head: They've left a mark on my brain

Eyebrow: I can't seem to get past my past

Side of Eye: It's still with me

Under Eye: I want to get beyond it

Under Nose: I want to be free of my past

Under Mouth: But I don't know if I'll ever be

Collarbone: It's so frustrating

Under Arm: It's okay to feel this way

Top of Head: I can choose peace even when I resist looking at my past

Eyebrow: All this stuff from the past

Side of Eye: It's been with me for so long

Under Eye: I can let myself feel this resistance to looking at my past

Under Nose: And I can let this resistance go

Under Mouth: I can release my resistance to looking at the past

Collarbone: I can feel peace when I think about looking at the past

Under Arm: Feeling quiet and calm in my body now

Top of Head: Choosing to feel peace around looking at my past

Take a deep breath. Again rate the intensity of your resistance to looking at the past. Keep tapping until you experience a greater level of peace.

MEET "BIG *T*" AND "LITTLE *T*"

I was seven years old, and my family had recently moved from Argentina to the United States.

I was new to Connecticut, new to my school, new to our home. The people, the language, the culture—everything felt strange. While I was (and still am!) incredibly fortunate to have a loving, supportive family, during that time, I was stressed and sad about being thousands of miles away from extended family and friends.

To make matters worse, I hated my new school.

To be clear, I *really* hated it—so much so that one morning I decided to boycott.

Once the car was parked in the school parking lot, I waited for everyone to vacate and then promptly locked myself inside. Sitting inside the car, I stared straight ahead, ignoring my great-aunt's desperate pleas from outside (she'd driven me to school that day—lucky her!).

I was determined not to go to school that day.

At this point in my life, I honestly don't remember that morning in detail, but I've heard the story enough times to feel as if I do.

By all accounts, I'd struggled with the transition to a new country. Fortunately, a couple of months later, my parents moved me to a different school. I loved it, quickly made friends, and soon felt right at home in our new life.

While that challenging period of time ended fairly quickly, that move, for me, started out as an ACE. Although that experience may not factor into my ACE score, it has likely stayed with me in some way. It may have even influenced my decision to live my adult life close to my childhood home.

Most of us lived through similarly challenging times in childhood.

Some of us survived trauma.

These experiences leave a mark on our brains, although to varying degrees. My move to the United States is what we call "little *t*" trauma. This category of experience covers a wide range, from moving to being bullied, neglected temporarily, having a critical teacher, a harsh coach, and more.

Major trauma, also called "Big *T*" trauma, has an undeniably more intense impact on health and well-being, as well as the brain. All kinds of abuse, neglect, extreme poverty, losing a parent, suffering disease, surviving natural disaster (earthquake, tsunami, mass shootings, and so on) are examples of "Big *T*" trauma.

What often happens is, without our conscious awareness, post-traumatic stress accumulates over time. Similar to how a glass eventually overflows if we continue to pour water in it, multiple "little *t*" and "Big *T*" traumas, even when they occur over a span of many years, will eventually cause our internal "glass" to overflow.

In other words, once our capacity for post-traumatic stress is exceeded, our brains operate at a higher level of stress across the board, or when certain memories or patterns in our life get triggered.

Have you ever attended a holiday family gathering and found yourself reeling backward, suddenly consumed by emotions around an event that happened when you were seven or eight?

It can be shocking how raw and real those memories still feel!

How, then, can we move forward once and for all?

Unless and until we create more space within our internal "glass," even when we don't consciously realize it, we can get stuck in unresolved emotional stress from painful childhood events.

THE ADAPTABLE ORGAN

What would your brain look and act like if all you did was think?

If you could barely move your body, weren't allowed to go anywhere or interact with anyone, how might your brain change?

Curious to find out, researchers looked at prisoners of war (POWs) who were kept in isolation for months and years at a time.

Since all these POWs could do during their isolated imprisonment was think, many developed incredible cognitive powers. Some trained themselves to quickly complete complex math equations entirely in their heads.

Another designed and built a house, board by board and nail by nail, completely in his mind. Once he was able to return home, he built that exact house.

In unimaginably bleak, often terrifying and traumatic circumstances, these POWs defied the odds and strengthened their brains in exceptionally powerful, positive ways.[2]

The news we've gotten so far about the brain and ACEs may seem bleak. The fact is, we *can't* rewind the clock and undo what happened in childhood.

Ready for the good news?

As you may recall, your brain, which is the driving force behind your health, wellness, and longevity, is *neuroplastic*, meaning that it can reorganize itself. In other words, it can change and create new neural connections that have an equally dramatic positive impact on health, well-being, and emotions, as well as mental abilities.

Because Tapping gets to the heart of the stress response, quieting the "primitive brain" that gets excessively activated by trauma and stress, it supports positive transformation in the brain at a faster rate than conventional "talk" therapy.

By using Tapping to release unresolved emotions, memories, and experiences from childhood, you give your brain a chance to reorganize around new, much more positive realities. In other words, with Tapping, you can begin to rewire the brain in ways that support your greatest self, rather than hinder and smother it.

ON "BIG T" TRAUMA

If you've suffered from "Big *T*" trauma, whether in childhood or adulthood, I highly recommend that you seek out a Tapping practitioner who can help you work through your experiences.

Tapping is one of the most powerful post-traumatic stress disorder (PTSD) treatment practices available, and a certified professional (many psychologists and psychiatrists have integrated it into their practices) can guide you through a healing process that doesn't require you to revisit the past in ways that feel intrusive or harmful.[3]

For a list of EFT practitioners, visit http://thetappingsolution.com/eft-prac titioners/.

To restore a sense of calm and safety in the present moment, you may also want to tap through the *All Is Well Tapping Meditation* script, which you'll find on page 308.

RELEASING A PAST EVENT

Although I don't remember that day when I locked my great-aunt out of the car, I've tapped on those early months of our move several times over the years. I haven't always experienced a huge shift, but I have sensed that the tapping has freed up energy. It's felt good to acknowledge and release the imprint of that time in my childhood.

That's our goal with the tapping we're about to do—to release an event from childhood that has gotten stuck inside you.

Take a moment now to focus on a childhood event you'd like to release.

Oftentimes, it's easiest to begin with a smaller event, like a critical comment from a teacher or coach, for example. You can also choose to focus on a more significant event, but only if it feels safe to do so.

Note: If, at any point, you feel extremely overwhelmed while tapping on the past, stop and breathe, tap on releasing your panic response, and wait to tap on that event with a qualified professional.

If you can't recall a specific childhood event, you can focus on a challenging period of time, including something as broad as puberty, middle school, and so forth.

You can also focus on repeat experiences from childhood, such as feeling left out socially or coming home from school to an empty house and having no one to talk to.

To begin, notice the emotions you experience when you focus on the event(s). Does the memory make you feel sad, lonely, angry, or something else?

This time, instead of rating the overall emotional charge of your story, focus on the specific, primary emotion(s) this story evokes. Give it a number of intensity on a scale of 0 to 10.

To clear this event, you'll tap through the points while telling the story of the event(s). Once again, here are general guidelines for tapping through a story:

- Make a point of adding in as many sensory experiences—sights, sounds, feelings—as you remember.

- Also tap on the emotions that this event made you feel at the time (if you remember), as well as the emotion(s) it evokes in you now.

- Don't worry about how you tell the story; just tap as the event(s) comes back to you, making your story as detailed as you can. There's no "right" or "wrong" way to tell your story, so don't worry about story chronology, structure, and so on.

- If, as you tap, your primary emotion shifts to a different one, notice that emotion and tap on feeling and releasing it.

Before you start tapping, take three deep breaths.

We'll begin by tapping three times on the Karate Chop point as you begin your story.

Keep telling your story as you tap through the rest of the points. You can speak it out loud, or just silently. If it comes up as a movie, just watch it. Whichever way feels natural to you.

Karate Chop . . . Eyebrow . . . Side of Eye . . . Under Eye . . . Under Nose . . . Under Mouth . . . Collarbone . . . Under Arm . . . Top of Head . . .

Karate Chop . . . Eyebrow . . . Side of Eye . . . Under Eye . . . Under Nose . . . Under Mouth . . . Collarbone . . . Under Arm . . . Top of Head . . .

Karate Chop . . . Eyebrow . . . Side of Eye . . . Under Eye . . . Under Nose . . . Under Mouth . . . Collarbone . . . Under Arm . . . Top of Head . . .

Continue tapping through the points until you've finished telling your story.

When you're ready, retell your story from beginning to end.

If, at any point in that retelling, you experience additional emotional charge, stop and tap through that part of the story until you feel relief.

Then when you're ready, begin the story again from the beginning.

Repeat this process until you can tell the entire story of the event(s) without experiencing emotional charge.

DAY 10 GREATEST SELF CHALLENGE: RELEASING THE PAST

Ugh. Not again.

That's the feeling a lot of us have when faced with the prospect of looking at the past. We'd prefer painful memories to just go away.

Your challenge, starting today, is to give yourself that gift. Using Tapping, you can finally let go of the past and the emotional pain it has caused you.

It's time to open up to this opportunity and heal old wounds for good.

By tapping on childhood events, you'll allow yourself the chance to step wholly and powerfully into your greatest self. Without these heavy emotional burdens, you'll have more energy and a new awareness of what's possible for you now and in the future.

Tapping on the past isn't about clearing it all at once. Most often it's a longer process, and little bits of tapping here and there can go a long, long way over time.

If you find yourself remembering events that feel overwhelming, tap on that overwhelm first and foremost. When you're ready, you can then tap through the event itself, but again, let it be a process, and don't ever force yourself to go "there" if it feels like too much.

Trust yourself and let the process unfold in its own time.

You can find the *Day 10 Tapping Meditation: Feeling Safe Releasing the Past* on page 272 of the Appendix.

◎ ◎ ◎

And look, I know we're covering a lot here, and you may be feeling a little worn-out. Take your time—there's no rush—but please do add Day 11 to your calendar now.

On Day 11 we dive even deeper into the primitive brain and use Tapping to release deep-seated fears. In the process, you'll experience big relief and even bigger *aha!* moments about why you sometimes act and react in certain ways.

Day 11

A Possum, a Polar Bear, and a Rabbit: Understanding the Freeze Response

It's a heartbreaking sight.

By all appearances, the polar bear, the rabbit, and the possum are dead. Their eyes are open, but their gazes are completely still. When a human approaches and moves their limbs, even rolling their entire bodies from side to side, none of the animals react. Their bodies are stiff, as if in rigor mortis.

Seconds turn into a minute, maybe longer, but still no visible signs of life.

With no warning, the polar bear's body begins to twitch, then shake. His eyes still appear fixed, as if in a trance. The shaking grows more intense. The bear's mouth begins making small biting movements, and his paws appear to be scratching at something. This enormous, powerful animal seems to be fighting off some kind of attack, yet he lies on his back, biting and clawing at thin air.

The shaking soon overtakes the bear's entire body. His massive frame convulses continuously, as if acting out his instinctive desire to fight back against attack.

It's quite a sight watching this animal in the throes of what seems like a seizure. Yet it's unclear exactly what's happening or what's coming next.

Will he "come to" when we least expect it?

Will he jump up and attack for real?

Will he return to a nonresponsive state?

It's impossible to tell.

His body's shaking and convulsing slow down, then stop. He takes a few deep inhalations and exhalations that appear purposeful as well as effective. Seconds later, the bear rises to his feet, resuming his normal stride without any indication of physical or mental damage.

Similarly, the possum and rabbit also lying on their backs, paws extended up in the air, their bodies completely still.

Without warning, their bodies begin to twitch. Each animal then rolls onto its stomach, gets up, and scurries away. Again, there is no sign that they've been hurt. In fact, they seem perfectly fine, as if the entire episode never happened.

Have you ever heard the expression "playing possum"?

When animals in the wild are threatened by predators but unable to fight or flee, some are known to play dead.

Also known as the *freeze response*, this reaction to trauma is a powerful survival technique. Some predators require a chase and/or fight to stimulate their hunger, and in its absence, they simply lose interest. By playing possum, potential prey are able to survive situations that would otherwise lead to certain death.

Once the need for playing possum has passed—the predator has lost interest and wandered off—animals literally shake off the trauma they've survived. This process of releasing the aftereffects of trauma from their bodies prevents long-term damage to their mental, emotional, and physical states.

The freeze response is an equally instinctive survival technique in humans when we feel powerless against attack, whether that attack is physical or emo-

tional. Unfortunately, unless and until we shake the trauma off, or release the trauma from the body and "primitive brain," we remain stuck, to varying degrees, in a traumatized state.

Yesterday we looked at releasing painful events from childhood. Today we move that process further along by examining where in your life you feel frozen, unable to take action, make changes, and/or show up as you want and expect to.

If you don't immediately recognize the freeze response in yourself, stay with me. It often takes a little digging around to notice the role it's playing in your life.

THE "FROZEN" BRAIN

It was a nice morning in September 1999 when Stan Fisher and Ute Lawrence, a professional couple in their 40s, set out to drive from their home in Ontario, Canada, to a business meeting in Detroit.

About halfway into their journey, visibility was suddenly reduced to zero by a wall of dense fog. Unable to see in front of the car, Stan hit the brakes, narrowly avoiding an enormous truck. Their car soon came to a standstill sideways on the highway.

The next several seconds were a blur of screeching and crashing sounds, some coming from their own car being hit and then jolted repeatedly in several directions.

Stan and Ute's car was number 13 in an 87-car pileup, the worst road disaster in Canadian history.

Following the deafening cacophony was an eerie silence. As soon as the car stopped moving, Stan sprang into action, desperately trying to open doors and windows. Nearby cars caught on fire, and both Stan and Ute heard people screaming for their lives. Neither could help, as they themselves were trapped inside their car, which was partially wedged underneath an 18-wheeler.

Eventually someone reached their car, fire extinguisher in hand, and smashed Stan and Ute's front windshield. After being lifted out, Stan reached in

to help Ute, who sat paralyzed in her seat, unable to move or speak. Eventually both of them were taken by ambulance to the hospital, where they were examined. Their cuts and bruises were bandaged, and both were deemed otherwise physically unharmed.

Three years passed before Stan and Ute sought out help for their recurring PTSD symptoms, which included difficulty sleeping, irritability, and increased alcohol intake to numb their painful memories.

To begin their trauma recovery treatment, Stan's and Ute's brains were scanned separately. Stan went first. As he was prompted to recall sights, sounds, and smells from the crash, he went into a full-fledged flashback. His brain quickly became overly activated in areas associated with fleeing and fighting. His heart also began to race, his body perspired, and his blood pressure rose to dangerously high levels.

Ute's brain scan showed something different altogether. Upon being prompted to recall sensory experiences from the crash, her brain showed decreased activity; it essentially went quiet. Her heart rate also slowed down. She didn't sweat or show any bodily signs of fleeing or fighting.

Both Stan and Ute were stuck in the trauma they'd survived, but each was having a different experience. While Stan's body went into an immediate, extreme fight-or-flight response, Ute froze. Her mind went blank, and her body was rendered immobile.

Ute's freeze response, her trauma therapists learned, dated back to early childhood. After Ute's father died when she was very young, Ute had been forced to live with her mother, a harsh and hypercritical woman. As a young child, Ute's only defense was to numb out and disappear mentally and emotionally from her circumstances. When faced with trauma as an adult, Ute reenacted this same response.

When the old brain takes over, it partially shuts down the higher brain, our conscious mind, and propels the body to run, hide, fight, or, on occasion, freeze . . . If for some reason the normal response is blocked—for example, when people are held down, trapped or otherwise prevented from effective action . . . the brain keeps secreting stress chemicals, and

114

the brain's electrical circuits continue to fire in vain. Long after the actual event has passed, the brain may keep sending signals to the body to escape a threat that no longer exists.[1]

Since the freeze response is most likely to happen when we feel powerless, it's especially common in children, including in situations that aren't life threatening. Lack of affection, harsh treatment, excessive punishment, and more can all *feel* traumatic to a child. The "primitive brain" then responds as if the situation is life threatening. Since fighting or fleeing often isn't possible for children, they're most likely to resort to the freeze response.

As adults this freeze response can play out in many different parts of our lives, preventing us from speaking out, being our true selves, confronting those who have betrayed us, responding to conflict, and more. The freeze response can also contribute to self-defeating behavior, including various forms of self-sabotage. It can also hold us back from making important life changes that we know we need to make . . . but somehow never do.

It's only when we release the freeze response on a somatic (body) level that we're able to move past it.

THAWING OUT

Whereas the polar bear, possum, and rabbit all instinctively understand that they have to release trauma from the bodies, often by trembling or shaking, as humans we're encouraged to numb out—to "get over it," "move on," or take medication intended to treat our symptoms.

Even those of us who have done our best to "do the work" may not have found relief. Recent research suggests that talk therapy alone often fails to resolve trauma symptoms and, in fact, may retraumatize survivors.

While these treatments can be important parts of the trauma healing process, none of them address the underlying imprint of trauma on the body and primitive brain. Because we're encouraged to suppress trauma rather than face it, the original helplessness we felt when we were first traumatized only magnifies.

Once we're able to let go of the somatic imprint that trauma leaves behind, we're once again free to respond, even defend ourselves when necessary. Think for a moment . . .

How would you feel if you could say what you've always wanted to say?

How would your body feel if you could strike out against someone who hurt you?

How powerful would you feel if you could fight back or escape from harmful people/ situations?

Repeatedly over the years, I've tapped with people who, decades later, are frozen by early "little *t*" as well as "Big *T*" trauma. As we've tapped through the memory, they've reenacted the action or spoken the words they meant to do or say but never could.

Once they do that, they're finally able to reinhabit their bodies and reclaim their power. At that point they no longer need to resort to the freeze response to defend themselves; they can protect themselves consciously and without carrying excess stress from past events.

The key to lasting relief from the freeze response, as we'll see, is to use Tapping to revisit the trauma or event that caused you to freeze. While tapping, you can take the action you wanted to take but couldn't, say the words you wanted to say but never did. Using this process, you can release the freeze response on emotional, mental, and somatic levels.

ON CREATING A SENSE OF SAFETY

The freeze response can result from a wide variety of experiences, especially when the response originates in childhood. If you are a "Big *T*" trauma survivor, keep in mind that trauma that happened decades ago may still be stuck in your body and primitive brain.

To heal from "Big *T*" trauma using tapping, I strongly suggest that you work with a certified EFT practitioner who can create a safe space for exploring and releasing the trauma you survived. For particularly challenging traumas, search out a psychologist or psychiatrist who is trained and incorporates tapping into their practice.

For a list of EFT practitioners, visit http://thetappingsolution.com/eft-prac titioners.

To restore a sense of calm and safety in the present moment, you may also want to tap through the *All Is Well Tapping Meditation* script, which you'll find on page 308.

FREEING YOURSELF FROM FREEZE

Now it's time to use Tapping to do what the polar bear, possum, and rabbit all knew they needed to do—release the event or trauma they'd survived on physical, emotional, and mental levels.

First, take a moment to notice where in your life you are having some kind of freeze response . . .

Do you hold back from speaking your mind in meetings?

Do you clam up with family, or fail to show up how you intend to?

Do you avoid talking about money or seeing a doctor when you know it's necessary?

Where in your life are you holding back—in your marriage, as a parent, in your career and/or finances, with certain people, or in specific situations?

Your freeze response may be as simple as being confronted about something and your mind going blank, or it may be looking forward to visiting family, only to find you're irritable and angry in their presence.

There may also be a specific event that caused you to freeze, such as an encounter, a conversation, and so on.

Identify one instance, relationship, or area in your life where you tend to freeze in some way.

Focus on that one person, circumstance, or event that does, or has, caused you to freeze. Imagine being in that moment, notice any sensations you experience, as well as emotions that come up.

Next rate the emotional intensity (or lack thereof, as we saw with Ute) on a scale of 0 to 10.

Take three deep breaths.

We'll begin by tapping three times on the Karate Chop point.

KC *(repeat three times)*: Even though I have this freeze response, and it feels so hard to overcome, I love myself and accept how I feel.

Eyebrow: This freeze response

Side of Eye: I freeze

Under Eye: I don't act/react the way I intend to

Under Nose: I freeze

Under Mouth: This freeze response

Collarbone: It's in my brain

Under Arm: It's in my body

Top of Head: When did it start?

Eyebrow: This freeze response

Side of Eye: Why does it happen?

Under Eye: When did it start?

Under Nose: Why do I freeze like that?

Under Mouth: This freeze response

Collarbone: It's safe to look at this

Under Arm: It's safe to look at when and where it started

Top of Head: I'm safe looking at my freeze response

Eyebrow: I can relax when I think about it

Side of Eye: I can stop judging myself for having this freeze response

Under Eye: It's safe to look at this

Under Nose: It's safe to feel safe

Under Mouth: Even though I freeze, it's safe to feel safe

Collarbone: I can feel calm when I look at this

Under Arm: I can feel safe in my body when I think about this response

Top of Head: Feeling relaxed and safe now

Take a deep breath. Again rate the emotional intensity (or lack thereof) on a scale of 0 to 10.

Keep tapping until you feel the desired level of safety with looking at your freeze response. You can use your own words, or continue with multiple rounds of the text above.

When you're ready, continue tapping as you tell the story of the event or person that caused you to freeze.

As you recall an instance or instances where you resorted to the freeze response, include any physical sensations, emotions, and sensory details—sights, sounds, smells—that come to mind.

While tapping through the story, also ask yourself questions like:

What do I need to say, but never did?

Are there actions I need to take to defend myself or express my emotions?

(If you have the urge to punch, kick, or physically strike out against someone who hurt you, make sure there's enough clear space around you that you don't hurt yourself or anyone else. And it probably doesn't need to be said, but we're doing this to release the trauma, not to hurt or attack anyone physically.)

Tap through the points as you let yourself release the words and fight-or-flight urges you have needed to experience but never did.

Karate Chop . . . Eyebrow . . . Side of Eye . . . Under Eye . . . Under Nose . . . Under Mouth . . . Collarbone . . . Under Arm . . . Top of Head . . .

*Karate Chop . . . Eyebrow . . . Side of Eye . . . Under Eye . . . Under Nose . . .
Under Mouth . . . Collarbone . . . Under Arm . . . Top of Head . . .*

*Karate Chop . . . Eyebrow . . . Side of Eye . . . Under Eye . . . Under Nose . . .
Under Mouth . . . Collarbone . . . Under Arm . . . Top of Head . . .*

Keep tapping until you can focus on that event or person and not experience any emotional charge.

DAY 11 GREATEST SELF CHALLENGE: RELEASING THE FREEZE RESPONSE

*The most potent stressors are loss of control and
uncertainty in important areas of life, whether personal
or professional, economic or psychological.*

— Gabor Maté

Few experiences make us feel as powerless and uncertain as the freeze response. We shut down and lose our ability to act, react, and respond appropriately. In the face of a threat, whether physical, emotional, financial, or other, we feel defenseless, unable to take hold of the situation, even our own brains and bodies.

Your challenge, starting today, is to take small, day-by-day steps to take back your power, to reprogram your brain to notice how much control you *do* have.

Begin by simply noticing where in your life you tend to freeze, in ways big or small. Just notice when you revert to the freeze response, and when possible, tap on feeling, and then releasing, your experience.

If, at any point, you feel numb or resistant to looking at your own version of freeze response, let me also say this. I've tapped with people on releasing their freeze response countless times over the years and seen them physically transform in front of me.

After tapping through *why* they freeze, their energy shifts noticeably, their bodies visibly relax. They walk taller, feel stronger. They've tapped through their internal equivalent of the Berlin Wall and walked away more powerful than ever. It's an incredible sight for me, and an even more powerful experience for them.

So if you ever notice yourself avoiding your own freeze response, stop and tap. You *do* matter, and you *are* worth it.

You can find the *Day 11 Tapping Meditation: Feeling Safe Unfrozen* on page 275 of the Appendix.

◉ ◉ ◉

Keep your momentum going by taking those 60 seconds right now to add Day 12 to your calendar. We're going to tap through one of our biggest and most primal emotions—anger. With tapping, you can finally let go of your anger, once and for all.

Day 12

Quieting the Storm: Letting Go of Anger

One day a samurai came to see master Hakuin.

"Master, tell me, is there really such thing as Heaven and Hell?" he asked.

Hakuin was quiet for a long time before asking the man, "Who are you?"

"I am a samurai swordsman, and a member of the Emperor's personal guard," the man replied.

"You are a samurai!" the master declared. "What kind of emperor would have you for a guard? You look more like a beggar!"

"What?" the samurai responded, his face reddening with anger as his hand moved toward his sword.

"Oho!" Hakuin replied. "So you have a sword, do you? I'll bet it's much too dull to cut off my head!"

Unable to contain his anger any longer, the samurai drew his sword and readied himself to strike.

"That is Hell!" Hakuin quickly exclaimed.

Understanding the lesson and the seriousness of the risk he had taken, the samurai sheathed his sword, and bowed.

"Now," Hakuin explained, "that is Heaven."[1]

Take a moment to think about this story. What does it bring up for you?

In the past couple of days, we've used Tapping to release wounds from childhood. In that process many of us encounter one of our biggest and most overwhelming emotions—anger.

Today we use Tapping to release that anger, whether it's from childhood or another part of your life experience.

THE FORBIDDEN EMOTION

He who angers you conquers you.
– Elizabeth Kenny

After 25 years of chronic knee pain, Bobbie was pain-free.

Her marriage was also growing stronger and more loving. Her relationship with her son was improving. Plus, her career was gaining momentum, and she'd lost more than 50 pounds.

Bobbie's entire life was transforming before her eyes, but the biggest and most important transformation was internal. For the first time Bobbie felt that she *was* good enough, that she *was* worthy of love, happiness, health, success, and peace.

That core belief in herself had been broken on the day of her fifth birthday party, when her abusive, alcoholic father announced in front of her friends that he wished that she'd never been born. Those hurtful words had devastated Bobbie's self-esteem, and they'd kept her stuck in physical and emotional pain for many years since.

It wasn't until a weekend in October 2013 that Bobbie's life began to change. It was also the first time I had the honor of tapping with her onstage.

As we tapped on the hurtful words that her father had spoken to her, Bobbie was overcome by the one emotion she'd never let herself feel fully—anger. I encouraged her to imagine herself as an ironclad five-year-old who couldn't be harmed by her father anymore.

She laughed and cried while envisioning her five-year-old self elbowing her father before throwing cake in his face. At one point she paused her tapping to physically make the movements to strike out against him.

After about 20 minutes of tapping, Bobbie's knee pain, as well as her anger and limiting beliefs, had dissolved. That evening she walked long distances, including walking up and down stairs, and felt no pain.

She was amazed.

Months later, the pain was still gone, and her life was transforming faster than ever.

Bobbie had spent more than two and a half decades in intense physical and emotional pain all because of the one emotion she'd never let herself feel—anger.

WATCH BOBBIE'S TAPPING LIVE!

You can watch Bobbie tapping onstage with me online at www.the tappingsolution.com/blog/painful-words/.

What might change for you if you could fully and safely release anger that's been in you for weeks, months, even years or decades?

Would your relationships improve?

Would your career take off?

Would your health and vitality be restored?

What would transform if that old anger was gone for good?

OUR EMOTIONS, OUR HEALTH

Did you know that, according to the Centers for Disease Control and Prevention, there's an emotional connection to 85 percent of all illnesses? That's a big number! Repressed anger is considered by many health and wellness professionals to be among the most toxic emotions, and a significant contributing factor to chronic physical pain, and possibly illness, as well.

TOPPLING THE TABOO

For Bobbie, and for many of us, anger is a taboo emotion. It's the emotion we work hardest to push away and tamp down. At the same time, it's an emotion we're hardwired to feel. It's part of our survival instinct, the fight-or-flight response.

Why do we resist anger so fiercely that, like Bobbie, we risk causing ourselves more pain in the process?

That habit often dates back to childhood. As children, most of us were punished and/or isolated for being angry, possibly sent to our rooms or left alone until we could "calm down" or "be nice."

The message we received was loud and clear—feeling and expressing anger is *not* okay. In fact, letting it out caused us more pain, not less. As a result, some of us learned to repress anger while others among us rebelled by lashing out in anger often.

Regardless of our patterns around anger, when we do let it out, we continually witness its power to damage relationships, destroy trust, and generally mess up our lives. It's yet more confirmation of what we already learned—feeling and expressing is *not* okay.

So what *do* we do with our anger?

If we can't avoid feeling angry, how do we handle it?

That's where Tapping comes in—letting us feel and express anger in ways that support our health and wellness without doing any harm to us, our lives, or our relationships.

Before we look at how to use Tapping to release anger, it's helpful first to do some Tapping on allowing ourselves to feel it in the first place.

LETTING ANGER BE ANGER

Think about how you tend to react to your own anger. Do you express it freely and often but find that you're still angry afterward?

If lashing out is your most common response to anger, notice how challenging it feels to let go of your anger fully, even after an outburst.

Give that sense of struggle a number of intensity on a scale of 0 to 10.

If, on the other hand, you tend to push anger away to avoid causing more problems, notice how unsafe it seems to feel and express your anger.

Give that sense of *un*safety a number on a scale of 0 to 10 now.

Take three deep breaths.

We'll begin by tapping three times on the Karate Chop point.

KC *(repeat three times)*: Even though anger doesn't feel safe, it's too overwhelming and too destructive, I accept how I feel and choose to let myself feel it now.

Eyebrow: This anger

Side of Eye: It's not safe

Under Eye: It's too destructive

Under Nose: This anger

Under Mouth: It doesn't feel safe

Collarbone: It's too destructive

Under Arm: This anger

Top of Head: I can't let it out

Eyebrow: When I do, it causes more problems

Side of Eye: Even after an outburst, I can't let it go

Under Eye: This anger

Under Nose: Either I can't let myself feel it

Under Mouth: Or I can't let it go

Collarbone: But I can't avoid it, either

Under Arm: It's in me

Top of Head: It's okay to feel it

Eyebrow: It's okay to let this anger come out

Side of Eye: I can accept this anger as a natural part of me

Under Eye: I can let go of my shame around feeling anger

Under Nose: I can let myself feel it

Under Mouth: It's here to protect me

Collarbone: It's safe to feel this anger now

Under Arm: I don't have to hold on to it any longer

Top of Head: It's safe to feel this anger

Take a deep breath. On a scale of 0 to 10, rate the intensity of your experience again. Keep tapping until you feel the desired level of safety with feeling your anger.

RELEASE FIRST, THEN PEACE

Visualize a tire being pumped with air, first to its maximum and then more, and more.

As the air forces its way inside, the tire's edges begin to bow out further, stretching beyond their intended limits. The rubber gradually thins out. The pressure is finally too much, causing the tire to burst.

Even if we've developed the habit of repressing anger, at some point the pressure of our anger grows too big and too intense to bear.

So we do what we have to do.

We burst.

In this exercise you're going to let yourself feel the pressure and notice where you experience it in your body. Instead of bursting, though, you'll release it using a simple but powerful tapping exercise that will allow you to experience authentic relief and peace.

This exercise is for you and you only, so go ahead and really let your anger out. This is the perfect opportunity to fess up to anger without experiencing repercussions!

This time we'll begin with tapping and then find specific people and events to focus on.

Start with three deep breaths, and then begin tapping on the Karate Chop point.

KC *(repeat three times)*: Even though I have all this anger in me, it's big and explosive and it still doesn't feel safe, I accept how I feel and choose to let it out now.

Next complete this same sentence over and over again while tapping through the points. Know that there's no issue too big or small to bring up. You can repeat things that make you especially angry, or fill in each blank with a different event or person.

Let it flow and keep tapping through the points, even if you struggle to complete the blanks at first.

Eyebrow: I'm angry about _____

Side of Eye: I'm angry about _____

Under Eye: I'm angry about _____

Under Nose: I'm angry about _____

Under Mouth: I'm angry about _____

Collarbone: I'm angry about _____

Under Arm: I'm angry about _____

Top of Head: I'm angry about _____

Eyebrow: I'm angry about _____

Side of Eye: I'm angry about _____

Under Eye: I'm angry about _____

Under Nose: I'm angry about _____

Under Mouth: I'm angry about _____

Collarbone: I'm angry about _____

Under Arm: I'm angry about _____

Top of Head: I'm angry about _____

Eyebrow: I'm angry about _____

Side of Eye: I'm angry about _____

Under Eye: I'm angry about _____

Under Nose: I'm angry about _____

Under Mouth: I'm angry about _____

Collarbone: I'm angry about _____

Under Arm: I'm angry about _____

Top of Head: I'm angry about _____

Take a deep breath. Notice how you feel.

Has your anger shifted, maybe growing bigger or getting smaller, becoming hotter or cooler?

Did you experience any sensations (pain, tingling, hot/cold) in your body as you tapped on your anger?

Now imagine your anger as a physical thing.

Does your anger have a color?

Gather your anger together and place it inside a box. How big and intense (or hot, or cold, and so on) does your box of anger feel on a scale of 0 to 10? Give it a number.

Tap through the points as you feel the full force and pressure of your box of anger. For example, your tapping might begin like this:

Eyebrow: This box of anger

Side of Eye: So much pressure inside

Under Eye: So much heat

Under Nose: This anger

Under Mouth: It's red hot

Collarbone: It burns

Under Arm: This anger

Top of Head: It wants to burst

Keep tapping until your box of anger feels calmer, less pressure-filled.

Then, when you're ready, tap while visualizing opening the box and releasing any remaining anger inside. That might look something like this:

Eyebrow: This box of anger

Side of Eye: Opening it now

Under Eye: Releasing the anger from inside

Under Nose: Letting it out

Under Mouth: It's getting calmer

Collarbone: I can let this anger go now

Under Arm: I can release it all now

Top of Head: Feeling calm and peaceful now

Continue tapping until you feel the desired level of peace.

If your anger doesn't dissipate, tap through the points while asking yourself questions like the following:

- *Why am I still angry?*

- *What am I really angry about?*

- *What's the emotion underneath my anger? Where do I feel that emotion in my body?*

Tap on what you discover and continue tapping until you experience the desired relief.

When your anger, and other related emotions, have been released, you can finish with some positive rounds of tapping.

Eyebrow: This anger

Side of Eye: All this anger

Under Eye: It felt like a storm inside me

Under Nose: So much pressure was building

Under Mouth: This anger

Collarbone: It's safe to let it go

Under Arm: It's safe to feel calm now

Top of Head: I don't need this anger anymore

Eyebrow: I can release it now

Side of Eye: I can let it out

Under Eye: I can release it from my body

Under Nose: And release it from my mind

Under Mouth: It's safe to let go of this anger

Collarbone: I'm safe without this anger

Under Arm: It was here to protect me

Top of Head: And I'm grateful for that

Eyebrow: This anger

Side of Eye: It was keeping me safe

Under Eye: I don't need it any longer

Under Nose: I can release it from every cell in my body now

Under Mouth: I'm safe without this anger

Collarbone: I can choose to feel calm and relaxed now

Under Arm: Choosing peace in my body

Top of Head: Feeling at peace now

Notice how you feel now. Repeat this entire exercise as many times, and as often, as you need to release your anger fully.

Also be mindful of how releasing anger impacts your emotional "load."

Do you feel lighter, less burdened, more energized, relaxed, or inspired?

How does your body feel?

Notice the different ways that releasing anger affects your daily experience.

DAY 12 GREATEST SELF CHALLENGE: LETTING ANGER GO

You're standing on a beach staring out at the ocean.

You watch as an enormous wave rises, gathering momentum as it gains in size. It's getting bigger, dangerously big, actually, and it's coming toward you, threatening to overtake the sandy ground you're standing on. You're awestruck by the wave's power, but also scared, if only for that split second, that it may come down on you.

Then, suddenly, it crashes down a few feet in front of you, displacing sand, hurling seaweed, causing nearby children to run away, screaming gleefully.

A few seconds later, in spite of the apparent danger that was just racing toward you, you stand in the same spot, wet but unharmed, at peace where you are. The force that, a few seconds ago, seemed to threaten your survival is now an expansive sea of serene beauty.

When we feel angry, we have a similar experience. We know the anger is there, we see it gaining momentum, we feel it rising, yet we underestimate our ability to withstand its force.

Your challenge, starting today, is to begin creating a new experience for yourself around anger. Whatever the root cause of your anger, your challenge is to get into the habit of noticing your anger when it arises.

Then, as soon as you can, tap on feeling and releasing your anger until you experience the deep and soothing peace you witnessed on that beach after that enormous wave crashed down before you.

I know, I know.

You don't always want to.

Tap anyway.

Release has to come first.

Then peace—aka the "heaven" Master Hakuin refers to—happens next.

How are you feeling? We've covered a lot of territory this week already.

Make sure to complete the *Day 12 Tapping Meditation: Releasing Anger*. You can find it on page 278 of the Appendix. As you do the tapping, really let yourself feel that anger so that you can finally and fully let it go. It's an incredible feeling when you're finally free of it.

◎ ◎ ◎

On Day 13 we dip into the past once more to give ourselves the gift of forgiveness. Ready to feel emotionally lighter and freer than you have in a long, long time? Pick a day when you'll read and tap through Day 13, and add it to your calendar right now.

If you're feeling overwhelmed by today and the anger you're feeling, don't rush it. Take three days, a week, or as much time as you need to tap through your anger. Give yourself the time you need, but do go ahead and add Day 13 to your calendar now. How about writing this? "Read Day 13: Emotional freedom day!"

You're doing great!

*Keep in mind as you move forward that some days
in the journey may resonate with you more than others.*

That's fine. That's normal.

*Whenever it feels right, go ahead and
change words within the Tapping scripts.*

*The point of Tapping is not to say "magic words,"
but to tap on your experience.*

*If changing a Tapping script
makes it feel more authentic to you, do it!*

*What matters is that you're doing the tapping
and releasing what no longer serves your greatest self.*

I'm proud of you! You're doing great. Keep it up!

Day 13

Letting It Go: Navigating Forgiveness

After two full hours of screaming and cursing at his father's grave, venting a lifetime's worth of rage, Wayne got back into his rental car. It seemed like time to return home. There wasn't much left to say.

Wayne's father had been an abusive alcoholic, womanizer, and criminal who'd spent time in prison. In the midst of the Great Depression, he'd walked out on his first two sons. At that time, his oldest son was just four years old and his youngest was 16 months old. The day he left, the boys' mother was in the hospital giving birth to her third son, Wayne. Both young boys were left home alone to fend for themselves.

Because of his father, Wayne spent the early years of his life being moved through a series of foster homes and into an orphanage. When Wayne was 10 years old, his mother was able to get her sons back.

The fact was, though, so much had gone wrong in Wayne's life, and he could trace it all back to his father.

As he first stood in front of his father's grave that day, the one thing Wayne knew for sure was that his father didn't deserve his love. As much as it hurt to hold on to his rage, Wayne was determined never, ever to forgive his father.

Have you ever felt that way? Who has earned years of your anger?

Anger is one of our biggest, most heated emotions. It's the proverbial hot lava of our inner volcano.

Still, though, we hold on to it, this emotion that repeatedly burns us.

Why do we do that?

Why do we insist on hurting ourselves with our anger when forgiveness would feel so much better?

These are important questions we began asking yesterday. Today we dive deeper into them and then take a fresh look at moving beyond anger into forgiveness.

"I REFUSE TO FORGIVE"

One of my most popular online Tapping scripts, which has been shared, liked, and passed around by tens of thousands of people around the world, is titled "I Refuse to Forgive."

The script begins like this:

Karate Chop: Even though I refuse to forgive them because of what they did to me, I deeply love and accept myself.

Deep down and in spite of your best and healthiest intentions, whom are you refusing to forgive?

Even when you tell yourself you're over it, all it takes is one harsh or unsupportive word, one unreturned call or e-mail to open the floodgates of your anger and your continued refusal to forgive.

Who is that person for you?

And why *is* it so hard to forgive them?

WHY WE SWALLOW THE BITTER PILL

Picture yourself standing at a crosswalk. Next to you there's a child innocently jumping around, not paying attention to traffic. You see an oncoming car driving too close to your side of the road just as the child jumps several critical inches beyond the safe zone. Without thinking, you reach out and grab the child's backpack, pulling her back to safety before the car passes.

That instinct to reach out and pull that child back to safety is how your primitive brain will react to your attempts to forgive someone who hurt you deeply.

To your primitive brain, holding on to anger is the smarter choice. Anger is hot, sure. Anger may even burn you, but anger is the emotional equivalent of self-defense. Anger will protect you.

To your primitive brain, forgiveness is too risky. It's the equivalent of that child jumping *toward* oncoming traffic *into* danger. Thor, the peace-loving caveman from Day 2, would choose forgiveness, and once again he would be devoured.

Your primitive brain wants you to be Grog, who would choose caution. Grog would choose fear, and when necessary, he would opt for anger. Although Grog may not enjoy his fear or his anger, he *will* survive.

As we learned on Day 2, survival is your primitive brain's job. Ensuring your survival is its reason for being.

When you try to forgive, your primitive brain reaches out and pulls you back into your anger so that you're not metaphorically "run over" by the pain of being hurt by that person again.

That's why forgiveness is so hard and why staying angry and refusing to forgive often comes more naturally.

But what if the so-called danger that your primitive brain thinks it sees isn't real?

What if the oncoming traffic that child appears to be stepping into is actually just a mirrored reflection, like a movie of the past that's on an endless replay loop?

What if the danger that your primitive brain is so busy avoiding is a mirage, or at least a threat that you can absolutely handle?

Is anger worth it, then, or is forgiveness the better choice?

"FROM THIS DAY FORWARD"

As Wayne sat in the car that day preparing to return home, his inner voice told him to do something he didn't expect. It told him to return to his father's grave.

Unsure why he was being led back to where he'd just been, Wayne got out of the car and stood once again in front of his father's tombstone.

The words he said next spilled out of him unexpectedly and without thought.

They began something like this: "From this day forward I will send you nothing but love. Who am I to judge you? Who am I to say you didn't do the best you could? I know nothing about your life. Starting now I send you nothing but love. Starting now I forgive you."

To Wayne's shock and relief, he hadn't just said the words; he had felt them at the core of his being.

Soon after that visit, Wayne flew to Fort Lauderdale, Florida, and spent 14 days in a motel. During those two weeks, he wrote his first book, *Your Erroneous Zones*.

He also transformed his lifestyle. In addition to beginning to run regularly, he lost a significant amount of weight. Most important, his entire daily experience changed. He had energy again. There was light in his life. Hope felt real, and his dreams became possible.

Your Erroneous Zones was first published in 1976. It spent 64 weeks on *The New York Times* bestsellers list, and has since sold more than 35 million copies. During the years that followed, Wayne went on to write dozens more books, including several other bestsellers. He also appeared repeatedly on PBS and inspired countless audiences around the world.

All that happened after Wayne released his rage and forgave his father. Without that heavy emotional burden, he was free to be his greatest self and realize his biggest hopes and dreams.

In the many years that followed, Wayne Dyer's work changed millions of lives.

What might happen in your life if you could forgive that person you've been refusing to forgive?

Whether that person is alive or has passed, what might shift for you if you finally let your anger toward him or her go?

WHOM DO YOU NEED TO FORGIVE?

You may want to take notes for this exercise, so grab a pen and paper or digital device before beginning.

When you're ready, take three deep breaths.

Imagine that the person you've been refusing to forgive is walking into the room where you are right now.

Notice how you feel when that person walks in.

Does your body tense?

Are you sad?

Are you angry?

What memories, ideas, and images come to mind when that person is in your presence?

Sit with these questions for a few minutes, and as things come up, feel free to write them down so you can tap on them later.

What you're searching for here is your current emotional response to that person, and how it brings up old memories or themes.

For example, you might say, "When my dad walks into the room, I instantly get angry and start thinking about how he was never around when we were growing up." Or "I'm so angry at my ex for cheating on me," or whatever else comes to you.

Trust that initial gut reaction and identify where you feel it in your body. Rate its intensity on a scale of 0 to 10.

Take another deep breath. We'll begin by tapping three times on the Karate Chop point.

Note: This tapping script uses general language. Change it as needed, use your own language, or do the tapping by yourself, without the script.

Karate Chop *(repeat three times)*: Even though I have <this feeling> toward my _____, I deeply and completely love and accept myself.

Eyebrow: <This feeling>

Side of Eye: This memory

Under Eye: When I see my _____

Under Nose: I feel _____ in my body

Under Mouth: And it's so hard to let it go

Collarbone: I've been holding on to this for so long

Under Arm: And I don't want to let it go

Top of Head: <This feeling>

Eyebrow: I feel it in my body

Side of Eye: This memory

Under Eye: When I see my _____

Under Nose: I feel _____ in my body

Under Mouth: And I can't let it go

Collarbone: I can't let this go

Under Arm: And I don't want to let it go

Top of Head: <This feeling>

Eyebrow: I've been holding on to this for so long

Side of Eye: It's exhausting

Under Eye: Maybe it's time to let this go

Under Nose: I can start to let this go

Under Mouth: I don't need this <emotion> anymore

Collarbone: It's hurting me

Under Arm: It's keeping me stuck in the past

Top of Head: Letting this <emotion> go now

Keep tapping through your experience. When you're ready, check in on the emotional intensity you experience when you imagine that person in the room with you. Again rate it on a scale of 0 to 10.

Note: If you're tapping on an abusive relationship or childhood, know that you will need to repeat this exercise multiple times, but that each time you do is a step in the right direction.

Repeat this process until you feel a sense of peace when you imagine that person in your presence.

DAY 13 GREATEST SELF CHALLENGE: FORGIVING *THAT* PERSON

I could tell you to start small and work up. I could ask you to give more forgiveness to the people who cut you off, blow you off, and tick you off in any given day.

That's one way to practice forgiveness.

Today, though, I'm not going to ask for that. I'm asking you instead to go for the gold.

I'm asking you to forgive that *one* person you're really, really angry at.

That one person who wronged you so deeply, he or she doesn't deserve your forgiveness.

I'm asking you to commit to healing *that* emotional wound.

It may feel impossible or like too much work. It may seem like too much to ask.

I don't know the details of your story, but I do know that you have every right to be *that* angry. You have good reason for refusing to forgive him or her.

But that anger and that refusal to forgive is a boulder that's lodged between you and your greatest self. Unless and until you can move it and let it roll away, you'll be limited in how you can show up, what you can do and how powerful, amazing, and inspiring you can actually feel.

If the person you're forgiving is still living, recognize also that forgiving him or her doesn't mean that person will change.

Forgiving someone doesn't mean we bring him back into our lives or assume that "this time will be different." Even after forgiving him, you may need to limit contact, perhaps even avoid him altogether.

What matters is that you use the process outlined in the previous exercise to forgive that person for what happened or didn't happen, for what was said or left unsaid.

Go back to the previous exercise a couple of times a day for as many days as it takes.

Acknowledge and tap on what comes up.

And, yes, this *is* a big topic. Expect to succeed, but know that you may, or may not, need more time than you'd like to take on this one.

This isn't a race, but do push yourself just enough to get to that place of release and peace.

Keep going until you feel that shift. It's a process. Trust and know that the results will come exactly when they're meant to.

As you heal that wound, also watch how other parts of your life transform.

Are you more patient or loving with your partner?

Do you finally attract the person you've been dreaming of, not the one who was put in front of you to try to heal this old stuff?

Do your financial patterns change? Does your body begin to heal?

Tap, forgive, and watch the new and amazing magic that unfolds in you and your life.

Congratulations on completing today! Forgiveness is central to healing deep emotional wounds and to becoming your greatest self. It's not always easy, and I'm proud of you for taking this on.

You can find the *Day 13 Tapping Meditation: "I Refuse to Forgive"* on page 281 of the Appendix.

◎ ◎ ◎

Now that you've shed this huge emotional weight, it's time to add Day 14 to your calendar! As we move forward to wrap up Week Two of the journey, we'll take some pressure off your self-development work, add some ease and flow, and check in on where you are now.

Day 14

What Stands Out?

Maxwell Maltz, a plastic surgeon in the 1950s, began noticing an interesting pattern in his patients.

After a cosmetic procedure, such as a nose job, it would take patients around 21 days to begin getting used to the changes in their appearance. Patients who'd lost a limb often suffered from phantom limb syndrome for approximately 21 days. Intrigued, Dr. Maltz soon began to notice that his own new habits took about 21 days to feel normal.

Twenty-one days.

It's long enough to seem credible, but short enough to feel doable.

Who *wouldn't* want to change their life in three weeks' time?

The idea is so appealing that it was adopted by self-improvement gurus over subsequent decades. As time went on, books, courses, and more began to definitively assert that it takes 21 days to adopt a new habit or get accustomed to a new reality.

You've probably heard that before, and clearly, so have I, given the timeline of this book!

The problem is, Maltz's finding has been misrepresented over time. He didn't assert that it takes 21 days to create new habits. He found that it often took *approximately* or a *minimum* of 21 days for a new habit or reality to feel normal.

Around 21 days. *At least* 21 days.

The 21-day mark was never absolute. It was a general guideline, and for bigger changes, a minimum. The actual length of time that change actually takes depends on multiple factors.[1]

You've spent the past five days tapping on the past, unearthing and releasing some of your deeper emotions and looking at how they impact some of your present choices. Today we look back at what you've discovered, revisit any especially useful parts, and also look at how to get the most from this journey by taking pressure off our 21-day timeline.

IT REALLY *IS* OKAY

Has it taken you 19 days to get to Day 14? More than 19 days? Fewer than 14?

Has it taken you two years? ☺

Are you tapping daily? Or are you busy feeling guilty because you've only been tapping here and there?

Over the years I've noticed a trend in the self-improvement industry, a subtle but persistent sense among audiences that they're not working hard enough or doing enough each day, month, and year to improve themselves.

These are people who read books, listen to audio, and attend events, but still feel that their efforts to improve themselves and their lives aren't measuring up.

The stress created by the belief that we are not doing enough is, unto itself, an impediment to progress.

Look, I want you to use this book.

I want you to tap daily, and complete a day each and every day.

I know the potential this book holds to support you in becoming your greatest self, and in turn, living your greatest life.

I believe in you, and I believe in Tapping.

I've seen people's entire lives transform in amazing and inspiring ways, thanks to consistent tapping. Even a few minutes each day can add up to powerful results!

I want that for you. I honestly can't wait to hear about how tapping supports you in manifesting your greatest self.

The thing is, change happens differently, at different times, and at a different pace, for each of us. The change process can be fickle. Our lives sometimes get complicated and slow us down.

That's all okay. That's normal.

Before we revisit your progress during this second week of the journey, let me say this:

You are *not* a project.

You do *not* need fixing.

If you feel like your life doesn't reflect your greatest self, know that you're in the right place.

Not feeling like your greatest self right now doesn't mean you're not great as you are. It means that you're feeling the pull of unrealized potential.

It *doesn't* mean that you're broken or that your life is a problem. You may *have* problems in your life. We all do. Having problems is different from seeing yourself as one of them.

So let me repeat myself:

You are *not* a problem. You are *not* a project. You do *not* need fixing.

This journey is about stepping into a new, deeper level of your greatest self. It's about realizing that unrealized potential in one or many areas of your life. And part of manifesting your greatest self is in fact accepting the parts of you that aren't "perfect."

If your journey so far has taken more, or even less, than 14 days, let's not make that into a problem. Let's trust that's been the right pace for you up until this point. You can change your pace going forward, or not. That's up to you, but feeling at peace with where you are in this journey is a critical part of moving forward.

RIGHT AS IS, RIGHT ON TIME

Remember in Week One how we focused on feeling peace versus panic?

Take a moment now to think about your journey so far, the tapping you've done up to this point, including the length of time it has taken you to get to Day 14.

How much "panic"—stress, worry, anxiety, guilt, discouragement, frustration, and so on—do you feel when you focus on where you are in your journey?

Give that sense of "panic" a number of intensity on a scale of 0 to 10 now.

Take three deep breaths.

Begin by tapping three times on the Karate Chop point.

KC (repeat three times): Even though I feel this panic about where I am in my life and in this journey, I choose to love myself and accept how I feel.

Eyebrow: This panic

Side of Eye: I feel like I'm not moving fast enough

Under Eye: Like I'm not making enough progress yet

Under Nose: I don't feel like my greatest self yet

Under Mouth: And that makes me feel panicked

Collarbone: I feel this panic in my body

Under Arm: I want to transform faster

Top of Head: I want to be my greatest self now

Eyebrow: This panic

Side of Eye: I feel it

Under Eye: It's in my body

Under Nose: I want big results now

Under Mouth: I need big results now

Collarbone: This panic

Under Arm: It's slowing me down

Top of Head: And it's freaking me out

Eyebrow: It's keeping me stuck, and I've had it for so long

Side of Eye: But what if I could let this panic go now?

Under Eye: What if I choose peace?

Under Nose: I can trust that I'm where I need to be

Under Mouth: I can trust that I am manifesting my greatest self

Collarbone: I can feel at peace with myself

Under Arm: I can see the problems in my life

Top of Head: And feel at peace with myself still

Eyebrow: I'm doing the work

Side of Eye: One step at a time

Under Eye: So it's safe to relax

Under Nose: And to forgive myself for not being "perfect"

Under Mouth: To trust in myself

Collarbone: And to know that everything is happening right on schedule

Under Arm: Feeling safe and calm in my body

Top of Head: Right now

Take a deep breath. Check back in on your sense of "panic" about where you are in your journey and your life. Give that "panic" a number of intensity on a scale of 0 to 10. Keep tapping until you experience the desired level of peace.

WHAT STANDS OUT FOR YOU?

I can't count the number of times clients and summit and course participants have had their most powerful breakthroughs by looking at seemingly disconnected events, memories, and emotions from the past.

Years of financial strain are resolved after tapping on a childhood memory of being bullied.

Decades of chronic physical pain end after tapping through a memory of a few harsh words from a teacher or coach.

At young ages the subconscious mind absorbs messages that stick with us, whether or not we're consciously aware of them as adults.

During this past week, you've used Tapping to discover some of the deeper emotional and mental programming that is likely influencing how you're showing up every day.

Without thinking too much about it, circle one or two days that stand out for you, either as being especially relevant or as feeling unresolved or incomplete:

Day 8: Planting the First Seed: A New Vision

You wake up to your divinely inspired mission. How do you feel? What will you do differently? Will you react and respond in new ways? How will your day feel?

Using Tapping, we plant that first seed, the vision of who your greatest self is and what your greatest self most yearns to feel.

We also use tapping to clear the slate from the fatigue of "working on ourselves" so that we can begin anew and create an authentic, inspired vision for the present and future.

Day 8 Greatest Self Challenge: Being Intentional (page 82)

Day 8 Tapping Meditation: Aligning with Your Intentions (page 266)

Day 9: Where Are Your Energy Leaks?

If you had a limited amount of energy to "spend" each day, how would you use it?

On this day we look at how much of our everyday energy reserves are being "spent" on the past.

As tempted as you may be to skip "all that old stuff," this, as a rule, is your fastest, most direct path toward your greatest self. Skip it at your own peril. ☺

Day 9 Greatest Self Challenge: Noticing Key Patterns (page 96)

Day 9 Tapping Meditation: Letting Go (page 269)

Day 10: Letting Go of the Past

Today we look at how Dr. Felitti's failed research project accomplished a far larger goal—helping us all unearth the impact of ACEs.

Using Tapping, which has been shown to be far more effective at trauma and PTSD relief than conventional therapies, we begin to look at past experiences, emotions, and beliefs that need more attention.

We also look at incredible stories of traumatized POWs who can inspire us all to move forward into a brighter, more inspiring future.

Before you decide to skip any and all opportunities to revisit this day, take a breath. I *know* that you don't want to go there. I get that, I really do, but I've worked with so many childhood trauma survivors over the years. Tapping has allowed them to heal at a level that simply wasn't possible without it.

Trust me on this one, will you? You won't regret it. If you're feeling called back to look at this again, trust that there's a big release waiting.

Day 10 Greatest Self Challenge: Releasing the Past (page 109)

Day 10 Tapping Meditation: Feeling Safe Releasing the Past (page 272)

Day 11: A Possum, a Polar Bear, and a Rabbit: Understanding the Freeze Response

What do a polar bear, a possum, and a rabbit have in common?

And what do we, as humans, have in common with them all?

On this day we explore a primal response to deep-seated fear, as well as trauma, known as the freeze response. We also look at the many little and big ways this response plays out in our lives, and then use Tapping to release it.

Almost everyone I know can relate to this chapter, including people who haven't undergone trauma. It's amazing what unfreezing can to do liberate your greatest self!

Day 11 Greatest Self Challenge: Releasing the Freeze Response (page 120)

Day 11 Tapping Meditation: Feeling Safe Unfrozen (page 275)

Day 12: Quieting the Storm: Letting Go of Anger

On this day we look at unearthing and unleashing anger, one of our most primal and necessary, yet taboo, emotions.

We also learn about Bobbie, who regained her mobility after decades of chronic physical pain, thanks to tapping on releasing deep-seated anger at her abusive father.

It's a big day that provides huge relief!

Day 12 Greatest Self Challenge: Letting Anger Go (page 133)

Day 12 Tapping Meditation: Releasing Anger (page 278)

Day 13: Letting It Go: Navigating Forgiveness

Whom are you refusing to forgive? What might open up in you and your life if you could forgive *that* person?

As we examine the power of forgiveness, we'll look at a story about the transformative power of deep, lasting forgiveness.

Using Tapping, we then begin to experience that same process and the deep relief and freedom it produces.

This is a big, and hugely important, topic. You'll be amazed by how much energy you'll set free once you can truly forgive.

Exercise: Whom Do You Need to Forgive? (page 140)

Day 13 Greatest Self Challenge: Forgiving *That* Person (page 142)

Day 13 Tapping Meditation: "I Refuse to Forgive" (page 281)

Pick one of the two days that you circled, and jot down some quick notes on what stands out for you about that day. Try to be specific in your answer. So instead of writing "it struck a chord," write *why* it struck a chord. For example, "Day 13 made me realize that my challenges with saying no date back to kindergarten, when my teacher punished me for saying no."

Day ### stands out for me because _____

Do some (or more) tapping on this, both tapping through your memory, as well as the emotions it created, until the event carries less emotional charge for you.

Next ask yourself:

What did this event make me believe I can't do or be?

Perhaps, for instance, your kindergarten teacher yelling at you created the belief that saying no is bad.

Write down the limiting belief that that event created in you:

_____

Take a deep breath. How true does your belief feel on a scale of 0 to 10? Give it a number now.

Next do some tapping on your limiting belief. In my example, that tapping might look something like this:

KC *(repeat three times)*: Even though my kindergarten teacher yelling at me created this belief that I'm not allowed to say no, I love myself and accept how I feel.

Eyebrow: I can't say no

Side of Eye: I'm not allowed to say no

Under Eye: I know that's not actually true

Under Nose: It still feels true, though

Under Mouth: My kindergarten teacher yelled at me

Collarbone: I felt so scared

Under Arm: I felt shame around saying no to her

Top of Head: I learned I shouldn't say no

Eyebrow: But that's not true anymore

Side of Eye: My conscious brain understands that

Under Eye: But my primitive brain is still scared to say no

Under Nose: I freeze when I need to say no

Under Mouth: So I say yes instead

Collarbone: In that moment saying yes feels easier

Under Arm: It's only later on that I wish I'd said no

Top of Head: I'm sick of saying yes when I mean no

Eyebrow: I can let go of this fear around saying no

Side of Eye: I can make my own choices now

Under Eye: I can let go of the fear I felt that day

Under Nose: I can feel safe saying no

Under Mouth: No

Collarbone: I'm saying no

Under Arm: I can say no whenever I need to

Top of Head: It's safe for me to say no

When you're ready, take a deep breath, and again rate how true your limiting belief feels on a scale of 0 to 10. Keep tapping until it no longer feels true.

You can repeat this same process for other days in Week Two, as needed, until you feel ready to move to Day 15.

DAY 14 GREATEST SELF CHALLENGE: SURPRISE!

Surprise! There is no challenge today. You've made it to Day 14. Congratulations!

Take some extra time to smell the roses, make your favorite cup of tea, call a friend, or just gaze at a beautiful flower.

Whatever makes your heart sing today, go and enjoy it.

You'll find the *Day 14 Tapping Meditation: I Don't Need Fixing* on page 284 of the Appendix.

◎ ◎ ◎

Also take a minute right now to add Day 15 into your schedule. Write something like, "Read Day 15—it's a fun one!"

Creating a Life You Love by Manifesting Your Greatest Self

Day 15

Dr. Seuss and Aristotle on the Best Little Choice You'll Ever Make

As I've shared, this is my fourth book.

I've always wanted to write, and I often tell people that I enjoy it. Which I usually do, expect when I'm busy dreading the writing itself, the process of actually *doing* the work, the thinking, the rewriting.

That's when I'd rather work on my next chapter . . . well, later.

At those times I remind myself that I have calls to make and e-mails to reply to—especially calls to make (I'm good at talking on the phone, plus it's an entertaining way to be productive). I tell myself that I'm having another busy day, that I can't take time to sit quietly and work on that chapter, not now, not today.

Ugh.

My deadline is set. I *have to* write today.

(You're not familiar with procrastinating, are you? I'm probably the only one . . .)

It was during one of these ugh-my-deadline moments while writing my first book that I asked myself a question that has since changed my approach to writing. That question was this:

What can I do to make my writing time a little more pleasant?

I didn't set a grand goal. I aimed for a bit more ease, a touch more joy.

I started asking myself similar questions every time I sat down to write, questions like:

What would make writing more enjoyable right now?

How can I give myself five minutes of happiness to get me started?

Sometimes it's the right cup of tea, coffee, or green smoothie. At other times it means moving to a favorite chair or writing outside. Oftentimes it includes listening to a 55-minute background audio that helps me focus and working for at least that amount of time.

These tiny tweaks to my writing routine have changed everything. While I still occasionally dread getting started on my writing, asking these simple questions (and making the resulting changes to my old routine) often allows me to continue writing past the end of that 55-minute audio.

More important, I'm *enjoying* writing again.

That shift happens because of a simple acknowledgment that I need to bring my own happiness into the equation.

What might happen in your life if you could make slight tweaks to your day that made you feel a little better, a bit more joyful, a tad closer to your happy place?

We've spent the first two weeks of this journey clearing panic and letting go of the past. This week we look at how to move forward, becoming more of your greatest self day by day.

To begin our final week, Week Three of the journey, we're going to look at simple ways to create five minutes of happiness in your day. Just five minutes of presence, pleasure, and enjoyment can change a lot.

ONE WORD, MANY EXPERIENCES

The Greeks have many words to describe what we call "happiness." It makes sense, given how many different kinds of "happiness" we experience.

Oftentimes authentic happiness happens in little moments that we can choose to savor.

Right now, at this very moment, what does happiness look and feel like for you?

Sometimes happiness is about feeling peaceful while reading a great book or enjoying nature.

Sometimes it's the excitement of a great night out with friends.

At other times it's spending time working on a favorite hobby or project.

What do your happy moments look and feel like? How many different feelings and experiences do those moments encompass?

Here's a list of possible happy moments to get you thinking:

Time spent with family and friends	A favorite hobby— cooking, gardening, woodworking, knitting, and so on
Enjoying nature	
A challenging but gratifying workout	Savoring a beautiful morning
A funny joke	Sipping a favorite beverage
Finishing a big project or task	Rocking out to music in the car
Feeling engrossed in a project or task	A big, warm hug

Talking to loved ones

Meditation

Dancing in the rain

Tapping

Laughing

Taking a relaxing bath

Celebrating holidays, birthdays, and so on

Receiving good news

Helping others

Running into someone you haven't seen in a while

Watching a great movie

Spending time with pets

Playing with children

Taking the scenic route

Watching a great video online

Dancing to a great song

Doing a favorite yoga pose

Having an *aha!* moment

Each of these pursuits can lift your mood and add more joy to your day.

How many of these happy moment experiences ring true for you? What others can you add to the list?

Take a moment now to list a few of your more recent happy moments:

_____

_____

_____

Read your list and notice how much (or how little!) appreciation and joy you feel.

LITTLE CHOICES

The Greek word that's closest to "happiness" is *eudaimonia*. It translates literally as "having good demons," but its actual meaning is closer to "human flourishing."

Unlike happiness, which is often fleeting, eudaimonia is a way of living. While it involves pleasure and leisure, Aristotle suggested that the pursuit of learning is equally, if not more, important.

Eudaimonia is not the product of external circumstances, such as wealth, love, or achievement. Similarly, having eudaimonia does not require any specific external circumstances. Instead, it's a goal that we, as humans, inherently seek to achieve.

In many ways eudaimonia is also what this book is about—being your greatest self, and in turn, living your greatest life.

To thrive at that level, Aristotle asserted that we have to *choose* our own flourishing. To be our greatest selves living our greatest lives, we have to pursue fulfillment and self-actualization rather than wait for "it"—joy, money, love, purpose, passion, spiritual life, and so on—to come to us.

Eudaimonia may sound like a big idea, but it boils down to the little choices we make every day. Do we choose to live well in this moment, or do we routinely choose something less fulfilling?

When I make a favorite cup of tea before sitting down to write, I'm choosing my own flourishing. In addition to being more productive, I enjoy the process of writing more. It's the ultimate win-win.

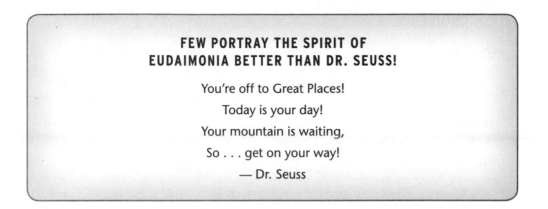

**FEW PORTRAY THE SPIRIT OF
EUDAIMONIA BETTER THAN DR. SEUSS!**

You're off to Great Places!
Today is your day!
Your mountain is waiting,
So . . . get on your way!

— Dr. Seuss

Making tea and pressing "Play" on that audio track is me choosing eudaimonia over the stress of "the deadline." In the words of Dr. Seuss, it's me choosing my great places and getting on my way.

My external circumstances haven't changed. My deadline is still fixed, and I still have the same amount of work to do, but the experience of meeting my deadline no longer feels burdensome. Instead, it feels like a challenge that I'm excited about meeting.

Already you've chosen this book, and you've chosen to get to Day 15. That's a commitment to your own flourishing, to realizing your greatest self and living your greatest life.

What other great places await? What is standing in *your* way?

SOUR IS SOUR . . . ARE YOU SO SURE?

Life handed him a lemon,

As Life sometimes will do.

His friends looked on in pity,

Assuming he was through.

They came upon him later,

Reclining in the shade

In calm contentment, drinking

A glass of lemonade.

That poem was originally printed in a 1940 issue of *The Rotarian*, and it of course refers to the well-known expression about turning lemons into lemonade.

Let's be honest about something, though. When we're in a negative space, when we're feeling bogged down by stress, making lemonade doesn't feel possible. At those moments we convince ourselves that it's our life circumstances—our finances, relationships, health, family, and so on—that need to change first.

The problem is, when we focus on "fixing" our external circumstances or only doing what we have to do, we resort to stress and panic.

When we bring our own enjoyment and fulfillment into our everyday experiences, we choose eudaimonia. And when we make that choice, we find that our circumstances change as a result of our new perspective, not the other way around.

By allowing little (and big!) bursts of happiness into our everyday experience, life feels lighter and more fulfilling, so it is.

DAY 15 GREATEST SELF CHALLENGE: ADDING EASE TO A TASK

I know it is wet and the sun is not sunny.
But we can have lots of good fun that is funny.
– Dr. Seuss

We tick off tasks on our to-do list only to find it growing longer.

We do more and note that we're *still* not doing enough.

Select one task that you know you need to do. Maybe on some level you even want to do it, but the fact is, you're also dreading it.

Your challenge for today is to write down, either on a piece of paper or on a digital device, three ways you could make that task more appealing.

Can you listen to music?

Light a candle?

Do a little dance before and after?

Sing as you go?

JUST NOT FEELING IT?

If just thinking about the task fills you with dread and fear, do a few minutes of tapping through the points while you think about it. Notice what comes up, and keep clearing it. You'll often find once you do that, the "happiness ideas" flow more freely!

Once you've got your list, assign a day and time (yep, go ahead, put it on your calendar right now) for you to complete, or at least make noticeable progress, on that task.

When the time comes, make sure to use *at least one* of the pleasure-enhancing adds-ons from your list to make the experience more enjoyable.

Then notice how it feels. Does doing the task actually feel more pleasant? Do you dread finishing it less? Are you more productive?

Add as much pleasure to the task as you need to make it feel less like a burden, and notice how your experience of getting it done shifts.

You'll know you've found the right combination when you're getting more done and enjoying it a lot more!

You'll find the *Day 15 Tapping Meditation: Choosing Happiness* on page 287 of the Appendix.

◎ ◎ ◎

Take that minute also to add Day 16 to your calendar. You can keep up with your current pace, or adjust it to fit where you are now.

You're into Week Three now. We'll be making more big strides, so be sure to keep tapping along! On Day 16 you unearth the heart of your greatest self—how you relate to yourself. We also take a fresh and somewhat surprising look at self-acceptance.

Ahhhhh!

Have you felt that yet?

If not, that deep sense of relief is coming.

*The more tapping you do, the faster
and more fully you'll experience it.*

*Tapping is the most effective and fastest way to — finally!
— shed what's no longer supporting your greatest self.*

So keep tapping and keep reading.

You're doing great!

*And one more thing . . . sometimes the shift with Tapping can be hard
to notice over the long term. You're happier, but you don't remember what
you felt like before. You're calmer, but it just feels natural.*

*So take a moment to really think, How am I different now,
in big and small ways, then I was when I started this book?*

Acknowledge your amazing progress, big or small!

Day 16

At the Core of It All: A Fresh Look at Self-Acceptance

It's pitch-black out, and the birds shriek and squawk loudly, as if reclaiming the outside world as their own. The surrounding mountains appear as enormous, dark masses, visible only by their jagged outlines.

It's not yet 5 A.M. when the first monk rises to strike the gong that awakens the monastery.

Three hours of morning meditation follow.

Afterward a bell rings, signaling the start of the day's main meal. The monks are served first, followed by the novices, and later the helpers.

There is time in the morning for self-care, including exercise, but there is also work to do. Without access to technology or creature comforts, the monks must tend to the temple and its grounds by hand each day.

There is another meal at midday, which consists mainly of leftovers from the first. The food is simple, the portions unremarkable. At some monasteries

food is forbidden after the midday meal, only hot beverages permitted until the following day.

After an afternoon spent learning and studying, as well as doing chores, the monks gather in the evening for a few more hours of meditation. They then go to bed so they can rise early and repeat the same schedule day after day.

That's a day in the life of a Buddhist monk, or a taste of it anyway.

There are, of course, no bills to pay. There's no traffic to contend with, no one demanding return calls. There are no devices beeping and little, if any, contact with the outside world.

Some monks leave the monastery periodically to speak and teach, but they always meditate for several hours each day, and they always return to the simple, structured life at the monastery.

It's this schedule, these priorities, and the many hours dedicated to meditation that may explain why monks' brain scans have shown increased capacity for joy and compassion, slower aging, and more.

Understandably, we read about monks and also want to age more slowly. We, too, want to experience meditative bliss. We read and hope to gain more mastery over mind and body.

But in the midst of our overcrowded, overscheduled, technology-infused lives, do these grand visions of idyllic spiritual purity bring us closer to that place of peace, or push us further away from it?

To be clear, I'm not suggesting that you want to forsake all worldly possessions and attachments to become a Buddhist monk. However, I am suggesting that many of us may be aspiring to visions that are so far removed from our lives that they risk pushing us away from a place of peace rather than toward it.

Now that we've begun to bring more happiness and enjoyment into daily life, we're going to take it one step further. We're going to look at how we can practice greater self-acceptance, within the context of our current, modern, real-life experiences.

RESETTING THE BAR

We live in a culture that idolizes extremes. We're subtly taught that being spiritual means striving to be more like monks, that success means having a "perfect" life. Similarly, to practice self-acceptance and self-love, we're told to learn to love *all* of ourselves.

The thing is, we wake up with bad breath sometimes. We have crazy days when we don't meditate or tap. We may feel great occasionally, but stressed, anxious, and bored more often. Some nights we can't even get enough sleep for our bodies to function at their best.

It's life. We're human.

To be your greatest self, it's important to practice more self-acceptance and self-love.

Here's the thing, though.

Striving for *total* self-acceptance and unconditional self-love is overwhelming, and simply setting yourself up to fail way too easily.

Do you unconditionally love your morning breath?

Do you unconditionally accept your bad moods?

Probably not.

You're probably more likely to brush your teeth each morning, and call a good friend, or do some tapping on your "off" days.

That's great! You're taking positive steps to change things that you choose not to accept.

Practicing total self-acceptance and unconditional self-love is a wonderful idea, but when we aim for those ideals, we're often drifting further away from true self-acceptance and true self-love than closer to them.

Most of us don't live atop mountains. Our schedules aren't always predictable, and we constantly encounter people who don't meditate for five or more

hours per day, including our own selves. (Encountering people who meditate for five minutes a day is a gift enough!)

It's life. We're human.

It's okay if you don't always tap or meditate as often as you intend to. It's also okay to notice that your relationship, your finances, or your house is a big mess that needs your attention.

The question is, in the midst of the messes in your life, what *can* you accept about yourself?

Here's what I'm getting at.

It's time to lower the bar on self-acceptance, for our own sakes!

So know that I'm not going to ask you to love and accept everything about yourself.

We all have characteristics, habits and quirks that we're not in love with, things we'd like to change about ourselves and our lives. Authors, gurus, mentors, and counselors—myself included!—have those same issues with themselves.

How can we practice authentic self-acceptance anyway?

JUST A PINCH MORE

You know when you're cooking, and you realize that you need a pinch more salt, a touch more seasoning?

That's how we're going to approach self-acceptance.

We're going to aim to be a bit nicer to ourselves, a touch more accepting.

What one little (or big!) thing can you accept about yourself right now?

I mentioned yesterday that I like to talk on the phone. I'm good at it. I also enjoy it. It's hardly an award-winning skill. Some might (understandably) say that it's silly of me to even mention it.

But it's the kind of easy feel-good thing I want you to focus on right now about yourself. Something you're good at, something that comes naturally, and something you just don't give yourself enough credit for.

JUST ONE THING

Can you take a moment to notice your infectious laugh, your gardening skills, your flair for texting with creative, entertaining emojis?

Pick one positive attribute or skill that you're willing to accept about yourself.

When you focus on that one thing, what's your gut reaction? Do you subtly blow it off as meaningless, insignificant, or a given?

On a scale of 0 to 10 how true is the statement, *this one thing I can accept about myself is too insignificant to matter*? Give it a number now.

Take three deep breaths, and begin tapping on the Karate Chop point.

KC *(repeat three times)*: Even though this <one thing> I can accept about myself seems too insignificant to matter, I choose to feel good about it now.

Eyebrow: This <one thing>

Side of Eye: It seems insignificant compared to everything else

Under Eye: There are so many other, more significant things I can't accept

Under Nose: There are so many things about me that I don't like

Under Mouth: This <one thing>

Collarbone: It's hard to make it feel important

Under Arm: It's just <one thing>

Top of Head: There are so many bigger issues I need to fix

Eyebrow: This <one thing>

Side of Eye: It doesn't seem that significant

Under Eye: It actually seems pretty meaningless

Under Nose: There are bigger, more important issues I need to address

Under Mouth: This <one thing>

Collarbone: Maybe I can let myself feel good about it

Under Arm: Maybe I can let it matter more than I usually would

Top of Head: This <one thing>

Eyebrow: I can let it matter now

Side of Eye: I can let myself feel genuinely good about it

Under Eye: This <one thing>

Under Nose: I can let it matter

Under Mouth: I can let myself feel good about it now

Collarbone: I can stop discounting its importance

Under Arm: And feel genuinely good about <one thing>

Top of Head: Letting myself feel good about this now

Take another deep breath, and rate on a scale of 0 to 10 how insignificant your one positive attribute or skill feels now. Keep tapping until you feel the desired level of self-acceptance and peace around it.

FINDING YOUR LIFE'S LIGHT SWITCH

Now that you've begun to appreciate one thing about yourself, try to notice one thing about your life that you can feel good about.

Think of it like a light switch, something you can use to add light to your life.

It can be as simple as the fact that you're *not* a monk and therefore you *do* get to sleep on a pillow in a comfortable bed each night.

Pick one positive thing about your life that you can accept right now.

Again notice how insignificant that one thing feels relative to everything in your life that you'd like to transform. Rate its relative insignificance on a scale of 0 to 10 now.

Take three deep breaths, and begin tapping on the Karate Chop point.

KC *(repeat three times)*: Even though this <one thing about your life> feels like no big deal compared with everything I want to transform, I choose to feel good about it now.

Eyebrow: This <one thing about your life>

Side of Eye: It seems like nothing

Under Eye: It seems small compared with the things I need to change

Under Nose: This <one thing about your life>

Under Mouth: It doesn't seem that important

Collarbone: It doesn't seem worth my attention

Under Arm: It doesn't feel worthwhile

Top of Head: This <one thing about your life>

Eyebrow: I can accept this

Side of Eye: Even though it seems insignificant

Under Eye: I can accept it

Under Nose: I can feel good about it

Under Mouth: This <one thing about your life>

Collarbone: I can let myself feel good about it

Under Arm: I can appreciate it now

Top of Head: Even though it seems so insignificant

Eyebrow: I can feel good about it now

Side of Eye: Maybe I can let this good feeling grow

Under Eye: Maybe I can nurture this good feeling

Under Nose: Maybe I can notice other things about my life that I can accept

Under Mouth: There are things in my life that I want to change

Collarbone: But there are also things I can accept as they are

Under Arm: And I can feel good about them

Top of Head: I can nurture this good feeling about my life

Take a deep breath and again rate how insignificant your one thing that you accept about your life feels on a scale of 0 to 10. Keep tapping until you feel the desired level of acceptance and peace around it.

DAY 16 GREATEST SELF CHALLENGE: MIRRORING YOUR SELF-TALK

If I asked you what you don't like about yourself, I'd bet you could quickly list off several things.

If I asked you what you can love about yourself, would you hesitate?

If you answered yes or maybe to that last question, that's your brain's negativity bias skewing your perspective.

That bias is part of your survival instinct, so you don't ever want to get rid of it. However, it is important to continue noticing the different ways it's working against you.

Today your challenge is to notice how that negativity bias may be impacting how you view yourself.

And you're going to do that in a different way, using mirror talk and tapping.

If mirror talk seems too weird, I get it. Honestly, I've been a fan and friend of Louise Hay for years, but it was only recently that I challenged myself to use mirror talk, which is one of Louise's favorite techniques.

My first experience with mirror talk started out feeling awkward. Once I relaxed, though, it was also incredibly powerful.

So first find a mirror and look into your own eyes.

Try saying something nice to yourself. If negativity or blankness surface, let those experiences happen, and begin tapping until you experience relief or clarity.

Continue repeating that one positive thing to yourself while looking in your own eyes and tapping through the points. Keep doing this until you believe what you're saying, until hearing it feels good.

Cultivate this one positive seed in your relationship with yourself. Let it feel big. Then see what else can grow.

Take some time to complete the *Day 16 Tapping Meditation: Filling Your Cup*. You'll find it on page 290 of the Appendix.

◎ ◎ ◎

First, though, make sure to add Day 17 to your schedule. Pick a day and commit to reading and tapping through it. You'll discover the power of a single word that can transform your relationship with yourself and others.

Day 17

You're Not Chocolate!

It was a beautiful summer morning when my wife, Brenna, walked into my office to chat. She had a decision to make and wanted to talk it through.

It was a Monday, and she was scheduled to take our daughter to a morning playdate at a friend's house. We'd had a fun but busy weekend, though, and Brenna was tired. She also wanted to use the morning to get organized for the week ahead.

After Brenna shared her hesitation on the phone, her friend had urged her to hop in the car and come over anyway. Since Brenna had already rescheduled this playdate, saying no another time felt awkward.

The fact was, though, as much as Brenna wanted to see her friend, she wasn't feeling up to it on this particular day.

Choices, choices, choices!

We face big and small ones every day. As simple as they may seem, even the little ones aren't always easy to make. Unless and until we're able to set healthy boundaries, unless we can decide what we really want for ourselves and our

lives, everyday choices can create stress that accumulates, eventually increasing tension in us and in our relationships.

Now that we've begun to create a new relationship with ourselves, today we look at our relationships with others. In the process, we get clearer on the critical role that setting healthy boundaries plays in those relationships.

THE FORBIDDEN WORD

As a Harvard Business School (HBS) student, Don felt obligated to go out every night. Some students loved the constant social buzz, but for him, having such an active social life felt depleting. But even one night at home was noticed and judged. "Where were you?" people would ask. "Why weren't you out last night?"

The expectation at HBS was that successful students would graduate with top grades and a huge social network. If students failed to establish that network, they were considered failures. As one of Don's friends put it, "Socializing here is an extreme sport."

During a summer job in China, to Don's great relief, he discovered that his keen listening skills and thoughtful input were valued above all else. He didn't need to socialize or speak up constantly in China. He could simply be himself. It was the first time since beginning his studies at HBS that he'd felt comfortable.

Once back at Harvard that fall, Don was again forced to pretend to be far more outgoing than he actually was. He had to continue to say yes to socializing night after night, even though he wanted and needed to say no.

Don's story is one of the many from Susan Cain's culture-shifting book *Quiet* that highlights a dilemma most of us face at various times, whether or not we're introverts.

Like Don, many of us have felt thrust into saying yes when we wanted, even needed, to say no.

Like Don, most of us have hesitated at the potential consequences of saying no. We fear that saying no will hurt people or cause us to miss out on important

opportunities. So instead of honoring our own need to say no, we say yes to avoid conflict and other undesirable consequences.

Unfortunately, by saying yes when we need to say no, we also deprive ourselves of peace and self-acceptance.

So how can we establish a healthier balance between saying yes and saying no? It begins with first being able to see clearly.

CLEARING THE PANES

It's another beautiful day—or at least, it should be. You wake up, open your eyes, and look out the window. Once again, to your dismay, the world outside looks gloomy.

It's dark, dreary, almost foggy, and the world looks just plain miserable.

It's not until years later that you make a simple but life-changing discovery.

The panes of glass that you've been attempting to look through day after day are caked with dirt and grime!

No matter how hard you look or how much you hope for sun, you can't, and won't, see it. There's simply too much dirt on the window for you to see that the sun is shining and the flowers are in bloom.

An entire world of wonder and delight is right outside your window, but all you've been seeing is gloom.

If only you had noticed how dirty those panes were earlier . . . there was nothing wrong with the glass itself or the world outside it.

That's often how we experience our lives when we're in the habit of saying yes when we yearn to say no. Because we're not honoring our own needs and desires, we can't see the beauty in front of us. With so much dirt in our way, we can't be our greatest selves or live our greatest lives.

As Louise Hay says, when we say no to others when we need to, we're actually saying yes to ourselves. By saying yes too often, we're actually saying no to ourselves, and that lack of self-care clouds our view.

Until we clear away the emotions and beliefs that cause us to say yes when we want to say no, our internal windowpanes remain clouded. (And this metaphor, while particularly relevant here, applies to many aspects of our lives where our belief systems and patterns are keeping us from experiencing the joy we most deserve and desire.)

So how can we clear our view? Let's try an exercise that I've seen time and again completely shift people's experiences around saying no, especially when that no is actually a yes to ourselves.

RELEASING OVERWHELM

Think of a situation where you felt compelled to say yes, even though you wanted to say no.

Was there an invitation or opportunity you felt you had to accept?

A friend or loved one you felt you had to say yes to?

And if you can't think of a past one, think of an upcoming one that you felt unsettled about.

Let yourself feel the emotional push and pull of saying yes when you wanted to say no.

On a scale of 0 to 10, how overwhelmed do you feel around saying yes when you want to say no? What other feelings are coming up for you? Note them and rate their intensity.

Take three deep breaths.

We'll begin by tapping three times on the Karate Chop point. As you tap, beyond saying the words, make sure to visualize or think about the event, and also to feel the feelings. Make it as real as you can.

KC *(repeat three times)*: Even though I felt that I had to say yes when I wanted to say no, I love myself and accept how I feel.

Eyebrow: I had to say yes

Side of Eye: I couldn't say no

Under Eye: I wanted to say no

Under Nose: I needed to say no

Under Mouth: But I had to say yes

Collarbone: I was stuck

Under Arm: I couldn't say no

Top of Head: I had to say yes

Eyebrow: Thinking about this, I feel so overwhelmed

Side of Eye: I couldn't say no even though I needed to

Under Eye: So much overwhelm

Under Nose: This overwhelm

Under Mouth: So overwhelmed about having to say yes

Collarbone: Sometimes I want to say no

Under Arm: But I have to say yes

Top of Head: All this overwhelm

Eyebrow: All this overwhelm about having to say yes

Side of Eye: I can feel it now

Under Eye: And I can let it go now

Under Nose: I can learn to set new boundaries

Under Mouth: It's a process

Collarbone: I can release this overwhelm now

Under Arm: I can feel peace

Top of Head: And trust that I can change this

Take a deep breath. On a scale of 0 to 10, how overwhelmed do you feel about making this choice now? Give it a number now.

Keep tapping, either continuing to use the previous script multiple times, or by just closing your eyes and tapping through the points as you think about the event. Let your mind wander around the event, visualizing it as you tap.

Notice how you feel. Notice what it reminds you of, and what else comes up. Keep tapping until you feel the desired relief.

RE-CREATING EQUILIBRIUM

I logged on to Facebook one morning and couldn't help but laugh when I saw this quote:

. . . .

Stop trying to make everyone happy.
You're not chocolate.

. . . .

Are you working overtime to please everyone *but* yourself? Where in your life are you trying to be chocolate?

The reality is, we can't continue to say yes as often, but we can't say no too much, either.

When we step back, we also notice that the people who ask for our time and attention often have good intentions. Brenna's friend wanted to connect with her and enjoy a summer morning together. HBS was pushing Don to socialize in order to accelerate his future career.

Both are positive intentions.

If we can't respect our own boundaries, though, we inevitably end up feeling overwhelmed, regardless of our own or others' best intentions. And while there may be times when you do have to say yes, I can almost guarantee that there are many other parts of your life where you can say no more often.

Before we use Tapping to get more comfortable with saying no, let me remind you of something you probably know, but may, at times, push aside.

Other people's happiness is not your job.

I know, shocking revelation. Here you are, thinking you could save the world by trying to make everyone else happy.

Of course this doesn't mean that your loving, caring, emphatic approach is all bad.

You *can* care for people. You *can* nurture and love your family and friends, but if that time and effort is always coming from a place of self-sacrifice, overwhelm, anger, or resentment, that negative energy will inevitably outweigh your positive, loving intentions.

You're not chocolate.

None of us can please everyone, especially if we're not meeting our own basic needs for time, space, and rejuvenation.

By honoring your need to say no, you give yourself more time and space for tapping, exercising, connecting, napping, creating—the many different pursuits that feed your soul and support you in becoming your greatest self.

VISUALIZING SAYING NO

Focus on a person or part of your life where you're trying to be chocolate.

Again, let the emotional tension, that push-pull energy of wanting to say no but feeling compelled to say yes, rise up inside you.

Picture yourself with that person, or in that circumstance. Really put yourself in that moment where you're being asked something that you want to say no to but feel like you have to say yes to.

Picture the other person's face or the text message or e-mail or phone call you need to respond to. Re-create that moment in your mind, incorporating as many sensory experiences as possible.

Also notice any sensations you experience in your body—pain, tightness, tension, heat/cold, and so on—when you imagine saying yes when you want to say no.

These are all ways that your heart, mind, and body are resisting your saying yes.

On a scale of 0 to 10, how much emotional, mental, and physical discomfort do you experience around making this choice?

Take three deep breaths.

Begin by tapping three times on the Karate Chop point.

KC *(repeat three times)*: Even though I feel so much resistance around saying yes, but I feel like I have to say yes, I love myself and accept how I feel.

Eyebrow: I have to say yes

Side of Eye: But I want to say no

Under Eye: All this resistance to saying yes

Under Nose: All this obligation around saying yes

Under Mouth: Saying no feels impossible

Collarbone: Saying no feels dangerous

Under Arm: I have to say yes

Top of Head: I can't say no

Eyebrow: I want to say no

Side of Eye: I need to say no

Under Eye: But I have to say yes

Under Nose: Saying no feels too hard

Under Mouth: Saying no feels too dangerous

Collarbone: I have to say yes

Under Arm: I usually say yes

Top of Head: They expect me to say yes

Eyebrow: Letting myself feel this tension around wanting to say no

Side of Eye: Letting myself see that it's time to say no more often

Under Eye: Even though it feels dangerous

Under Nose: I can learn to say no more often

Under Mouth: I'm scared to say no

Collarbone: But I'm angry about saying yes so often

Under Arm: Letting myself feel all this tension now

Top of Head: It's safe to feel it all

Take a deep breath.

Once again return to your visualization. Put yourself in that moment with the person or in the circumstance where you want to say no but feel obligated to say yes.

Imagine yourself being asked to do the thing you want to say no to. Whether it's a request in person, an e-mail, a text, or a phone call. Picture yourself receiving the request or knowing that you need to respond.

What is the primary emotion you feel? Are you angry, afraid, or resentful?

Begin tapping through the points, talking through that emotion, as you let yourself feel it.

Karate Chop . . . Eyebrow . . . Side of Eye . . . Under Eye . . . Under Nose . . . Under Mouth . . . Collarbone . . . Under Arm . . . Top of Head . . .

Karate Chop . . . Eyebrow . . . Side of Eye . . . Under Eye . . . Under Nose . . . Under Mouth . . . Collarbone . . . Under Arm . . . Top of Head . . .

Karate Chop . . . Eyebrow . . . Side of Eye . . . Under Eye . . . Under Nose . . . Under Mouth . . . Collarbone . . . Under Arm . . . Top of Head . . .

Continue tapping. When you're ready, begin talking through the choice you need to make, including your desire to say no and your feeling that you have to say yes.

Karate Chop . . . Eyebrow . . . Side of Eye . . . Under Eye . . . Under Nose . . . Under Mouth . . . Collarbone . . . Under Arm . . . Top of Head . . .

Karate Chop . . . Eyebrow . . . Side of Eye . . . Under Eye . . . Under Nose . . . Under Mouth . . . Collarbone . . . Under Arm . . . Top of Head . . .

Karate Chop . . . Eyebrow . . . Side of Eye . . . Under Eye . . . Under Nose . . . Under Mouth . . . Collarbone . . . Under Arm . . . Top of Head . . .

When you're ready, visualize yourself saying no. If saying the word *no* feels harsh, you can say something like the following:

It's not a good time.

Let's figure out a different time.

Today's not a good day for that.

Thanks, I just can't do that right now.

No, thank you!

As you continue to see yourself in that moment, tap through the points as you say no.

Karate Chop . . . Eyebrow . . . Side of Eye . . . Under Eye . . . Under Nose . . . Under Mouth . . . Collarbone . . . Under Arm . . . Top of Head . . .

Keep tapping while you practice saying no. Notice how it feels. Are you afraid of the response you'll receive? What consequences do you expect from saying no?

Keep tapping as you practice saying no and tapping through how you feel about saying no.

Karate Chop . . . Eyebrow . . . Side of Eye . . . Under Eye . . . Under Nose . . . Under Mouth . . . Collarbone . . . Under Arm . . . Top of Head . . .

Once saying no feels more comfortable, imagine the response you expect to get from saying it. Will people get mad at you or feel confused and rejected? Do you fear you'll lose an opportunity or not be invited in the future?

Keep tapping as you imagine others' response(s) to your saying no.

Karate Chop . . . Eyebrow . . . Side of Eye . . . Under Eye . . . Under Nose . . . Under Mouth . . . Collarbone . . . Under Arm . . . Top of Head . . .

Keep tapping as you digest others' response(s).

Karate Chop . . . Eyebrow . . . Side of Eye . . . Under Eye . . . Under Nose . . . Under Mouth . . . Collarbone . . . Under Arm . . . Top of Head . . .

Karate Chop . . . Eyebrow . . . Side of Eye . . . Under Eye . . . Under Nose . . . Under Mouth . . . Collarbone . . . Under Arm . . . Top of Head . . .

Karate Chop . . . Eyebrow . . . Side of Eye . . . Under Eye . . . Under Nose . . . Under Mouth . . . Collarbone . . . Under Arm . . . Top of Head . . .

When you can imagine others' response(s) while feeling calm, take a deep breath.

When you're ready, start tapping and begin the same visualization from the beginning. Run through the entire sequence—being asked, saying no, getting a response.

Karate Chop . . . Eyebrow . . . Side of Eye . . . Under Eye . . . Under Nose . . . Under Mouth . . . Collarbone . . . Under Arm . . . Top of Head . . .

Karate Chop . . . Eyebrow . . . Side of Eye . . . Under Eye . . . Under Nose . . .

Under Mouth . . . Collarbone . . . Under Arm . . . Top of Head . . .

Karate Chop . . . Eyebrow . . . Side of Eye . . . Under Eye . . . Under Nose . . .
Under Mouth . . . Collarbone . . . Under Arm . . . Top of Head . . .

Continue tapping through the sequence as many times as you need to. When you can tap through the entire sequence without feeling emotional intensity, you've successfully cleared it!

DAY 17 GREATEST SELF CHALLENGE: FEELING AT EASE SAYING NO

We nod our heads yes when we want to shake them no. We give the thumbs-up when we're not feeling it. We add "it" to our calendars when we crave more unscheduled time.

Saying yes feels easy.

It runs out of us like syrup, making our interactions feel sweet—until later when we're expected to fulfill promises that we never wanted to make in the first place.

For the next 24 hours your challenge is to take 60 seconds, just one full minute, before responding to requests for your time, attention, and energy. Do this for all requests, including ones that sound appealing or feel mandatory.

Use that time first to check in with yourself. Most of us experience some level of overwhelm, even to small requests. Whatever emotional response you have, stop and notice it.

Then begin tapping through that emotional response, and notice how you actually want to respond.

Take that time to notice and check in with yourself.

Just notice and check in. It doesn't mean say no to everything, it just means be conscious about your choices.

For Brenna, that "check-in" led to rescheduling that playdate one more time. Not only did she have a great Monday; she wholeheartedly enjoyed the playdate when it did finally happen.

Give yourself that gift. Be conscious about what you actually want to experience in your life. Be conscious about where you want to put your energy.

Just be conscious, and watch your life transform!

You can find the *Day 17 Tapping Meditation: I'm Not Chocolate!* on page 293 of the Appendix.

◎ ◎ ◎

And, of course, it's also time to add Day 18 to your calendar! Pick a day, whether it's tomorrow or three days from now, and commit to reading and tapping through it then. That's when you'll discover how transforming the story you're telling yourself can completely change your life.

Day 18

Creating Your "Version Two": Embracing Your Greatest Self

I'm going to tell you two equally true versions of the same story. As you read them, try to guess which public or historical figure I'm describing.

Here's version one:

The oldest of three children, X was in elementary school when his father left and his mother succumbed to substance abuse. Over the years his mother remarried several times, but it was X, her eldest son, who took care of the family.

In addition to doing his best to shield his siblings from the chaos in their home, X often ran errands for his mother, who for long periods of time refused to leave the house.

Many times she sent him to the pharmacy to beg for more painkillers, claiming that she had lost her pills. Years passed before X realized that she'd been lying in an attempt to cover up how many pills she was taking.

As X grew older, his mother's dependence on him turned violent. Terrified of losing him as her primary caretaker, she began resorting to new forms of abuse, including pouring dish soap down his throat until he threw up.

Fortunately, during his sophomore year of high school, a teacher singled X out. Recognizing his gift for communication, that teacher gave him a copy of a speech and asked him to read it. If the speech resonated with who he was, his teacher asked that he enter a speech contest. If the speech had no impact on him, X had no obligation.

X read the speech and cried his eyes out. The speech was about never giving up, and it spoke to his will to overcome a childhood lost to his mother's addiction, chronic food insecurity and abuse, as well as being abandoned by his father at seven years old.

X entered that speech contest and won first place. He entered another and another, winning each time.

Those successes gave him a seed of hope that he had found a way to reach people, but his home life, especially his mother's mental health, continued to decline.

Finally, when X was 17, she chased him out of the house with a knife. He left his mother's house that day and never returned.

Instead of attending college, X began working as a janitor. For a stretch of time, he was homeless, forced to live out of his car.

Fast-forward some years, X began working in event promotion, moving later into coaching. By his early 30s, X's wildly successful work had begun to impact millions of people around the world, including celebrities and thought leaders. His foundation has since helped to alleviate poverty, feeding millions of people in need every year.

Any idea who that is?

Here's the second version:

Known today as one of the world's most powerful motivational speakers, X's work has transformed the lives of millions of people around the globe. World leaders and icons, including Bill Clinton, Princess Diana, Mother Teresa, Mikhail Gorbachev, and Nelson Mandela, credit X with helping them achieve their potential. Many celebrities and sports stars do the same.

Each year he travels the globe, sharing his empowering message, which he's conveyed to more than 4 million people worldwide through his live events, and more than 50 million people through his best-selling books and online programs.

Some might argue that X's success has come in spite of his painful childhood, the cancer he fought in adulthood, as well as the end of his first marriage. X, however, believes that it's these challenges, especially those from childhood, that have shaped him most powerfully.

Growing up with an alcoholic mother who was also addicted to painkillers, he suffered physical and mental abuse, as well as chronic food insecurity. Rather than absorbing those experiences, he became determined to break out of the pattern of self-destruction he had witnessed in the adults around him.

Now the founder or partner in roughly a dozen different businesses whose combined revenue is $5 billion annually, X has a relentless drive to help people turn their lives around.

His foundation helps feed millions in need each year and is among his top priorities. A father of four, he is joyfully married to his second wife, and he is known for being as authentic in person as he is onstage.

X is . . .

Have you guessed it yet?

Should I tell you, or keep you guessing?

Just kidding! X is Tony Robbins.

Think for a minute, how did each version of his story impact you?

In the first version when you got to the section where he'd been chased out of the house and was homeless and working as a janitor, did part of your brain briefly go, *Uh-oh, it's game over for this guy . . . ?*

In the second version, did you feel differently? Was it comforting to know about the successful outcome right away? Did he seem more confident, capable, and powerful in version two?

Although those discrepancies in perception may seem obvious, they're important to notice.

At what points did he seem weak, even hopeless? When did he seem like a hero?

Storytelling is one of our most powerful communication tools. The bigger, more important question is, which version of your own story are you telling yourself?

Does your story emphasize how your past and your present are limiting you?

Or is your story about manifesting your greatest self after overcoming adversity?

What story do you tell yourself about who you are, who you can become, and what's possible in your life?

Today, as we continue to lay a foundation for moving forward as your greatest self, we're going to use Tapping to begin transforming your self-defeating "version one" story into an empowering and inspiring "version two."

POST-TRAUMATIC GROWTH

How do people who have undergone trauma not just bounce back (that's resilience), but come back at a higher level? It's called *post-traumatic growth*, and it's an area of study that's getting more attention.

Unknowingly, many of us first learned about post-traumatic growth as children through the story of a young boy who witnessed the horrific murder of his parents. Although devastated, he eventually grew into a man who dedicated his life to helping people victimized by injustice and crime. Through that work he saved countless people's lives.

His name? Batman.

The stories around post-traumatic growth are as incredible in real life as they are in fiction.

Scarlett Lewis is one of the most inspiring post-traumatic growth stories I've had the honor to witness. After losing her youngest son, Jesse, who was in first grade when he was shot in the Newtown school shooting of 2012, Scarlett and I tapped together several times.

After undergoing an intense grieving process, Scarlett was able to forgive the young man who shot Jesse. Today she radiates the healing love she wrote about in her book, *Nurturing Healing Love: A Mother's Journey of Hope & Forgiveness*. She has also since founded the Choose Love Movement, and is actively working to heal trauma survivors, including parents and educators, in and around her community.

Through The Tapping Solution Foundation, I have also worked with many other parents and educators whose lives came to a screeching halt after that shooting took 20 elementary school children from us.

Each survivor's story is both heartbreaking and inspiring. One after another, thanks to tapping through the incredible trauma they survived, they have returned to their lives and communities to contribute more than they ever had before.

To be fair, all of them would do anything to undo the trauma they survived—to get their lost family members back, turn back time and pay closer attention, and so on. Realizing that they can't undo the past, however, they instead make extraordinary choices.

What kinds of stories do you think they tell themselves about what's possible in their own lives?

TUNNELING TOWARD LIGHT

Remember yesterday when we did that exercise around finding the life switch in your life, focusing on that light and letting it shine inside you?

In order to get to that switch, you may have had to first fumble around in the dark, to travel through the parts of yourself and your life that feel dark.

When I work with people, that's often what happens. Using Tapping, they navigate through their own inner darkness—the challenging emotions, memories, and limiting beliefs that are keeping them stuck.

Once they release that, they find their own light, and the story they tell themselves naturally changes into an inspiring and empowering "version two" story.

When you look at your own past, what darkness is still there? Where in your own "version one" story are you stuck?

THE (UN)STICKING POINT

Think now of one area of your life—your relationship, family, health, finances, and so on—where you feel stuck, *least* able to become your greatest self.

When you focus on that area of your life, rate how stuck you feel on a scale of 0 to 10.

Take three deep breaths, and begin tapping on the Karate Chop point.

KC *(repeat three times)*: Even though I feel stuck in this part of my life, I love and accept myself.

Eyebrow: I feel stuck

Side of Eye: So stuck when it comes to <area of your life>

Under Eye: I don't know how to get unstuck

Under Nose: So stuck when it comes to <area of your life>

Under Mouth: I feel blocked

Collarbone: Like there's no good way to break through

Under Arm: Feeling so stuck here

Top of Head: There's a story in <area of your life>

Eyebrow: It's a story I need to tell

Side of Eye: Not sure I want to, though

Under Eye: This story

Under Nose: What's the story?

Under Mouth: I don't want to tell it

Collarbone: What if I get lost in that story?

Under Arm: Maybe I'm already lost in it

Top of Head: I'm stuck

Eyebrow: I need to tell this story

Side of Eye: I need to tell it all now

Under Eye: It's safe to tell this story

Under Nose: I have to let myself tell this story

Under Mouth: I can tell it now

Collarbone: It's safe to tell this story

Under Arm: I can tell it now and let myself feel what I feel

Top of Head: I can let myself feel it all now

Continue tapping through the points as you tell the story that's keeping you stuck in this part of your life.

Let yourself feel the emotions that old story brings forward.

Keep tapping as you tell the whole story, including what you believe is possible and not possible as a result of this story.

Continue tapping through your old story for as long as it takes to tell the whole story and release the darkness, especially the negative emotions and limiting beliefs this story has created.

When you can tell the story without feeling negative emotional charge, you've successfully released it.

That's when you can write your new "version two" story.

Keep tapping as you begin that now.

What's possible for you in this area of your life now?

Describe your most inspiring and empowering vision of your "version two" story.

Continue tapping through the points as you begin exploring this new story. Keep tapping until it feels more authentic and also possible.

OPTIONAL EXERCISE: CLEARING RESISTANCE AROUND YOUR "VERSION TWO" STORY

Struggling to create your new story? Try this exercise to get started.

Focus first on one area of your life that you'd like to transform. Usually, this is a "pain point" in your life—relationships, finances, health, career, and so on.

Fill in the blanks in this story:

I feel _____ *(positive emotion) with my*
_____ *(area you want to transform).*

I am now able to _____ *(positive action, such as "pay my bills with ease" or "communicate openly with my partner," "sleep through the night," and so on).*

That new experience frees me to _____
(positive action you can take because that area of life is no longer a problem, such as "exercise more" or "be a mentor," "pursue my passion for gardening/ woodworking/and so on").

Tap through that story, allowing yourself to feel and release any negative emotions it creates.

Keep tapping through the story until you can feel the positive emotion that you wish to feel.

You can apply this same process to other parts of your life, and gradually create a bigger picture of how your "version two" story feels throughout the different parts of your life.

TIME IS ON YOUR SIDE

Onstage Tony Robbins makes no secret of the fact that he *created* the Tony Robbins we all know. In the Netflix documentary movie *I Am Not Your Guru*, he openly shares that he spent the first part of his life trying to please people. It was only through work and determination that he became the best version of himself.

He didn't magically become *the* Tony Robbins. He worked at it. He re-created himself.

Telling your version two story and inhabiting your greatest self is also a process. Your new story won't always feel authentic.

Even after tapping through some of your own darkness, the new and empowering story you tell yourself may seem fake, too good to be true, or too far removed from where you are now.

That's okay. That's fear talking. Fear is here to protect you, but you don't have to let it stop you.

Time is on your side. You can choose to use it well.

STEPPING INTO YOUR NEW STORY

When fears around your new story creep in, stop and rate the intensity of your fear on a scale of 0 to 10.

Take three deep breaths, and begin tapping on the Karate Chop point.

KC *(repeat three times)*: Even though I'm feeling all this fear around my new and more empowering "version two" story, I love and accept myself as I am.

Eyebrow: This fear

Side of Eye: It's overwhelming

Under Eye: I can't believe this new story

Under Nose: It doesn't seem possible

Under Mouth: This story can't actually come true

Collarbone: It's too good

Under Arm: It's too great

Top of Head: I'm not like that

Eyebrow: My life isn't like that

Side of Eye: This new story

Under Eye: It doesn't feel real

Under Nose: It doesn't feel possible

Under Mouth: It feels like a fantasy

Collarbone: Like a movie I can't possibly star in

Under Arm: This new story

Top of Head: It feels too good to be true

Eyebrow: I'm scared to believe in it

Side of Eye: I'm scared to trust it

Under Eye: I'm scared to hope it will come true

Under Nose: What if it doesn't?

Under Mouth: What if it really is too good to be true?

Collarbone: What if it never comes true?

Under Arm: What if it could come true?

Top of Head: It's so scary to believe in this new story

Eyebrow: My old story is depressing

Side of Eye: But it's more comfortable than this new story

Under Eye: This new story sounds like a lot of work

Under Nose: What if it's too much work for me?

Under Mouth: What if I can't do that much?

Collarbone: So much fear

Under Arm: I'm scared to believe this new story

Top of Head: All this fear

Eyebrow: I can feel it in my body

Side of Eye: It's intense

Under Eye: This fear

Under Nose: It's trying to keep me safe

Under Mouth: But it's also keeping me stuck

Collarbone: This fear

Under Arm: I see it and I feel it

Top of Head: It's safe to release it

Eyebrow: I can invest in hope

Side of Eye: I can invest in me

Under Eye: I can create my greatest self

Under Nose: It's going to get uncomfortable

Under Mouth: And there may be lots of work to do

Collarbone: I can tap

Under Arm: I can trust in this new story

Top of Head: Letting myself feel relaxed and hopeful now

Take a deep breath. Again rate the intensity of your fear around believing in your new story. Keep tapping until you experience the desired level of peace.

DAY 18 GREATEST SELF CHALLENGE: LIVING YOUR NEW STORY

On Day 7 we learned about the power of repetition. What might happen if you repeated your new story to yourself over and over and over again?

Would you begin to believe it? Would you begin to *feel* it?

Your challenge starting today is to tell and retell yourself this new "version two" story.

(If your "version two" story takes some time to come to you, don't stress. Just get curious, notice what you'd like to transform, and let yourself imagine new possibilities.)

Through repetition, along with tapping, you're then going to re-create the story you tell yourself.

Day after day, multiple times each day, you're going to tell yourself this new story. You're going to tap through the story until it feels true, and you're going to do that over and over again.

Then stay tuned. Watch what happens. Notice how you feel.

And then repeat the process again and again.

Make sure to complete the *Day 18 Tapping Meditation: Becoming Your Version Two on page* 296 of the Appendix.

◎ ◎ ◎

Also take a moment to add Day 19 to your calendar now. That's when we begin to clear the slate for your greatest self to emerge.

*They say the final "leg"—that last 10 percent—
of any project or undertaking is the hardest part.*

Fortunately, by now you've already done a lot of deep clearing.

It's all "up" from here! ☺

*Keep tapping, and remember that you can (and should!)
change Tapping scripts whenever those changes make your
tapping feel more authentic to your experience.*

You're so close!

Keep it up!

Day 19

Embracing the Mess, Clearing the Clutter

When you think of clutter, what do you think of?

The answer is more personal than we tend to assume. Often it depends on the person, the time, the space.

A room piled high with books might be inspiring to a professor or writer but feel distracting, even depressing, to someone who thrives in clear, open space.

Someone who insists on keeping a neat house may also not feel bothered by the clutter in his or her car.

When we talk about clutter, we're not talking in clearly defined opposites like clean versus dirty, good versus bad, or messy versus neat.

In fact, clutter isn't just about our "stuff."

During this journey we've looked at stress and overwhelm (panic), as well as the past, and deeper emotions like anger and fear. Those are all examples of emotional clutter.

Mental clutter often looks like "busy thoughts" from unfinished business that distracts us from more fulfilling pursuits.

And let's not forget my personal (least) favorite, calendar clutter.

Today we're going to look at different kinds of clutter, how it differs from messiness, and then clear any clutter that's holding you back.

EMBRACING THE MESS

You're at home, but in the middle of an important work call when your kids announce that they're starving. Their insistent demands, of course, come minutes after you offered them a snack. Back then, all 13 minutes before your meeting started, they weren't hungry. Now that you're busy, they're ravenous.

You begin making them food, trying to cradle your phone on your shoulder, doing your best to focus your attention on what's being said in the call.

Then the doorbell rings. And the dog barks.

You accidentally spill the milk, and your phone falls to the floor with a loud bang.

The doorbell rings again. The dog barks more.

Your kids run screaming into the kitchen and accidentally kick your phone into the spilled milk.

Ugh.

You wipe off your phone, which is still working (phew!). You return to your call, and in spite of a bumpy start, you get the exact information you need to complete your project (yay!).

As it turns out, the doorbell rang because the UPS driver dropped off a package you've been waiting for (it's here, yessss!).

And your kids, of course, are the biggest and most glorious mess in your life (heart full of love . . . followed by frustration . . . followed by more love . . . and more).

While that period of time may have caused some short-term stress, most of the messiness you experienced was a reflection of the full life you're leading.

That's not clutter. That's an example of how life can get messy at times. It's not perfect, and neither is any one of us.

Getting rid of some of the clutter in your life isn't about making everything perfect. If there are kids around, your kitchen probably won't be spotless 24-7. That's okay.

So when we talk about clutter, what are we really talking about?

THERE'S NO "SHOULD DO" IN "WANT TO"

When I come home from speaking at Hay House events with other author/speakers in the healing/personal development space, I do what I've done since middle school, when I first discovered my mom's Tony Robbins CDs.

I put my earphones in and listen to more of my favorite audios from authors like Caroline Myss, Wayne Dyer, and Louise Hay.

I share that to say, I *love* this stuff. Since I was first introduced to the personal development/healing space as a teenager, it's been a central part of my life.

It's not surprising then, that in 2014 when I was invited to meet the Dalai Lama, my immediate response was an enthusiastic, "Yes! I'll be there!"

At the time I'd been traveling and speaking a lot, connecting and reaching out to people around the globe. I wanted nothing more than to continue expanding and growing this work that helps people transform their lives.

After accepting the invitation to meet the Dalai Lama, I wondered how it would feel to be in his presence. I envisioned showing him Tapping. And thought about how fun it would be to take a picture with him.

I was going to meet the Dalai Lama! It was the most unexpected and thrilling opportunity imaginable.

As the date got closer, though, a little voice inside me began stirring. It said, *You're tired . . . there is no such thing as a missed opportunity . . . stay home.*

My speaking schedule had been heavy for a while, and the deeper truth was that I was feeling pulled to slow down. I absolutely did want to continue expanding and growing my work, but first I needed some rest.

As the date approached, I also learned that meeting the Dalai Lama would mean missing a visit from my uncle. He lived in Argentina, so I typically only got to see him every five or so years.

Did I want to meet the Dalai Lama? Yes, of course I did.

At that particular time in my life, though, that additional trip felt like too much.

That trip *felt* like calendar clutter.

In the end I made the difficult decision to stay home that weekend. Of course, there was a part of me that tugged and said, "What if you made a mistake?" But when I did some tapping on it, I got real clarity and felt comfortable that I'd made the right decision.

The result?

A lovely evening with my family on a beautiful Connecticut night listening to stories from my uncle of decades past. There were stories about how my parents met (I knew the basics but got more details), and stories about the grandfather I never knew, as well as stories about me as a kid.

The stories I heard that night nourished a part of my soul like nothing else could. I connected with the people I love most and made memories that will last a lifetime.

I was so grateful to have made that decision and doubly so a year later when my uncle passed away unexpectedly. It put that special night, and my difficult decision, in context, highlighting what matters most and how life comes together when we eliminate clutter and get clear.

CLEARING ONE CLUTTER "PILE"

Is your e-mail in-box bursting?

Is your calendar overflowing?

Is your voice mail box filling to capacity?

Those all count as clutter!

Pick one area of your life where there's clutter.

Once you've decided on the one area of focus, take "it"—your calendar, in-box, and so on—out.

Look at it. *Really* look at it.

How does your body feel when you look at it? Do your shoulders tense up? Does your stomach tighten? Do you feel physical pain, pressure, hot, cold, or throbbing?

Is there one e-mail, one day on your calendar, one message or item that's causing the most stress?

Notice which primary emotion you feel when you think about that clutter. Are you scared, angry, worried, resentful?

Rate the intensity of your primary emotion on a scale of 0 to 10.

Take three deep breaths. We'll begin tapping on the Karate Chop point.

KC *(repeat three times)*: Even though I feel all this <primary emotion> when I focus on this clutter in my life, I love myself and accept how I feel.

Eyebrow: All this <primary emotion>

Side of Eye: I can feel it in my body

Under Eye: Whenever I think about this clutter

Under Nose: So much <primary emotion>

Under Mouth: I can feel it now

Collarbone: I don't want to deal with this clutter

Under Arm: I want it to go away

Top of Head: But it's there

Eyebrow: And that makes me feel so much <primary emotion>

Side of Eye: I don't want to do this

Under Eye: I want this clutter to go away

Under Nose: I want it gone

Under Mouth: Why do I feel so much <primary emotion>?

Collarbone: Are there other reasons I don't want to deal with this?

Under Arm: So much <primary emotion> around this clutter

Top of Head: I'm dreading the process of clearing this clutter

Eyebrow: But I also want it to go away

Side of Eye: It's okay to feel all of this

Under Eye: Maybe it's time to look at this

Under Nose: Maybe it's time to release it

Under Mouth: I can start to let go of this <primary emotion>

Collarbone: Releasing this <primary emotion>

Under Arm: From every cell in my body

Top of Head: Feeling calm when I think about this clutter

Take a deep breath. On a scale of 0 to 10 again rate the intensity of your primary emotion around clearing that clutter now.

Continue tapping until you feel the desired level of peace.

When you're ready, continue focusing on that clutter. Tap through the points as you ask yourself the following questions, answering each one as specifically as you can:

- *In a perfect world, how could I clear this clutter while feeling more ease in the process?*

- *What will it feel like once this clutter is cleared?*

Keep tapping through the points, and notice what comes up.

There may be clutter that you can't clear, and that's okay. Focus instead on noticing and releasing negative emotional charge around that clutter.

Keep tapping until you experience a greater level of peace.

Repeat this process on any other clutter that makes you feel dread, anxiety, fear, or other challenging emotions.

THE 100-POUND WALLET

"What is *that*?" I asked from across the table.

My wife, Brenna, and I were out to dinner with a group of friends. One friend Sue had pulled out her wallet. It was, by far, the largest, most stuffed wallet I'd ever seen.

Sue laughed lightheartedly. "My wallet!" she replied.

"Wait, let me see that. Can I see that?" I asked jokingly.

She nodded and handed her wallet over, clearly as amused as I was.

After getting her permission to glance through its contents, I found what amounted to a stack of expired coupons, multiple expired cards, including five years of AAA cards, only one of which was still valid. We all laughed.

After getting her permission, I tossed out her four expired AAA cards, and the evening ended on a jovial note.

Months later Sue traveled to Thailand, and she was stopped at security for an extra 20 minutes because they insisted on searching her wallet. She laughed to herself, remembering that night at dinner, wondering what I'd say if I saw

her sidelined at Thai security, dreaming about starting her beach vacation . . . as soon as they finished searching her wallet!

Granted, those 20 minutes didn't ruin her trip, but they did take some time out of her beach vacation. The clutter in her wallet was adding literal weight to her life. It was slowing her down, if only in small ways.

What clutter in your life or your surroundings is slowing you down?

CREATING MORE SPACE FOR JOY

After reading Marie Kondo's book *The Life-Changing Magic of Tidying*, Brenna taught me to ask one simple but powerful question when considering whether to keep or give away "stuff."

The question is:

Does this bring me joy?

It's a simple, powerful way to clear not just physical space but also mental and emotional clutter.

To begin, visualize or go to a physical space in your home or office that feels cluttered.

As you look around that area, look at the objects in it.

Ask yourself:

What in this space brings me joy?

Then ask:

What in this space doesn't bring me joy?

If it's helpful, physically separate the objects that bring you joy and those that don't into different sections or piles.

Pick up one object that no longer brings you joy. Notice any negative emotions or memories that come up when you focus on that object. Rate the intensity of that experience on a scale of 0 to 10.

Put the object down, take three deep breaths, and begin tapping through the points as you tell the story of that object—what it reminds you of, how that memory makes you feel, what feels true, and so on.

For example, if the object is an old toy or keepsake from your child's now grown, you might tap through your emotions around no longer needing that object in the house.

Alternately, if the object is something that you and your ex purchased, you might need to tap through any emotions that come up around that memory or the ending of that relationship.

Whatever emotional significance that object holds, keep tapping until you feel the desired level of peace around it.

Next ask yourself:

Am I ready to let go of this?

If you answer no, notice how intensely you feel that resistance. Rate it on a scale of 0 to 10.

Tap on that resistance until the thought of getting rid of that object causes less friction.

Keep clearing any clutter that feels heavy or negative in any way. You'll be amazed by how much clarity you'll gain once you've gotten rid of clutter!

DAY 19 GREATEST SELF CHALLENGE: CLEAR IT, DO IT, FINISH IT!

When was the last time you looked at the supplies for that project you were excited about but never found the time to actually finish?

What about that stack of papers you keep moving to the side?

And is that partially written book, story, or poem still sitting idly on your hard drive?

Beyond just your "stuff," what unfinished business is cluttering your life?

Pick one piece of unfinished business. One creative project, one closet, one corner of your garden, one e-mail in-box.

Pick one thing, and commit to finishing what you started. If you encounter that *ugh, I don't want to* feeling, stop and tap on it.

If, while tapping on it, you realize that it's a project you no longer care to finish, decide once and for all to table it. That's huge! By making that decision, you've removed that bit of clutter from your life.

If it is a project that you still want to finish, clear space in your calendar, dive in, and commit to getting it 100 percent done within a realistic but specific, defined timeline.

As you get back to it, play your favorite music, invite a friend over to keep you company, promise yourself a reward afterward. Do what you need to do to make it fun.

For some extra motivation, here are some great quotes:

> *Starting strong is good. Finishing strong is epic.*
> – Robin Sharma

> *Before you start anything, learn how to finish it.*
> – Unknown

> *Commitment means staying loyal to what you said*
> *you were going to do long after the mood*
> *you said it in has left you.*
> – Unknown

And let's not forget this Nike tagline:

Start strong. Finish stronger.

So go ahead—finish one thing. Notice how you feel while you're finishing and once you're done.

Wait, you're done? You're done! Time to celebrate!

You can find the *Day 19 Tapping Meditation: More Space, More Joy* on page 299 of the Appendix.

◎ ◎ ◎

You're almost at the end of our journey—kudos! Get ready because on Day 20 we take our greatest selves "out for a spin," so to speak.

Also take that minute right now to add Day 20 into your calendar. You're almost ready to launch!

Day 20

Will You Take My Hand?

It's a quiet Sunday. The weather is too extreme to enjoy, so instead of going on a long walk, you sit down on the couch and look out the window.

The sky is pretty, inspiring, even, in spite of the weather. The trees stand tall, clouds shift slowly but steadily into an endless number of new configurations. As you take it all in, you're suddenly overcome by an undeniable feeling of connection. It's as if Mother Nature or the Universe is speaking to you. It says something like this:

I am here, always.

Will you take my hand?

Will you ride the gentle, warm waves and the abrupt, bumpy ones and still hold on?

Take my hand. Will you trust unconditionally that I am here?

Will you get out in the world and create your magic, your wonder, so that I can support your flourishing?

Will you trust that, even when it seems as if you're alone, that you are safe, you are loved?

Come. Co-create with me.

Take my hand.
Will you take my hand?
Will you walk with me now and forever into your most fulfilling,
abundant future?

Suddenly you blink, shaking your head, as if to bring you back to the couch you're sitting on, the walls that surround you.

These are big questions, and your heart is thumping, your mind is churning, unsure how to answer.

Will I ride even the choppiest of waves and still trust?

Will I get out in the world and co-create my greatest self and brightest future?

Can I trust *that* fully, *that* deeply?

Big questions.

Exciting questions, but scary, too.

You've spent the past 19 days (or weeks or whatever it's been) letting go of stress, practicing choosing peace, and releasing the past, your deepest emotions, and your most ingrained patterns.

How do you feel?

Do you feel ready to move deeper into your greatest self?

Are you feeling called to shed more?

As the close of this journey approaches, we'll build more trust in the process and the fulfilling, abundant future that awaits us when we become active co-creators of our greatest selves and greatest lives.

HERE'S THE TRUTH

You know that moment in *A Few Good Men* where Colonel Jessup, played by Jack Nicholson, finally breaks while on the witness stand and blurts out his most famous line?

That line, of course, is this: *"You can't handle the truth!"*

It's a seminal moment, the point at which Jessup cracks under pressure, finally allowing the story to move forward.

Before you assume that I'm saying those words to you (I'm not, not at all!), please pause. Take a deep breath.

I mention that line because, in many ways, it describes the mythology that our culture has created around what we call "success."

Whether we define "success" on spiritual terms or more tangible ones, we often focus on the final outcome rather than the process it took to get there.

Here's the truth, as I've lived it and seen it play out similarly in others' lives.

As I sit here doing work that I love, surrounded by the people in this world I love most in a community that I feel deeply connected to, I am forever aware of the moments that got me here.

There have been many, to be fair, and many of them have felt blessed—by the Universe and its abundance, by family, friends, fans. The list is long.

But that's not the whole story.

The work I now get to do, the vision and purpose that lure me to my office each day, started with my documentary movie, *The Tapping Solution*.

It was the first film I'd ever made. There were many moments that led to its first showing to a small audience in Bethel, Connecticut.

There was a lot of work to do after that first showing.

There was a lot work to do always. Period.

For months we traveled around the country interviewing experts, and I suffered throughout that time from severe allergies and chronic insomnia. My health got so bad, in fact, that I took time that I didn't have to spare and traveled to India to do a cleansing fast.

When I returned two weeks later to resume progress on the film, I was faced with a devastating setback.

It was one of many huge setbacks I experienced before, during, and after making that movie.

The entire journey was intense and demanding. *Very* intense and *very* demanding.

There were numerous times when things seemed impossibly bleak, times when many different parts of my life seemed to be crumbling around me all at once.

Any number of times I easily could have given up. I could have told myself that it was too hard, that the Universe was trying to tell me something, that it was time to hang up my hat, admit defeat.

Any number of times I could have walked away and had legitimate reasons for doing so.

The thing was, in my heart this crazy dream of making this film had taken root. I had no idea how to make a movie, and almost no relevant experience to fall back on, but I was committed.

As tempted as I was to give up at those times when bad news was rolling in a lot faster than good, some little voice inside told me not to.

Like I said, this dream had taken root inside me.

So I kept moving—okay it felt more like limping sometimes, but I kept going all the same.

And I tapped. Oh wow, did I tap! Nearly every day of this journey I've taken you on is a page from my own journey.

There's no way I could have followed through on my dream of making that movie if I hadn't tapped on my limiting beliefs, unresolved events, emotions, and ingrained patterns.

If I hadn't shown up to notice and heal how I was *being*, I would have abandoned the movie project that eventually led me to where I am now, sitting here at my desk, writing this book.

That's the truth.

And unlike Jessup, I *know* you can handle that truth.

I'm not suggesting that you should expect hardship on your journey. But expecting never-ending ease and uninterrupted flow isn't realistic, either.

When we expect all unicorns and all rainbows all the time, we're coming from a place of fear.

When we work that tirelessly to paint pretty pictures all around us, we're trying to whitewash deep-seated fears that we *can't* handle the truth.

That's why we need Tapping, to unearth that fear, anger, and other forms of resistance that have hardened into limiting beliefs about what we "can't" do and how we "will never" be.

When we use Tapping to shed this baggage that always has the potential to crop up, we're free to continually step more wholly and deeply into our greatest selves.

And *that's* when we can co-create our greatest lives.

Which is why, if we want sustainable results, being always has to come *before* doing.

I can't say that enough.

Being *before* doing.

If we start by focusing on doing and push aside how we're being, we give up, self-sabotage, procrastinate. Whatever our old patterns are, they step in, take over, cloud, then crush what might have been.

So tell me, as you continue to become your greatest self, what will you co-create?

Can you trust that even the setbacks you experience are meant to be? That the lessons you have yet to finish learning are divinely inspired? That you can handle them in new ways now, thanks to Tapping and the clearing and releasing you've done through this process?

Let's tap on it!

CULTIVATING DEEPER FAITH

How much negative emotional charge do you experience when you think about continuously co-creating your greatest self and your greatest life?

How much stress and anxiety do you feel about exiting your comfort zone to do that?

Rate the intensity of your emotions now on a scale of 0 to 10.

Take three deep breaths and begin tapping on the Karate Chop point.

KC *(repeat three times)*: Even though I'm not sure about continually co-creating my greatest self and greatest life, it sounds scary, I love myself and accept how I feel.

Eyebrow: This fear

Side of Eye: I can feel it

Under Eye: What if I'm not up to this?

Under Nose: What if I fail at being my greatest self?

Under Mouth: This fear

Collarbone: I can feel it in my body

Under Arm: I'm afraid

Top of Head: It's all so unknown

Eyebrow: That scares me

Side of Eye: It's okay to feel this fear

Under Eye: I'm safe feeling this fear

Under Nose: This fear is just here to get my attention

Under Mouth: *Hey, this is new!*

Collarbone: That's what my fear is saying to me

Under Arm: *This is new!*

Top of Head: But what if I can't do new stuff?

Eyebrow: It's easier to go back to my old stuff

Side of Eye: At least I know that stuff

Under Eye: This is new

Under Nose: And new feels scary

Under Mouth: It's okay to feel this fear

Collarbone: It's safe to feel this fear in my body

Under Arm: I can feel this fear now

Top of Head: And I can let it go

Eyebrow: New can be amazing!

Side of Eye: New doesn't equal bad

Under Eye: I can do this!

Under Nose: I can shed this fear

Under Mouth: And keep tapping on it

Collarbone: It may crop up again

Under Arm: That's okay

Top of Head: I'm safe

Eyebrow: I can handle this!

Side of Eye: I don't know what's next

Under Eye: No one knows that

Under Nose: My fear is trying to protect me

Under Mouth: Thank you, fear!

Collarbone: I don't need you right now, though

Under Arm: I'm safe

Top of Head: New is okay

Eyebrow: I can brave this newness!

Side of Eye: I'm safe with these unknowns

Under Eye: I already am my greatest self

Under Nose: And I can keep shedding this fear

Under Mouth: And the other layers that cloud my view

Collarbone: I don't know what's ahead

Under Arm: But I'm safe and I'm loved

Top of Head: And I can trust that and relax now

Take a deep breath. Again rate your stress, anxiety, and other resistance. Keep tapping until you experience the desired level of peace.

YOU'RE ALREADY A PRO AT THIS

Name one big dream that you've made into your reality. I know you've got *at least* one.

Stop and think. Think back to years ago, months ago, whatever timeline is most relevant.

Can you remember when that dream was first born inside you?

Did it feel exciting? Energizing?

And then, as dreams tend to do, did it seem to deflate? Did that big dream somehow turn into the impossible dream?

What was your dream?

Did you want your own business, a family, that house? Did you dream of taking that trip, mastering that new skill or sport, living abroad, becoming a parent? What was it?

Remember back to the entire journey you went on, from the inception of that dream to its realization.

What hurdles did you have to overcome before, during, and after? What lessons did you have to learn and relearn to realize that dream?

I know, I know. It's no big deal now. Everything you went through to realize that dream seems insignificant now that you've done it. Almost as soon as you realized that dream, you moved on to your next big dream.

Think about that for a moment.

You had a big dream. So exciting!

But then that big dream then started to feel like the impossible dream.

Things got hard, maybe confusing.

You were tempted to give up. *Really* tempted.

But then . . . drumroll . . . *you did it.*

You made your dream into your reality.

Did you get that part? You kept going. You made the impossible, possible.

Amazing!

The fact that you soon blew off what a big deal realizing that dream was is yet another example of your negativity bias kicking in.

Don't worry—it's not you. We all do that. It's hardwired into our brains.

Your negativity bias kicked in so fast, you didn't even notice how much joy it stole from you.

YOU'VE GOT THIS!

Look, I may not know you personally, but here's one thing that I do know.

This whole being your greatest self and co-creating your greatest life "thing"—you've got this! It you're not feeling that yet, it's only because there's still some "stuff" clouding your view. Tap on it!

Trust me; you've got this.

Keep tapping. Keep trusting.

The Universe is wise and loving, here to grant your wishes and teach you the necessary lessons along the way.

You've got this. Really, you do.

Keep tapping. Keep moving forward. You can always start this journey again. You can always revisit any parts that feel unfinished.

You've so got this!

Will you trust that?

SO . . . WHAT'S NEXT?

Yes, I know you know it, but I'll say it anyway.

This journey is never over. I'm still in it every single day. The scenery changes, the weather changes, but what changes most of all is inside you.

Your inner climate.

That's what eventually transforms most.

The more tapping you do, the more practice you have with releasing what's no longer serving you, the more grounded and peaceful you feel.

So even when it's raining, you find reasons to dance.

Because inside, once you've tapped, you see it, that ray of light peeking in through the far corner.

And you know what you once overlooked, that beyond that temporary layer of gloom, the sun is always shining.

And thanks to your tapping throughout this journey, you can now see and feel that sunshine.

Yes, even when it's raining.

DAY 20 GREATEST SELF CHALLENGE: STEPPING INTO CO-CREATION

It's time.

You're ready to take your greatest self out for a spin. To begin co-creating your greatest life.

Pick one area of your life where you want to focus on co-creating a new reality.

Do you want a more fulfilling career?

An intimate relationship?

More financial abundance?

What is it you really want more of in your life?

Select one action step you can take toward making that transformation happen.

Can you finally ask for a raise?

Take that course to learn new skills or test-drive a passion?

Be more open to new people and experiences?

What concrete action step can you take toward co-creating your greatest life?

Commit to it, and do it.

That's your challenge for today, tomorrow, this week, and onward, to practice co-creating by taking one step forward.

Tap when it feels scary or hard or boring, or when things don't turn out how you want, when you hoped they would.

Tap, and then get out there again. Go co-create. Just do it.

You'll find the *Day 20 Tapping Meditation: At Peace in the Light* on page 302 of the Appendix.

◎ ◎ ◎

Just one day to go! Take a minute to add Day 21 into your calendar now. Write: "Read Day 21—time to move toward my greatest life. Here's how!"

Day 21

Which Lane Are You In?

Once upon a time there was a spiritual seeker named Seeker One. Above all, she craved enlightenment, to feel deeply connected with the divine source and true joy.

Seeker One spent days, nights, and weekends on this quest. Before long, she felt more peaceful and joyful, far less caught up in the everyday stressors that once seemed all consuming.

All who knew Seeker One noticed these changes. Many were impressed at how close she seemed to her goal of achieving spiritual enlightenment and pure joy.

Seeker One also felt the seeds of true transformation blooming inside her. However, she could also still feel the limitations of her mind and her past holding her back.

After much contemplation, she decided to double her commitment to her spiritual practice. Hoping to hold herself accountable, Seeker One shared this intention with her close and trusted friend, Seeker Two.

Seeker One and Seeker Two had long been friends. To many their friendship seemed an odd pairing. Seeker Two, after all, was far less focused and motivated. Unlike Seeker One, Seeker Two often got distracted from his goal of achieving enlightenment.

Hearing Seeker One's ambitions, Seeker Two resolved that he, too, would commit more fully to his spiritual practice. But, as all who knew him predicted, as the days turned into weeks, Seeker Two got distracted. Although he continued his practice, he did so at a far slower pace than Seeker One.

Several months later, after an unusually long time apart, the two friends arranged to meet once more.

The moment Seeker One sat down, Seeker Two was shocked to feel how frantic and unsettling her energy seemed. She looked tired and stressed out.

After an awkward moment passed between them, Seeker Two spoke.

"My dear friend, last we met, you were committed to doubling your efforts to achieve spiritual enlightenment. What I see in your face and feel in your energy now, though, is quite different. I must ask, what happened?"

Seeker One hung her head. "Yes, you are right. I failed."

"But what happened?" Seeker Two asked again.

"I did what I said I'd do. I doubled my practice. I worked tirelessly to attain enlightenment. After a few months, however, I felt depleted, so I gave myself a break. I promised myself a few days of rest. However, I was so tired that I found a few days wasn't enough. Those days turned into weeks, and now I am further away from enlightenment than I have ever been."

"Oh, I see," Seeker Two replied. "You can start again. It is never too late."

Seeker One nodded despondently. "Maybe, but dear friend, I must say, you do seem transformed. Your energy is the most peaceful and joyful I have ever seen. How did you do it?"

Seeker Two smiled a smile that radiated pure joy. "Huh, I guess that is true. I do feel more peaceful and more joyful. I do not have your discipline, though, or your drive. I did not practice as rigorously as you did."

"So how did you do it?" Seeker One implored.

"I practiced a little each day, or most days, that is. I practiced a little in the morning and sometimes at night. I practiced on plane rides and train rides, before meetings, and between appointments. I did what I could, but you must know, dear friend, never for so long as you. I do not have your tenacity, your ambition."

"And yet it is you who are enlightened."

Recognize that story?

If I called Seeker One the Hare and Seeker Two the Tortoise (and then admitted that I tweaked more than a few details), would you recognize it?

You already know what I'm going to say, but I'll say it anyway.

From this moment forward, be the Tortoise. Take steps toward your greatest self every day, or most days, but never while racing, never while panicking. Move forward in peace, tapping as you go.

WITHOUT FURTHER ADO . . .

Can you hear the fireworks? Do you have your dancing shoes?

Congratulations!

I am blown away, and so very proud of you! You made it to Day 21, so yes, it's time to celebrate already. That's huge progress and a substantial commitment to your greatest self and most fulfilling, rewarding future.

I hope you're beginning to feel what I've known all along. Your greatest self has been inside you the whole time. All you've needed is the chance to shed stress and unload the past so you walk a little lighter and feel a lot brighter.

You are not, and never will be, alone. Revel now in the beauty, light, and wonder that surrounds you . . .

> *When I look into the future, it's so bright it burns my eyes.*
> – Oprah Winfrey

And besides you doing your own celebrating, I want to take a moment to personally celebrate *you*.

It takes a special kind of person to commit to reading this whole book, doing the tapping, and immersing yourself in this work around manifesting your greatest self.

The fact that you made it here lets me know, 100 percent, that you can manifest your greatest self, that you can create the life of your dreams.

It doesn't mean it's all done. It doesn't even mean that it will ever be done. But it does mean that within you, that spark of joy, of abundance, of freedom, of kindness, of compassion is shining brightly and is already making a difference in the world.

I honor you.

I honor how you are showing up in the world.

I honor your commitment to manifesting your greatest self.

As I sign all my e-mails . . .

Until next time . . . Keep Tapping!

Much, much love and a big, big hug,

Nick

P.S. You'll find the *Day 21 Tapping Meditation: Let's Celebrate!* on page 305 of the Appendix. Since you've completed the journey, there is no challenge today.

So . . . how do you feel? Don't worry, this journey is always here for you. You can make it your annual New Year's gift to yourself, or launch it again around your birthday each year.

Read and tap through it anytime. You'll reap new rewards each time you do. To make that review process easier, I've added *Your 21-Day Journey Map*, where you'll find a summary of each day of the journey all in one place.

Your 21-Day Journey Map

Congratulations! Now that you've been through all 21 days, here's a summary of each day of the journey so that you can easily refer back, as needed.

Quick Start: Let's Get Tapping!

Are you new to Tapping? If so, this is the place to start. We go through the how-to and do some quick tapping to get you started. It's an easy-to-follow process, and you'll love the results it will produce throughout the journey.

Even if you're already a "tapper," don't miss the beginning of this chapter. There's brand-new science around how Tapping impacts gene expression.

WEEK ONE: CHOOSING PEACE

Day 1: Peace or Panic?

To kick off the journey, we look at how we feel on any given day. Are we going through our days from a place of peace or a place of panic?

In that process we also examine the subtler ways that we "panic" and what peace looks and feels like. We also look at the effort and daily practice that positive people put into choosing peace, and use Tapping to experience more of it.

Day 1 Greatest Self Challenge: Practicing Peace (page 12)

Day 1 Tapping Meditation: From Panic to Peace (page 245)

Day 2: Negativity, Hardwired: A Look at the Primitive Brain

Remember Grog and Thor? They sit perched at the edge of a cave, and only one of them gets eaten by the tiger. Who is it, and why?

Through that story, we learn about the brain's negativity bias. This is also where we learned a bit more about the science of Tapping, and how it communicates with the body and primitive brain to balance our negativity bias.

Day 2 Greatest Self Challenge: Redirecting Your Brain (page 18)

Day 2 Tapping Meditation: Turning toward the Positive (page 248)

Day 3: The Upsides of Us: Harnessing the Power of Community

Can you be surrounded by people yet still feel lonely?

On this day we look at how loneliness impacts us, and how community can support us in taking this journey and feeling more fulfilled in our daily lives.

We also learn about Dr. Zak, aka Dr. Love, and his surprising prescriptions for overcoming feelings of isolation.

Day 3 Greatest Self Challenge: Come Join Us! (page 27)

Day 3 Tapping Meditation: Letting Go of Loneliness (page 251)

Day 4: Tell the Truth: Accepting What Is

On this day we get inspired to take an honest look at our lives, to see the "dirt" we need to see in order to clean it and begin moving into our greatest selves.

For many this day is a powerful eye opener, and important day for establishing a foundation for the journey ahead.

Exercises:

Opening the Door (page 35)

Telling Your Truth (page 37)

Day 4 Greatest Self Challenge: Telling Your Truth (page 39)

Day 4 Tapping Meditation: Accepting Your Truth (page 254)

Day 5: Practicing Peace, Welcoming Joy

Three climbers summited Mount Everest, yet each had a very different experience. Which climber do you most resonate with?

On this day we begin to pay more attention to how much joy we let into our lives, and use Tapping to see more opportunities to celebrate the little everyday victories we all experience.

Exercise:

Savoring the Smaller Wins (page 46)

Day 5 Greatest Self Challenge: Celebrating Your Wins (page 50)

Day 5 Tapping Meditation: Positive Tapping (page 257)

Day 6: What's It Saying? Listening to the Body

Is your lower back trying to tell you something? (Not to worry, I haven't gone off the deep end!)

On this day we look at how the body communicates with us, and use Tapping to begin tuning in to what it's saying.

We also look at limiting beliefs about the body, and begin to practice cultivating positive beliefs and emotions about the body.

Exercises:

Discovering Limiting Body Beliefs (page 54)

Oh, What a Pinkie Toe (page 56)

Day 6 Greatest Self Challenge: Tuning In to the Body (page 60)

Day 6 Tapping Meditation: Body Attunement (page 260)

Day 7: Ritual and Repetition: Making Transformation Stick

What do Michael Jordan, Benjamin Franklin, and Wade Boggs all have in common?

To wrap up the end of Week One, we did some quick review and looked at how the two R's can support us in moving forward.

Day 7 Greatest Self Challenge: Adding New Tools (page 67)

Day 7 Tapping Meditation: Peace & Patience (page 263)

WEEK TWO: EXPERIENCING LASTING RELIEF

Day 8: Planting the First Seed: A New Vision

You wake up to your divinely inspired mission. How do you feel? What will you do differently? Will you react and respond in new ways? How will your day feel now?

Using Tapping, we plant that first seed, the vision of who your greatest self is and what your greatest self most yearns to feel.

We also use Tapping to clear the slate from the fatigue of "working on ourselves" so that we can begin anew and create an authentic, inspired vision for the present and future.

Exercises:

I Want To Feel _____ (page 75)

Clearing the Slate (page 78)

Feeling at Peace with Your Intentions (page 80)

Day 8 Greatest Self Challenge: Being Intentional (page 82)

Day 8 Tapping Meditation: Aligning with Your Intentions (page 266)

Day 9: Where Are Your Energy Leaks?

If you had a limited amount of energy to "spend" each day, how would you use them?

On this day we look at how much of our everyday energy reserves are being "spent" on the past.

As tempted as you may be to skip "all that old stuff," this, as a rule, is your fastest, most direct path toward your greatest self. Skip it at your own peril. ☺

Exercises:

Choosing Self-Acceptance and Self-Love (page 89)

Seeing the Story (page 93)

Releasing the Story (page 94)

Day 9 Greatest Self Challenge: Noticing Key Patterns (page 96)

Day 9 Tapping Meditation: Letting Go (page 269)

Day 10: Letting Go of the Past

Today we look at how Dr. Felitti's failed research project accomplished a far larger goal—helping us all unearth the impact of ACEs.

Using Tapping, which has been shown to be highly effective at treating PTSD, we begin to look at past experiences, emotions, and beliefs that need more attention.

We also look at incredible stories of traumatized POWs who can inspire us all to move forward into a brighter, more inspiring future.

Before you decide to skip this day, I *know* that you don't want to go there. I get that, I really do, but I've worked with so many childhood trauma survivors over the years. Tapping has allowed them to heal at a level that simply wasn't possible without it.

Trust me on this one, will you? You won't regret it.

Exercises:

Ugh! Ick! Anything *but* the Past! (page 102)

Releasing a Past Event (page 107)

Day 10 Greatest Self Challenge: Releasing the Past (page 109)

Day 10 Tapping Meditation: Feeling Safe Releasing the Past (page 272)

Day 11: A Possum, a Polar Bear, and a Rabbit: Understanding the Freeze Response

What do a polar bear, a possum, and a rabbit have in common?

And what do we, as humans, have in common with them all?

On this day we explore a primal response to deep-seated fear, as well as trauma, known as the freeze response. We also look at the many little and big ways this response plays out in our lives, and then use Tapping to release it.

Almost everyone I know can relate to this chapter, including people who haven't undergone trauma. It's amazing what unfreezing can to do liberate your greatest self!

Exercise:

Freeing Yourself from Freeze (page 117)

Day 11 Greatest Self Challenge: Releasing the Freeze Response (page 120)

Day 11 Tapping Meditation: Feeling Safe Unfrozen (page 275)

Day 12: Quieting the Storm: Letting Go of Anger

On this day we look at unearthing and unleashing anger, one of our most primal and necessary, yet taboo, emotions.

We also see learn about Bobbie, who regained her mobility after decades of chronic physical pain, thanks to tapping on releasing deep-seated anger at her abusive father.

It's a big day that provides huge relief!

Exercises:

Letting Anger Be Anger (page 126)

Release First, Then Peace (page 127)

Day 12 Greatest Self Challenge: Letting Anger Go (page 133)

Day 12 Tapping Meditation: Releasing Anger (page 278)

Day 13: Letting It Go: Navigating Forgiveness

Whom are you refusing to forgive? What might open up in you and your life if you could forgive *that* person?

As we examine the power of forgiveness, we look at a story about the transformative power of deep, lasting forgiveness.

Using Tapping, we then begin to experience that same process and the deep relief and freedom it produces.

This is a big, and hugely important, topic. You'll be amazed by how much energy you'll set free once you can truly forgive.

Exercise:

Whom Do You Need to Forgive? (page 140)

Day 13 Greatest Self Challenge: Forgiving *That* Person (page 142)

Day 13 Tapping Meditation: "I Refuse to Forgive" (page 281)

Day 14: What Stands Out?

Does it really take 21 days to establish a new habit?

Today we look back at what Dr. Maxwell Maltz discovered about this time frame, and what his finding does (and doesn't) mean for the duration of our own journey.

We also look back and notice what stands out for you from Week Two.

It's a great chance to wrap up an intense week, take a little pressure off, and resolve any unfinished issues.

Exercises:

Right as Is, Right on Time (page 148)

What Stands Out for You? (page 150)

Day 14 Greatest Self Challenge: Surprise! (page 155)

Day 14 Tapping Meditation: I Don't Need Fixing (page 284)

WEEK THREE: MANIFESTING YOUR GREATEST SELF

Day 15: Dr. Seuss and Aristotle on the Best Little Choice You'll Ever Make

Are you allowing yourself to flourish and thrive each and every day?

After two weeks of clearing, we take a deeper look at choosing joy and supporting our own flourishing on a day-in-day-out basis.

Are you ready? You're getting ready to shine, and this is an important next step.

Exercise:

One Word, Many Experiences (page 161)

Day 15 Greatest Self Challenge: Adding Ease to a Task (page 165)

Day 15 Tapping Meditation: Choosing Happiness (page 287)

Day 16: At the Core of It All: A Fresh Look at Self-Acceptance

By this point in the journey, we're feeling more grounded, but still unsure what our greatest selves look and feel like.

Today we get to the core of it all, and take a new, and surprisingly fresh, look at self-acceptance.

This day will not only leave you feeling renewed and relieved; it will give you an entirely new way to relate to yourself.

Exercises:

Just One Thing (page 173)

Finding Your Life's Light Switch (page 174)

Day 16 Greatest Self Challenge: Mirroring Your Self-Talk (page 176)

Day 16 Tapping Meditation: Filling Your Cup (page 290)

Day 17: You're Not Chocolate!

Are you trying to be chocolate? Always trying to please others, even when it doesn't please you?

After the preceding several days spent looking at the past, we return to the present and look at how self-worth issues can cause us to sacrifice ourselves to please others.

We then use Tapping to release overwhelm and look at ways to set healthier boundaries that support more caring, supportive relationships with ourselves and others.

Exercises:

Releasing Overwhelm (page 181)

Visualizing Saying No (page 184)

Day 17 Greatest Self Challenge: Feeling at Ease Saying No (page 189)

Day 17 Tapping Meditation: I'm Not Chocolate! (page 293)

Day 18: Creating Your "Version Two": Embracing Your Greatest Self

Are you telling yourself your version one or version two story?

On this day we experience the power of story, and then notice how the story we tell ourselves impacts us.

We also learn about post-traumatic growth and stories of how adversity can become the source of our deepest, most enduring strength.

In that process we also begin to create a solid foundation for moving forward into our greatest selves and greatest lives.

Exercises:

The (Un)Sticking Point (page 196)

(Optional) Clearing Resistance Around Your "Version Two" Story (page 198)

Stepping into Your New Story (page 200)

Day 18 Greatest Self Challenge: Living Your New Story (page 202)

Day 18 Tapping Meditation: Becoming Your Version Two (page 296)

Day 19: Embracing the Mess, Clearing the Clutter

How clean and clear do you and your life really need to be?

Today we look at clutter in your physical surroundings and your life. We also look at the difference between messiness and clutter.

Then we use Tapping to clear clutter and create more space for thriving.

Exercises:

Clearing One Clutter "Pile" (page 209)

Creating More Space for Joy (page 212)

Day 19 Greatest Self Challenge: Clear It, Do It, Finish It (page 213)

Day 19 Tapping Meditation: More Space, More Joy (page 299)

Day 20: Will You Take My Hand?

Can you trust, *really* trust, that you're worthy, loved, and supported?

Today we deepen faith in our greatest selves, and begin to co-create our greatest lives. First, though, there's one more rock to turn over . . . are you ready?

This is an important day for getting even more grounded in the journey, and accepting the invitation to step into your greatest self and co-create your greatest life.

Exercise:

Cultivating Deeper Faith (page 221)

Day 20 Greatest Self Challenge: Stepping into Co-Creation (page 226)

Day 20 Tapping Meditation: At Peace in the Light (page 302)

Day 21: Which Lane Are You In?

Congratulations! You made it. I'm so proud of you!

So . . . how will you move forward in the world? We begin with a story to illustrate the different options available to you.

This day sets the tone for every day coming up. Don't miss this—it's time to celebrate!

Day 21 Tapping Meditation: Let's Celebrate! (page 305)

APPENDIX

Days 1–21 Tapping Meditations

DAY 1 TAPPING MEDITATION: FROM PANIC TO PEACE

This is a great Tapping Meditation to use when you're feeling the negative effects of stress, like when you're struggling to relax and slow down at the start or end of a busy day. It's also great when you feel stressed or anxious but aren't exactly sure why.

To begin, take a deep breath, and check in with yourself.

How are you feeling emotionally? Do you feel stressed or anxious? Worried or overwhelmed? Impatient? Notice what comes up for you.

Also notice your physical experience. Do you feel tension, tightness, or pain anywhere? Do you feel any clenching, tingling, heat, or cold?

After noticing these different aspects of your present-moment experience, visualize putting it all in a "panic sack." On a scale of 0 to 10, with 10 being impossibly heavy, rate how heavy your panic sack feels right now.

Take three deep breaths. We'll begin by tapping on the Karate Chop point.

KC *(repeat three times)*: Even though I'm feeling all this panic and stress, my panic sack is so heavy right now, I love myself and accept how I feel.

Eyebrow: All this panic

Side of Eye: So much stress

Under Eye: It's such a heavy load

Under Nose: I feel overwhelmed

Under Mouth: It's too much

Collarbone: All this stress

Under Arm: All this panic

Top of Head: I can feel how heavy it is

Eyebrow: It's safe to feel this panic now

Side of Eye: Really feeling this stress now

Under Eye: I don't have to fear it

Under Nose: I can let myself feel how heavy it all is

Under Mouth: This panic sack

Collarbone: It's too heavy to carry

Under Arm: I have to put it down now

Top of Head: It's hard to do, though

Eyebrow: I'm used to carrying it

Side of Eye: It's been with me for a long time

Under Eye: I'm used to this panic sack

Under Nose: Even though I don't like it

Under Mouth: It's too heavy to carry

Collarbone: I can put it down now

Under Arm: It's weighing me down

Top of Head: I can put it down now

Eyebrow: I can let myself rest

Side of Eye: But what if I need this panic sack?

Under Eye: What if it's keeping me safe?

Under Nose: I'm not sure I'm ready to put it down

Under Mouth: This panic sack

Collarbone: It's so familiar

Under Arm: But it's gotten too heavy

Top of Head: So I'm putting it down now

Eyebrow: Giving myself a break

Side of Eye: Releasing this panic sack

Under Eye: I don't need it right now

Under Nose: I can let myself rest

Under Mouth: I can give myself this break now

Collarbone: And put the panic sack down

Under Arm: I don't need it right now

Top of Head: I'm safe without this panic sack

Eyebrow: Releasing this panic sack now

Side of Eye: Gently putting it down

Under Eye: I can relax and feel safe

Under Nose: I can let my mind rest

Under Mouth: I can let my body rest

Collarbone: I can breathe more deeply and slowly now

Under Arm: I can put this load down now

Top of Head: Feeling peaceful now

Take a deep breath, and check back in with yourself, emotionally as well as physically. Notice any shifts you experience by rating the weight of your "panic sack" again on a scale of 0 to 10. Keep tapping until you get the desired relief.

TAPPING TIP

Tapping is also a great self-discovery tool. If, while tapping, you have an *aha!* moment about something specific that's bothering you, tap on releasing that. Whether it's an emotion, memory, or something else, your fastest path to peace is always by releasing the weight of your present-moment experience.

DAY 2 TAPPING MEDITATION:
TURNING TOWARD THE POSITIVE

This is a great meditation to use when you're struggling to feel and see the positive. With repeated use, it can help your brain be more balanced, less prone to always resorting to the negativity bias.

To begin, take a deep breath, and check in with yourself.

Now that you've noticed your brain's negativity bias at work, what emotions do you feel about whatever caused your brain to go negative?

Also notice your physical experience. In this negative state of mind, do you feel tension, tightness, or pain anywhere? Do you feel any clenching, tingling, heat, or cold?

After noticing these different aspects of your present-moment experience, notice how intensely negative you feel on a scale of 0 to 10, with 10 being extremely negative.

Then take three deep breaths. We'll begin by tapping on the Karate Chop point.

KC *(repeat three times)*: Even though I'm feeling all this negativity, it's so hard to feel positive, I love myself and accept how I feel.

Eyebrow: All this negativity

Side of Eye: So much negativity in my brain

Under Eye: It feels so real

Under Nose: This negativity seems like the truth

Under Mouth: It seems so real

Collarbone: All this negativity

Under Arm: It's encoded in my brain

Top of Head: It's meant to help me survive

Eyebrow: This negativity bias

Side of Eye: It's trying to protect me

Under Eye: It feels so real

Under Nose: It feels so true

Under Mouth: This negativity bias

Collarbone: It's very convincing

Under Arm: It's here to keep me safe

Top of Head: But it also makes my world feel dark

Eyebrow: This negativity bias

Side of Eye: It squashes the light

Under Eye: And makes things feel dark

Under Nose: It feels so true, though

Under Mouth: It feels so real

Collarbone: This negativity bias

Under Arm: It's so convincing

Top of Head: It's just trying to protect me

Eyebrow: But it's too dark

Side of Eye: I don't need it right now

Under Eye: I can let myself feel the light

Under Nose: And see it, too

Under Mouth: I can trust the light

Collarbone: I can move toward the light

Under Arm: The light is real, too

Top of Head: I can let more light into my life

Eyebrow: It's safe to feel this light

Side of Eye: And let it seep into my brain

Under Eye: I can let it into my body

Under Nose: And feel the joy it brings me

Under Mouth: I can trust this light

Collarbone: And let it fill me now

Under Arm: It's safe to trust this light

Top of Head: I can let more light in

Eyebrow: Relaxing into this light now

Side of Eye: Allowing myself to open to this light

Under Eye: I can feel safe with this light

Under Nose: I can see this light and feel safe

Under Mouth: Letting myself feel peaceful now

Collarbone: I can trust that this beautiful light is all around me

Under Arm: I can trust that this beautiful light is real

Top of Head: Feeling peaceful within this light now

Take a deep breath, and check back in with yourself, emotionally as well as physically. Notice any shifts you experience by rating the intensity of your negativity again on a scale of 0 to 10. Keep tapping until you get the desired relief.

DAY 3 TAPPING MEDITATION: LETTING GO OF LONELINESS

This meditation will help you release feelings of loneliness that can arise even when you're surrounded by people. In so doing, it will also support you in opening up to more and deeper connections.

To begin, take a deep breath, and check in with yourself.

Now that you've looked at how all-consuming loneliness can be, take a moment to notice when and how often you feel lonely. Do you tend to feel lonely at certain times of day or at certain times of the year? Do you feel lonely in certain circumstances or around certain people?

As you focus on that loneliness, also notice your physical experience. When you feel lonely, do you feel tension, tightness, or pain anywhere? Do you feel any clenching, tingling, heat, cold, or hunger?

After noticing these different aspects of your present-moment experience, give your loneliness a number of intensity on a scale of 0 to 10, with 10 being extremely lonely.

Then take three deep breaths. We'll begin by tapping on the Karate Chop point.

KC *(repeat three times)*: Even though I feel really lonely sometimes, I deeply and completely love and accept myself.

Eyebrow: This loneliness

Side of Eye: It's all consuming

Under Eye: It's so intense

Under Nose: I feel so alone

Under Mouth: Even when I'm with people

Collarbone: I feel so lonely sometimes

Under Arm: This loneliness

Top of Head: It feels bigger than me

Eyebrow: This loneliness

Side of Eye: It's all-consuming

Under Eye: It's overwhelming

Under Nose: It feels bigger than me

Under Mouth: It's safe to feel this loneliness

Collarbone: I can let myself feel it

Under Arm: Even though it's scary feeling lonely like this

Top of Head: I don't like how it feels

Eyebrow: I feel so alone

Side of Eye: It's safe to feel this loneliness now

Under Eye: I can feel it

Under Nose: And I can let it go

Under Mouth: This loneliness

Collarbone: It's inside me

Under Arm: I can release it now

Top of Head: And make more space for connection

Eyebrow: This loneliness

Side of Eye: It's been holding me in

Under Eye: Preventing me from connecting

Under Nose: It wants to protect me

Under Mouth: But it's hurting me

Collarbone: And I can let it go now

Under Arm: I can let this loneliness go now

Top of Head: And let myself be more open to connection

Eyebrow: It feels risky, though

Side of Eye: I might get hurt

Under Eye: But this loneliness is hurting me, too

Under Nose: So I'm going to let it go now

Under Mouth: I'm going to free myself from this loneliness

Collarbone: And let myself connect more

Under Arm: It's safe to make more space for connection

Top of Head: I don't need this loneliness anymore

Eyebrow: I can see that I'm not all alone

Side of Eye: I can connect with people and feel safe

Under Eye: Letting go of this loneliness

Under Nose: It's okay if my relationships aren't perfect

Under Mouth: It's okay if connecting with people doesn't always work perfectly

Collarbone: I'm safe letting go of this loneliness now

Under Arm: I can seek out new ways of connecting

Top of Head: It's safe to feel safe connecting with people

Take a deep breath and notice how intense your loneliness is now on a scale of 0 to 10. Also notice any shifts you experience in your body. Keep tapping until you get the desired relief.

DAY 4 TAPPING MEDITATION: ACCEPTING YOUR TRUTH

This is a great meditation to use when you're struggling with the truth, such as a realization that you have had, but prefer to resist because looking away from it feels easier. By tapping through this, you'll feel better equipped to see this truth and also feel more peace around it.

As you tell your present-moment truth, notice again how you feel emotionally and in your body. Rate the intensity of your experience on a scale of 0 to 10.

Take three deep breaths.

We'll begin by tapping on the Karate Chop point.

KC *(repeat three times)*: Even though I feel all this discomfort around telling my truth, I deeply and completely love and accept myself.

Eyebrow: This truth

Side of Eye: It's uncomfortable to tell

Under Eye: I don't want to see it

Under Nose: It brings up too many big emotions

Under Mouth: This truth

Collarbone: It's overwhelming

Under Arm: I don't want to see it

Top of Head: I don't want to feel it

Eyebrow: This truth

Side of Eye: It's overwhelming

Under Eye: That's okay

Under Nose: I can let myself see it

Under Mouth: I can feel the emotions it brings up

Collarbone: I can trust my truth to guide me

Under Arm: This truth is showing me what I want to transform

Top of Head: It's showing me where to focus

Eyebrow: What I see, I can change

Side of Eye: This truth is helping me

Under Eye: I can relax when I tell this truth

Under Nose: I can look at this truth and feel calmer now

Under Mouth: I don't have to avoid this truth anymore

Collarbone: I can see it

Under Arm: And I can feel the emotions it brings up

Top of Head: I can trust that this truth is helping me move forward

Eyebrow: This truth

Side of Eye: It's my guide

Under Eye: I don't have to fear it anymore

Under Nose: I can hear it

Under Mouth: I can see it

Collarbone: And still trust that I'm safe

Under Arm: Relaxing into this truth now

Top of Head: It's safe to see this truth

Eyebrow: I'm safe seeing this truth

Side of Eye: I can relax when I tell this truth

Under Eye: And trust that I can transform what I choose to

Under Nose: It may not happen this second

Under Mouth: It may take a little time

Collarbone: But I can still relax and trust

Under Arm: I can transform what I choose to

Top of Head: Relaxing with this truth now

Eyebrow: Feeling safe with what is

Side of Eye: I don't have to be afraid

Under Eye: I can see clearly

Under Nose: And trust that I'm safe

Under Mouth: Relaxing my entire body now

Collarbone: This truth is my guide

Under Arm: I can trust myself to move forward

Top of Head: Feeling safe with this truth now

Take a deep breath. Notice the intensity of your resistance to this truth now, and rate it again on a scale of 0 to 10. Keep tapping until you get the desired relief.

Your truth, as well as your feelings about it, may change from one day or one moment to the next. That's fine. Trust the process, and allow yourself to continue tapping through the discomfort to experience a deeper, more authentic sense of peace.

DAY 5 TAPPING MEDITATION: POSITIVE TAPPING

This meditation will support you in feeling more joy. It's a great one to use when you're starting to feel more positive and want to magnify that feeling.

When you notice a win, stop and notice how much positive emotion you feel.

Give that positive emotion a number on a scale of 0 to 10, with 10 being the most positive you can imagine feeling.

Take three deep breaths.

We'll begin by tapping on the Karate Chop point.

KC *(repeat three times)*: Even though it sometimes feels weird celebrating these everyday wins, I can feel good now and enjoy celebrating <state your win here>.

Eyebrow: <State your win here>

Side of Eye: I can feel good about this!

Under Eye: I can let go of the weird feeling around celebrating this

Under Nose: And just feel good in my body now

Under Mouth: I can let myself feel full of joy

Collarbone: And full of gratitude

Under Arm: It's safe to feel all this joy

Top of Head: And let my body be flooded with gratitude

Eyebrow: I can let these positive feelings grow

Side of Eye: I can let them flood my mind

Under Eye: And overtake my body

Under Nose: It feels good to feel this!

Under Mouth: It's fun noticing these everyday wins

Collarbone: It gives me energy to feel these positive bursts

Under Arm: I can nurture these positive feelings

Top of Head: I can feel more positive more often

Eyebrow: It's safe to feel more joy

Side of Eye: It's safe to trust there will always be more to celebrate

Under Eye: I can let myself feel good now

Under Nose: I can let it feel really good

Under Mouth: I can relax into this positive emotion now

Collarbone: I can let this positive emotion grow

Under Arm: Feeling this joy now

Top of Head: Letting myself relax now

Eyebrow: Letting this good feeling in

Side of Eye: I can feel good now

Under Eye: It's safe to trust my joy

Under Nose: I can let it grow

Under Mouth: I can trust this joy

Collarbone: I can trust this good feeling

Under Arm: And let it expand inside me

Top of Head: It feels good!

Eyebrow: This good feeling

Side of Eye: It's expanding inside me

Under Eye: Supporting my body

Under Nose: Allowing healing to happen

Under Mouth: I can feel this in my body

Collarbone: And let it expand

Under Arm: This good feeling

Top of Head: I can let it expand now

Eyebrow: It's another guide

Side of Eye: Showing me where to find my joy

Under Eye: I love this feeling!

Under Nose: And I can let it expand now

Under Mouth: Jumping into my joy

Collarbone: And letting it feel amazing

Under Arm: I can feel it in my body now

Top of Head: I can let this joy expand inside me

Take a deep breath. Rate the intensity of your positive emotion again on a scale of 0 to 10. Keep tapping until you get the desired effect.

As you get comfortable with your new habit of celebrating everyday wins, notice how your overall mood and energy shifts over time.

DAY 6 TAPPING MEDITATION: BODY ATTUNEMENT

This is a great meditation to use to get back in touch with your physical body. If you're feeling disconnected, numb, or struggling with physical symptoms, this can be a good way to begin hearing what your body is trying to tell you.

If you can, find a quiet place to take three deep breaths. Scan your body, beginning at the top of your head, down into your neck, your shoulders, down both arms, to your wrists, your hands, then your fingers.

Move your attention to your back and into your stomach and solar plexus. Notice your hips, your thighs, your knees. Continue down to your ankles, your feet, then into your toes.

Feel the sensations, the tension or tingling, hot or cold, ease or discomfort in your body. If there's one feeling that's especially noticeable, give it a number on the 0–10 scale of intensity.

Take three deep breaths.

We'll begin by tapping on the Karate Chop point.

KC *(repeat three times)*: Even though I don't always stop to listen to my body, I can feel quiet and receptive now.

Eyebrow: My body

Side of Eye: It has so much to tell me

Under Eye: I can stop and listen to what it's saying

Under Nose: I can hear its messages

Under Mouth: And let it speak its truth

Collarbone: I can listen without judgment

Under Arm: I can feel what my body needs me to feel

Top of Head: I can remember what it needs me to remember

Eyebrow: I can open to my body's wisdom now

Side of Eye: It's safe to notice my body in these ways

Under Eye: It's safe to hear what it's telling me

Under Nose: I can focus my attention on my head

Under Mouth: And go down my neck

Collarbone: To my shoulders

Under Arm: I can hear what they're telling me now

Top of Head: Down to my upper back

Eyebrow: What's it saying?

Side of Eye: And my arms

Under Eye: How do they feel?

Under Nose: Into my hands

Under Mouth: Then back to my chest

Collarbone: And my stomach

Under Arm: What do they need me to know?

Top of Head: I can focus on my solar plexus

Eyebrow: Is it talking to me?

Side of Eye: And then move my attention to my lower back

Under Eye: And into my hips

Under Nose: What do they need me to hear?

Under Mouth: I can listen to my thighs

Collarbone: My knees

Under Arm: My lower legs and ankles

Top of Head: And my feet

Eyebrow: I can hear what they're saying to me

Side of Eye: I can experience what my body is experiencing

Under Eye: I can allow it all to come forward

Under Nose: And I can release it

Under Mouth: I can listen

Collarbone: And I can let it go

Under Arm: Allowing myself to trust what my body is saying

Top of Head: And let go of any discomfort

Eyebrow: I can release it

Side of Eye: I can give my body that relief

Under Eye: I can relax my body now

Under Nose: I can let these feelings pass through my body

Under Mouth: I can feel safe in my body

Collarbone: I can listen to what my body needs to tell me

Under Arm: It's safe to listen to my body

Top of Head: Letting myself relax and feel peace in my body now

Take a deep breath. Notice what you're feeling in your body now. If you rated a feeling before tapping, again give it a number on scale of 0 to 10. Keep tapping until you get the desired relief.

DAY 7 TAPPING MEDITATION: PEACE & PATIENCE

This is a great meditation to use when you're struggling to feel peace around the pace of change and transformation. Tap and feel more at peace with how, and how quickly, you and your life are transforming.

Either transformation doesn't seem to happen fast enough, or it's happening really quickly and all we want is more, faster.

When it comes to creating positive change, enough rarely feels like enough.

More often than not, we want positive transformation to happen faster. We don't want to work on ritual. We don't want to use repetition. We want results, and we want them now.

Impatience with the change process is understandable, but it's also an obstacle to progress. Ironically it's often when we stop resisting tools like Tapping, as well as powerful structures like ritual and repetition, that change actually does happen faster than we imagined possible.

When you find yourself feeling bogged down by the current pace of change in your life, or just yearning for more, faster, take a moment to check in with yourself.

First rate your frustration or anxiety around the current pace of change in your life on a scale of 0 to 10.

Take three deep breaths.

Begin by tapping on the Karate Chop point.

KC *(repeat three times)*: Even though I'm struggling with the pace of change right now, I love myself and accept how I feel.

Eyebrow: I want more, faster!
Side of Eye: I want things to change for the better right now!

Under Eye: I don't have time for ritual

Under Nose: I don't have time for repetition

Under Mouth: I need things to transform now

Collarbone: This impatience with the pace of change

Under Arm: It's stressing me out

Top of Head: I want more, faster

Eyebrow: This impatience

Side of Eye: So much impatience

Under Eye: This impatience

Under Nose: It's slowing me down

Under Mouth: It's stressing me out

Collarbone: But it doesn't feel safe to relax

Under Arm: I need big changes now!

Top of Head: But change is scary, too

Eyebrow: I want more

Side of Eye: And I want it faster

Under Eye: All this impatience

Under Nose: I don't have time for patience

Under Mouth: Or for repetition

Collarbone: Or ritual

Under Arm: I need big changes now!

Top of Head: But change is scary, too

Eyebrow: I only want certain changes

Side of Eye: I don't have time for all of this

Under Eye: I need positive change now

Under Nose: I can't wait

Under Mouth: All this impatience

Collarbone: It's stressful

Under Arm: This stress is slowing me down

Top of Head: Maybe it's time to let it go

Eyebrow: And trust that change is happening at the perfect pace

Side of Eye: I can relax into what is happening now

Under Eye: Even though everything isn't how what I want it to be

Under Nose: I can feel safe with this pace of change

Under Mouth: I can relax my body now

Collarbone: And feel calm when I think about the current pace of change in my life

Under Arm: I can feel calm in my body

Top of Head: And trust that change is happening at the perfect pace

Eyebrow: Ritual and repetition are important

Side of Eye: They'll support me in transforming

Under Eye: I can let myself slow down enough to use them

Under Nose: I can trust that change is happening at the right pace

Under Mouth: I can relax about the current pace of change

Collarbone: I can trust in this transformation process

Under Arm: And relax my body when I think about it

Top of Head: I can feel calm, safe, and relaxed now

Take a deep breath, and on a scale of 0 to 10, rate your resistance—frustration, anxiety, and so on—around the current pace of change in your life. Keep tapping until you experience the desired level of peace.

DAY 8 TAPPING MEDITATION: ALIGNING WITH YOUR INTENTIONS

This is a great meditation to use to get into deeper, clearer alignment with your vision for yourself and your life.

When you notice yourself feeling resistance to your feeling intentions, notice first how this resistance is showing up. Is it a physical sensation, like tightness in your jaw or stomach? Is it emotional resistance, such as fear or doubt?

When you're clear on how your resistance is showing up, rate its intensity on a scale of 0 to 10.

Take three deep breaths.

Begin by tapping on the Karate Chop point.

KC *(repeat three times)*: Even though I feel all this resistance around realizing this vision and these intention(s), I accept how I feel and choose to feel peace now.

Eyebrow: All this resistance

Side of Eye: I'm struggling with this intention

Under Eye: I want it to become true

Under Nose: I want to feel this way

Under Mouth: But I feel all this resistance around it

Collarbone: I'm not sure I believe it's possible

Under Arm: I'm not sure it will ever happen

Top of Head: I do want it to happen, though

Eyebrow: But I still feel all this resistance

Side of Eye: I don't like how it feels

Under Eye: I want to shed this resistance

Under Nose: It's okay to feel this resistance

Under Mouth: It's safe to feel this resistance

Collarbone: I can feel it now

Under Arm: And I can let it go

Top of Head: I can release this resistance from my body now

Eyebrow: And feel peace when I think of this intention

Side of Eye: I can feel at ease in my mind

Under Eye: I can trust that this intention is possible

Under Nose: I can feel safe believing in this intention

Under Mouth: I choose to feel peace when I focus on this intention

Collarbone: I can feel safe in my mind and body now

Under Arm: Trusting in this intention

Top of Head: Feeling peace around this intention now

Eyebrow: I can imagine it

Side of Eye: I can feel it!

Under Eye: This intention

Under Nose: It feels so good!

Under Mouth: I'm scared to trust it could come true

Collarbone: But I want it to

Under Arm: I can trust this intention

Top of Head: I can feel safe

Eyebrow: I can see it!

Side of Eye: I can feel it!

Under Eye: This intention

Under Nose: It fills me with positive emotions

Under Mouth: I can feel them in my body

Collarbone: They're part of me now

Under Arm: I can let them in

Top of Head: And trust this intention can be manifested

Eyebrow: I can enjoy envisioning it

Side of Eye: And trust myself to take action toward it

Under Eye: I can feel peaceful and joyful about it now

Under Nose: I can accept these good feelings

Under Mouth: And let them flow throughout my body now

Collarbone: It's safe to dwell in them

Under Arm: And let them flood my mind and body now

Top of Head: Feeling the love and warmth of this intention now

Take a deep breath. Again rate the intensity of your resistance to this intention now. Keep tapping until you experience a greater level of peace around your feeling intention.

DAY 9 TAPPING MEDITATION: LETTING GO

This is a great meditation to use when you notice yourself resorting to old leaky patterns. It will support you in releasing them and in moving toward new and healthier ones.

When you notice yourself reverting to an old leaky pattern, rather than resisting what's happening, stop and acknowledge how frustrated or stressed you feel about your inability to get over this pattern.

Give that resistance a number of intensity on a scale of 0 to 10.

Take three deep breaths.

Begin by tapping on the Karate Chop point.

KC *(repeat three times)*: Even though I feel this frustration and stress around this recurring pattern, I love and accept myself, and choose to feel peace now.

Eyebrow: This pattern

Side of Eye: This old leaky pattern

Under Eye: I can't seem to overcome it

Under Nose: It's so frustrating

Under Mouth: This old leaky pattern

Collarbone: Why won't it go away?

Under Arm: I really want to move past it

Top of Head: But it keeps coming back

Eyebrow: This old leaky pattern

Side of Eye: It's so ingrained in me

Under Eye: I want to move past it

Under Nose: I'm frustrated that I can't seem to do that

Under Mouth: All this frustration around this old leaky pattern

Collarbone: I feel it in my body

Under Arm: But I can choose peace now

Top of Head: I can love myself even when I fall back into it

Eyebrow: This old leaky pattern

Side of Eye: It's been with me for so long

Under Eye: That's okay

Under Nose: I can feel safe even when it comes back

Under Mouth: I can choose peace anyway

Collarbone: I can relax when this pattern reappears

Under Arm: Feeling quiet and calm in my body now

Top of Head: Choosing peace now

Eyebrow: This old leaky pattern

Side of Eye: It doesn't have the same power over me now

Under Eye: I can notice it

Under Nose: And make a new choice

Under Mouth: This old leaky pattern

Collarbone: I can recognize it now

Under Arm: I can step back and choose a new way forward

Top of Head: It doesn't have the same power over me now

Eyebrow: This old leaky pattern

Side of Eye: It doesn't rule me anymore

Under Eye: Because I can see it

Under Nose: And I'm making a new choice now

Under Mouth: I'm taking a new path

Collarbone: And this path is better for me

Under Arm: I'm free now

Top of Head: I can take a new and better path now

Eyebrow: I can decide what this path will be

Side of Eye: I can make it what I want it to be

Under Eye: I'm free now

Under Nose: I can make new choices

Under Mouth: I'm free now

Collarbone: And I can feel good

Under Arm: I can make different choices now

Top of Head: And feel at peace with where I am now

Take a deep breath. Again rate the intensity of your resistance to this old leaky pattern now on a scale of 0 to 10. Keep tapping until you experience a greater level of peace around your pattern. When you're ready, tell the story around this pattern until you feel an even deeper sense of relief.

DAY 10 TAPPING MEDITATION: FEELING SAFE RELEASING THE PAST

This is a great meditation to use when you're resisting looking at unresolved events and emotions from the past. By tapping through this, you can begin to face the past and experience a deeper sense of peace and acceptance.

When you notice yourself resisting the opportunity to tap on past events and emotions, first acknowledge how you're feeling. If, for example, you're frustrated that the years of work you've already done on your past haven't brought you resolution and peace, notice and accept that frustration.

Give your resistance, and any emotions associated with it, a number of intensity on a scale of 0 to 10.

Take three deep breaths.

Begin by tapping on the Karate Chop point.

KC *(repeat three times)*: Even though I don't want to look at the past, it's too much and I'm sick of it, I choose to feel safe now.

Eyebrow: All this stuff from the past

Side of Eye: Why won't it go away?

Under Eye: I'm sick of dwelling in the past

Under Nose: But it's still with me

Under Mouth: I can feel it in my mind and body

Collarbone: All these emotions from the past

Under Arm: These past events I can't seem to get rid of

Top of Head: They've left a mark on me and my brain

Eyebrow: I can't seem to get past my past

Side of Eye: It's still with me

Under Eye: I want to get beyond it

Under Nose: I want to be free of my past

Under Mouth: But I don't know if I'll ever be

Collarbone: It's so frustrating

Under Arm: It's okay to feel this way

Top of Head: I can choose peace even when I resist looking at my past

Eyebrow: All this stuff from the past

Side of Eye: It's been with me for so long

Under Eye: I can let myself feel this resistance to looking at my past

Under Nose: And I can let this resistance go

Under Mouth: I can release my resistance to looking at the past

Collarbone: I can feel peace when I think about looking at the past

Under Arm: Feeling quiet and calm in my body now

Top of Head: Choosing to feel peace around looking at my past

Eyebrow: I can see how things were

Side of Eye: And notice how they're still affecting me

Under Eye: It's safe to acknowledge the past

Under Nose: And see how it's still affecting me

Under Mouth: I can trust this new awareness

Collarbone: I can let it guide me

Under Arm: I can let go of my fear around looking at the past

Top of Head: And let this awareness carry me forward

Eyebrow: This awareness will be my bridge

Side of Eye: It will carry me toward peace

Under Eye: It will take me toward my greatest self

Under Nose: I can trust it

Under Mouth: I can cross this bridge

Collarbone: And know that I'm safe

Under Arm: There's a new me waiting

Top of Head: My greatest self is calling

Eyebrow: And I can take this leap of faith

Side of Eye: I can look at my past

Under Eye: And know that it will carry me forward

Under Nose: It's safe to go there

Under Mouth: I can feel safe going there

Collarbone: Letting go of this fear now

Under Arm: I am safe going there

Top of Head: Letting this calm awareness grow in me now

Take a deep breath. Again rate the intensity of your resistance to looking at the past. Keep tapping until you experience a greater level of peace. When you're ready, tap through the points as you tell the story of any past event(s) that you're ready to release.

DAY 11 TAPPING MEDITATION: FEELING SAFE UNFROZEN

This is a great meditation to use when you're struggling to release the freeze response, however it plays out for you.

When you notice yourself resorting to some kind of freeze response, first acknowledge how you're feeling.

If you can tie it to a specific event, or several, focus on it or them, one at a time. If it's just a general feeling and you can't really pinpoint what's going on, start with general tapping and then move toward the specific.

Then give your freeze response a number of intensity on a scale of 0 to 10.

Take three deep breaths.

Begin by tapping on the Karate Chop point.

KC *(repeat three times)*: Even though I still have this freeze response encoded in me, preventing me from acting and being the way I intend to, I choose to feel safe now.

Eyebrow: This freeze response

Side of Eye: It's encoded in my brain

Under Eye: It's my brain's way of keeping me safe

Under Nose: It's encoded in my body

Under Mouth: I don't have to judge my freeze response

Collarbone: I can simply accept that it's in me

Under Arm: It's meant to keep me safe

Top of Head: This freeze response

Eyebrow: It's in my brain and body

Side of Eye: I don't want it

Under Eye: But it's encoded in my brain and body

Under Nose: It was meant to keep me safe

Under Mouth: I'm grateful for that

Collarbone: But now it's time to let it go

Under Arm: I can look at this freeze response

Top of Head: I can notice why it happens, with whom and when

Eyebrow: And I can feel safe letting it go

Side of Eye: This freeze response

Under Eye: I don't need it anymore

Under Nose: I can let it go

Under Mouth: I can feel safe without this freeze response

Collarbone: Feeling relaxed and calm in my body

Under Arm: Feeling safe letting this freeze response go

Top of Head: Choosing to feel peace now

Eyebrow: I don't need to freeze

Side of Eye: I can thaw out

Under Eye: I'm safe now

Under Nose: It's hard to trust that it's safe to unfreeze

Under Mouth: That's okay

Collarbone: Even though I'm still a little scared, I'm safe now

Under Arm: I can feel this fear around unfreezing

Top of Head: And I can let it go

Eyebrow: Releasing this fear from every cell in my body

Side of Eye: Letting it all go now

Under Eye: I am safe now

Under Nose: I can trust that

Under Mouth: Feeling peaceful in my body now

Collarbone: Freeing myself from this freeze response

Under Arm: Letting it go

Top of Head: Feeling relaxed and aware now

Eyebrow: I can let my body relax now

Side of Eye: I can feel safe

Under Eye: It's safe to feel safe

Under Nose: Letting my body feel fluid now

Under Mouth: Relaxing my mind now

Collarbone: I can let any remaining fear go now

Under Arm: It's safe to feel safe

Top of Head: Feeling safe and peaceful in mind and body now

Take a deep breath. Again rate the intensity of your freeze response on a scale of 0 to 10. Keep tapping until you experience a greater sense of safety and peace. If other events or realizations came to mind while you were tapping, tap through the points as you tell that story or express those emotions until you're able to release them fully, as well.

DAY 12 TAPPING MEDITATION: RELEASING ANGER

This is a great meditation to use when you're struggling to let go of anger, once and for all.

When you feel angry, notice where you feel anger in your body. Give it a number of intensity on a scale of 0 to 10.

Imagine yourself as ironclad. Imagine that you can do and say anything to let your anger go without experiencing any repercussions.

Take three deep breaths.

Begin by tapping on the Karate Chop point.

KC *(repeat three times)*: Even though I have all this anger in me, I can feel it in my body, and it feels bigger than me, I love myself and choose to feel this anger now.

Eyebrow: This anger

Side of Eye: It's in me

Under Eye: I can feel it in my body

Under Nose: This anger

Under Mouth: It feels bigger than me

Collarbone: It's explosive

Under Arm: This anger

Top of Head: I can let myself feel it now

Eyebrow: I'm safe feeling this anger now

Side of Eye: I can let myself really feel it

Under Eye: Feeling this anger now

Under Nose: I can let this anger get bigger

Under Mouth: I can really feel it now

Collarbone: I'm so mad!

Under Arm: All this anger

Top of Head: It's safe to really feel it now

Keep tapping through the points as you do or say what you need to in order to release your anger.

If you need to punch or kick someone, you can physically make any necessary gesture(s), as long as there's enough space around you that you don't hurt yourself or anyone else.

If there are words you need to say, do so out loud while tapping through the points.

Karate Chop . . . Eyebrow . . . Side of Eye . . . Under Eye . . . Under Nose . . . Under Mouth . . . Collarbone . . . Under Arm . . . Top of Head . . .

Karate Chop . . . Eyebrow . . . Side of Eye . . . Under Eye . . . Under Nose . . . Under Mouth . . . Collarbone . . . Under Arm . . . Top of Head . . .

Keep tapping until you feel relief; then proceed to the following positive round.

Eyebrow: This anger

Side of Eye: It was keeping me safe

Under Eye: But I'm safe without it

Under Nose: Releasing any remaining anger now

Under Mouth: Letting it go from every cell in my body

Collarbone: It's safe to release it fully now

Under Arm: I don't need it anymore

Top of Head: Letting it all go

Eyebrow: I'm safe without this anger

Side of Eye: Releasing it all now

Under Eye: Choosing peace now

Under Nose: Feeling relaxed and calm in my body now

Under Mouth: It's safe to feel this peace

Collarbone: And let it grow inside me

Under Arm: I can relax my body

Top of Head: And feel peaceful now

Rate your anger now on a scale of 0 to 10. Keep tapping until you experience the desired relief.

DAY 13 TAPPING MEDITATION: "I REFUSE TO FORGIVE"

This is a great meditation to use when you're struggling with forgiving someone. It's the only one in this book that has been published previously (on my blog), and it's one of the most widely shared ones I've put out there. Try it, and let yourself open up to the experience of forgiving someone who has hurt you deeply.

First identify who or what you are having trouble forgiving. Get really specific about what happened, what they said, what they did, how they acted, and bring that memory clearly to mind.

How do you feel when you think of that? What's the emotion? Where do you feel it in your body? Rate the intensity on a scale of 0 to 10.

Take three deep breaths.

Begin by tapping on the Karate Chop point.

Karate Chop *(repeat three times)*: Even though I refuse to forgive them because of what they did to me, I love myself and accept how I feel.

Eyebrow: I can't believe they did that

Side of Eye: I'm so angry

Under Eye: It's not right

Under Nose: It's not fair

Under Mouth: And I refuse to let it go

Collarbone: All this anger

Under Arm: All this ____ (fill in the blank with how you feel)

Top of Head: In every cell of my body

Eyebrow: I can't let this go

Side of Eye: Because they don't deserve that

Under Eye: They don't deserve my forgiveness

Under Nose: And I refuse to let this go

Under Mouth: So much anger

Collarbone: About what happened

Under Arm: About what they did

Top of Head: About what they said

Eyebrow: I can't let this go

Side of Eye: I don't deserve what they did to me

Under Eye: And they don't deserve my forgiveness

Under Nose: I deserve better

Under Mouth: All this anger

Collarbone: I can't let it go

Under Arm: I'm so angry

Top of Head: All this anger

Eyebrow: I can't live with what they did

Side of Eye: But this anger is hard to live with, too

Under Eye: I can't let this anger go, though

Under Nose: But I don't want to keep it, either

Under Mouth: All this anger

Collarbone: Maybe I can let some of it go

Under Arm: Maybe I can release part of it

Top of Head: Letting it go

Eyebrow: Releasing it now

Side of Eye: From every cell in my body

Under Eye: I don't need this anger anymore

Under Nose: I'll be stronger without it

Under Mouth: I can protect myself without this anger in me

Collarbone: Letting this anger go now

Under Arm: Even though it still feels hard

Top of Head: It still feels like I'll need this anger to keep me safe

Eyebrow: I can't live with what they did

Side of Eye: But this anger is hard to live with, too

Under Eye: Releasing this anger now

Under Nose: Letting it go now

Under Mouth: I don't need it anymore

Collarbone: I'm safe without this anger

Under Arm: It's safe to forgive them

Top of Head: Letting myself feel peaceful and safe now

Take a deep, cleansing breath and let it go.

Think of what happened again, and notice how your experience has changed. Rate its intensity again on a scale of 0 to 10.

Keep tapping until you experience the desired level of peace around that person or event.

DAY 14 TAPPING MEDITATION: I DON'T NEED FIXING

This is a great meditation to use when you're feeling overwhelmed by the number of emotions, events, and behaviors that you want to transform. Through this tapping, you'll feel more at peace with who, what, and where you are now.

You're not a project. You don't need fixing.

Do you believe that, really?

If not, notice how intensely you feel like you and/or your life needs "fixing." Rate the intensity of that feeling on a scale of 0 to 10 now.

Take three deep breaths.

We'll begin by tapping on the Karate Chop point.

KC *(repeat three times)*: Even though I feel broken, like my life needs a big makeover, I choose to accept how I feel.

Eyebrow: I feel broken

Side of Eye: There are so many issues I need to tap on!

Under Eye: My life feels like a huge mess

Under Nose: I feel like it needs a huge makeover

Under Mouth: I'm exhausted by how much fixing I need to do

Collarbone: And how much "stuff" I need to tap on!

Under Arm: It's too much

Top of Head: I just want it all to go away

Eyebrow: It's too intense to deal with

Side of Eye: There's too much of it

Under Eye: I want it all to just go away

Under Nose: It's too much

Under Mouth: Too intense

Collarbone: And dealing with it will be too much work

Under Arm: I need it to just go away

Top of Head: I want it to go poof in the night and never come back

Eyebrow: I'm tired just thinking about all the things I need to tap on

Side of Eye: And about how much fixing my life needs

Under Eye: It's too much

Under Nose: Too intense

Under Mouth: Too much work

Collarbone: I don't want to do it

Under Arm: That's okay

Top of Head: Maybe I don't have to

Eyebrow: Maybe I'm putting too much pressure on myself

Side of Eye: Creating urgency I don't need

Under Eye: All this pressure

Under Nose: I don't like it

Under Mouth: Why am I in such a rush?

Collarbone: This is a process

Under Arm: It's safe to slow down when I need to

Top of Head: Releasing this pressure

Eyebrow: Maybe I don't need fixing

Side of Eye: I can become more aware

Under Eye: And transform what I choose to

Under Nose: But I'm not broken

Under Mouth: And my life is not a project

Collarbone: I'm good as I am

Under Arm: I can appreciate myself now

Top of Head: I don't need fixing

Eyebrow: I can relax about where I am

Side of Eye: I can make progress also

Under Eye: And enjoy the process

Under Nose: Releasing any remaining pressure

Under Mouth: I don't need fixing!

Collarbone: I'm not a project

Under Arm: I can trust that things are unfolding perfectly

Top of Head: And feel good now

Take a deep breath. Again rate how intensely you feel like you need fixing on a scale of 0 to 10. Continue tapping until you experience the desired release.

DAY 15 TAPPING MEDITATION: CHOOSING HAPPINESS

This is a great meditation to use to continue training yourself to consciously choose your own happiness each and every day, including when it seems far away.

When your world is wet and the sun isn't sunny (to quote Dr. Seuss once again), happiness doesn't feel like a choice. It feels out of reach, beyond the limitations of your current life, finances, career, relationship, and so on.

When that feeling overtakes you, notice how out of reach happiness feels. On a scale of 0 to 10, rate how true the statement I can only feel happy once my life circumstances change feels.

Take three deep breaths.

Begin by tapping on the Karate Chop point.

KC *(repeat three times)*: Even though I feel like happiness is out of my reach, like it can only come after my circumstances change, I love myself and accept how I feel.

Eyebrow: Happiness

Side of Eye: It seems so far away

Under Eye: My world feels wet

Under Nose: And the sun doesn't feel sunny

Under Mouth: Happiness

Collarbone: It seems too far away

Under Arm: There are too many problems

Top of Head: I can't feel happy right now

Eyebrow: Happiness

Side of Eye: It feels so far away

Under Eye: So out of my reach

Under Nose: There are too many obstacles in my life

Under Mouth: Too many real life problems to deal with

Collarbone: I can't be happy right now

Under Arm: I can't be happy when my life is like this

Top of Head: Happiness

Eyebrow: It feels out of my reach

Side of Eye: I can't get there now

Under Eye: I can't get there yet

Under Nose: Not until my circumstances change

Under Mouth: Not until things are different

Collarbone: Happiness

Under Arm: It feels so far away

Top of Head: That makes me sad

Eyebrow: I don't like feeling this way

Side of Eye: I feel powerless

Under Eye: Like I can't control my life or my happiness

Under Nose: It's stressful

Under Mouth: And I don't feel happy

Collarbone: It's okay to feel this sadness

Under Arm: Letting myself really feel it now

Top of Head: I can let this darkness fade

Eyebrow: I can let myself see light

Side of Eye: I can let this shift happen

Under Eye: I can let myself enjoy a single moment

Under Nose: I can feel good for one moment

Under Mouth: It's safe to feel good

Collarbone: Even though it may pass

Under Arm: It's safe to feel good in this moment

Top of Head: I can let myself enjoy this moment

Eyebrow: And be fully present in my own enjoyment

Side of Eye: I can release fear and resistance

Under Eye: And let this moment feel good

Under Nose: It's safe to feel good now

Under Mouth: It's safe to let this moment feel happy

Collarbone: I can enjoy myself now

Under Arm: And be fully present in that enjoyment

Top of Head: Feeling fully present in this moment now

Take a deep breath, and again rate how true the statement *I can only feel good once my life circumstances change* feels on a scale of 0 to 10.

Keep tapping until you experience the desired level of joy.

DAY 16 TAPPING MEDITATION: FILLING YOUR CUP

This is a great meditation to use when you're struggling to accept and love yourself, including when you notice your own negative self-talk. Your relationship with yourself is the true foundation of all transformation, and a great area to revisit whenever you're feeling called toward it.

When you're struggling to feel good about yourself, notice which emotion you feel most intensely. Are you feeling shame about who you are? Sad about what you feel you can't do or be?

Identify your primary emotion and rate its intensity on a scale of 0 to 10.

Take three deep breaths.

Begin by tapping on the Karate Chop point.

Note: We're all at different places in our relationships with our own selves. If the language in this script doesn't fit, change it in ways that best reflect your experience.

KC *(repeat three times)*: Even though I can't feel good about myself, it seems impossible, I choose to feel peace now.

Eyebrow: I can't feel good about myself

Side of Eye: There's too much bad

Under Eye: Too much I need to change

Under Nose: I can't feel good about myself

Under Mouth: I can't accept all of myself

Collarbone: I can't love myself

Under Arm: I'm not feeling it right now

Top of Head: There's too much that needs to change

Eyebrow: There's too much I'm not happy with

Side of Eye: So much I need to change

Under Eye: I can't feel good about myself

Under Nose: I can't love or accept myself

Under Mouth: There's too much I have to change

Collarbone: I have to change first

Under Arm: And then I can really love and accept myself

Top of Head: There's too much to change

Eyebrow: I can't love how I am now

Side of Eye: I can't accept who I am now

Under Eye: I have to change first

Under Nose: I don't deserve love or acceptance when I'm like this

Under Mouth: It hurts to say that

Collarbone: I can hear how mean that sounds

Under Arm: Would I say that to someone else?

Top of Head: Would I say that to a child?

Eyebrow: Those are harsh words I'm saying to myself

Side of Eye: Do I really mean them?

Under Eye: These harsh things I say to myself

Under Nose: It's too easy to be mean to myself

Under Mouth: I can be a little gentler

Collarbone: I don't have to be this harsh

Under Arm: I can be a little gentler with myself

Top of Head: It hurts, though

Eyebrow: It's hard to see the good

Side of Eye: The bad is so much more visible

Under Eye: It's hard to see the good in me

Under Nose: Maybe I can notice a little bit more good in myself

Under Mouth: Maybe I can be a bit gentler

Collarbone: I can make tiny shifts

Under Arm: And be a little gentler with myself

Top of Head: It's safe to be a little kinder to myself

Eyebrow: I can be a bit nicer

Side of Eye: A bit gentler

Under Eye: A bit kinder

Under Nose: It's safe to be a bit nicer to myself

Under Mouth: I can make little changes

Collarbone: And be a bit nicer to myself

Under Arm: It's safe to say nicer things to myself

Top of Head: Letting myself relax and feel safe now

Take a deep breath, and again rate the intensity of your primary negative emotion you were feeling about yourself on a scale of 0 to 10.

Keep tapping until you experience the desired level of relief and peace.

DAY 17 TAPPING MEDITATION: I'M NOT CHOCOLATE!

This is a great meditation to use when you're struggling to overcome a tendency toward pleasing others at your own expense. Through this tapping, you can begin to establish healthier boundaries for yourself and in your relationships.

Anytime you notice yourself trying to be chocolate—saying yes to please others even though you want to say no—stop and notice what you're really feeling.

On a scale of 0 to 10, rate how difficult it feels to say no.

Take three deep breaths.

Begin by tapping on the Karate Chop point.

KC *(repeat three times)*: Even though I'm trying to be chocolate again, saying yes to please others when I want to say no, I love myself and accept how I feel.

Eyebrow: I'm trying to be chocolate again!

Side of Eye: It's a tough habit to break

Under Eye: I'm trying to be chocolate again

Under Nose: I've been doing this for so long

Under Mouth: But I can't be chocolate

Collarbone: I'm not chocolate

Under Arm: I'll never be chocolate

Top of Head: But I'm still trying to be chocolate

Eyebrow: Why am I still trying to be chocolate?

Side of Eye: I'm not chocolate!

Under Eye: Saying no will taste sweeter

Under Nose: I'm not chocolate!

Under Mouth: I can say no

Collarbone: It's a little scary, though

Under Arm: People might not always like it

Top of Head: But I'm not chocolate

Eyebrow: I don't need to be chocolate

Side of Eye: I can be me!

Under Eye: Sometimes I'll need to say no

Under Nose: I can do it calmly

Under Mouth: I can say no graciously

Collarbone: But still say no

Under Arm: Because I don't need to be chocolate!

Top of Head: I can be me

Eyebrow: I can trust that it's okay to say no

Side of Eye: I can take a little more time for myself

Under Eye: And know that it's the best thing to do

Under Nose: I don't have to try to be chocolate anymore

Under Mouth: I can be me!

Collarbone: It's safe to take care of myself

Under Arm: To take time when I need it

Top of Head: And enjoy every second!

Eyebrow: I can enjoy taking more time for me

Side of Eye: Letting myself enjoy taking time for me

Under Eye: I don't have to please everyone

Under Nose: I can take time for myself

Under Mouth: And enjoy it!

Collarbone: I can make decisions that work for me

Under Arm: And take more time for myself

Top of Head: I can say no when I need to

Eyebrow: Saying no more often will taste a lot sweeter

Side of Eye: It's safe to stop trying to be chocolate

Under Eye: I'll never succeed at being chocolate

Under Nose: And saying no more often tastes sweeter

Under Mouth: It's safe to stop trying to please everyone

Collarbone: It's safe to say no more often

Under Arm: Letting myself relax and feel calm now

Top of Head: Letting myself feel safe saying no

Take a deep breath. Rate again the emotional intensity of your resistance around saying no on a scale of 0 to 10. Keep tapping until you experience the desired level of peace.

DAY 18 TAPPING MEDITATION: BECOMING YOUR VERSION TWO

This is a great meditation to use when you're struggling with releasing an old story about who you are and what is possible in your life. Through this tapping, you can begin to feel more ready to occupy your new and more empowering "version two" story.

To grow into a beautiful flower, a seed must first sit alone in the dark soil, never knowing when water will come or when it will see the sun.

That seed doesn't dig itself up because it's dark, scary, and lonely in there. It stays. It trusts in the process of life. Sure enough, one day it breaks through the surface, grows into a flower, and becomes a contributing member of a larger garden.

Imagine your story as that seed. It's buried inside you, still enveloped in darkness, not knowing what's next, when it will see light, drink water, or join the other flowers that are already blooming in the garden.

Notice how far off the blooming of your seed into a flower seems. Rate the intensity of that "too far away/would never happen/not really in the cards or me" feeling on a scale of 0 to 10.

Take three deep breaths.

Begin by tapping on the Karate Chop point.

KC *(repeat three times)*: Even though this story is buried in so much darkness, so much uncertainty, I can relax and let myself trust that it will bloom.

Eyebrow: This story

Side of Eye: It's covered in darkness

Under Eye: So much fear

Under Nose: It's a seed buried in dark soil right now

Under Mouth: And I don't know if it will ever bloom

Collarbone: All this darkness around me now

Under Arm: So much work to do

Top of Head: It feels impossible

Eyebrow: I don't know if I can trust this new story

Side of Eye: I'm scared to trust this new story

Under Eye: I'm scared to hope that it could come true

Under Nose: All this fear

Under Mouth: It's bigger than me

Collarbone: This fear

Under Arm: It feels bigger than me

Top of Head: It's safe to feel this fear

Eyebrow: I can feel it now

Side of Eye: And I can let it go

Under Eye: I can make room for hope

Under Nose: I can release this fear

Under Mouth: I can see this new story

Collarbone: I can let myself feel it, too

Under Arm: I can feel this hope

Top of Head: I can commit to this new story

Eyebrow: I can let myself become it

Side of Eye: I can release my old story

Under Eye: Even though that old story feels safer

Under Nose: That old story is also limiting

Under Mouth: That old story is keeping me stuck

Collarbone: I can let it go now

Under Arm: I can feel my fear around this new story

Top of Head: And I can let that go, too

Eyebrow: I can trust in this new story

Side of Eye: I can feel the hope it inspires in me

Under Eye: I can commit to this new story

Under Nose: I can manifest my greatest self

Under Mouth: I can tell myself this new story

Collarbone: And repeat it to myself over and over again

Under Arm: I can tell and retell this story

Top of Head: I can trust and love this new story

Eyebrow: I can become my greatest self

Side of Eye: And tap on my fear when it arises

Under Eye: This new story

Under Nose: I can let it feel good

Under Mouth: I can move into it now

Collarbone: I can trust the joy and how it makes me feel

Under Arm: I can be my greatest self

Top of Head: Letting myself trust fully in this new story now

Take a deep breath. On a scale of 0 to 10, again rate how far off your new story feels now.

Keep tapping until you feel the desired level of connection with your new story.

DAY 19 TAPPING MEDITATION: MORE SPACE, MORE JOY

This is a great meditation to use when you're resisting the opportunity to clear physical, mental, and/or emotional clutter from your life. You'll feel less dread and more willingness to take care of the things that need your attention.

As you focus your attention on clutter and the different ways it shows up in your life, you'll undoubtedly encounter resistance.

When that happens, stop and notice how intensely you experience that resistance on a scale of 0 to 10.

Take three deep breaths.

Begin by tapping on the Karate Chop point.

KC *(repeat three times)*: Even though I'm not really ready to look at this clutter in my life, it's too overwhelming, I love myself and accept how I feel.

Eyebrow: This clutter

Side of Eye: It's stressful

Under Eye: I don't want to deal with it

Under Nose: I want to push it aside

Under Mouth: This clutter

Collarbone: It's too much work

Under Arm: I can't face this

Top of Head: This clutter

Eyebrow: I know it's weighing me down

Side of Eye: And slowing me down

Under Eye: I can feel it

Under Nose: But I can't face it

Under Mouth: It's too hard to deal with

Collarbone: Taking care of it sounds exhausting

Under Arm: I'd rather shove it aside

Top of Head: I'd rather ignore it

Eyebrow: Can't I just forget about it?

Side of Eye: Bury it for good?

Under Eye: I can't deal with this

Under Nose: It's too overwhelming

Under Mouth: It's too much

Collarbone: But it's slowing me down

Under Arm: I don't like this clutter

Top of Head: It's stressful

Eyebrow: And it's keeping me stuck

Side of Eye: It's safe to see how much stress this clutter makes me feel

Under Eye: It's safe to feel how this clutter affects me

Under Nose: I can let myself feel how heavy it is

Under Mouth: I don't like how it feels

Collarbone: I can let myself see this clutter

Under Arm: And I can release the overwhelm it causes

Top of Head: Releasing this overwhelm

Eyebrow: Letting go of my resistance around clearing this clutter

Side of Eye: I can take care of this

Under Eye: I can feel excited about finally finishing it

Under Nose: Letting myself feel energized about clearing this clutter

Under Mouth: Allowing myself to imagine finishing it

Collarbone: Allowing myself to feel the relief that will bring

Under Arm: I can clear this clutter

Top of Head: I can take charge of my life

Eyebrow: I can have more control over the clutter in my life

Side of Eye: Letting myself feel energized about clearing more space!

Under Eye: The more mental, emotional, and physical space I can clear

Under Nose: The more room my greatest self has to grow!

Under Mouth: Feeling energized about clearing more space!

Collarbone: That means more room for joy

Under Arm: More space for pleasure

Top of Head: Letting myself feel energized about clearing this clutter

Take a deep breath and again rate the intensity of your resistance around clearing this clutter on a scale of 0 to 10.

Keep tapping until you feel more energized about clearing it.

DAY 20 TAPPING MEDITATION: AT PEACE IN THE LIGHT

This is a great meditation to use when you're feeling scared about stepping out of your comfort zone to manifest your greatest self and co-create your greatest life. Tap and remember, you can do this!

When you think of this ongoing journey, of becoming your greatest self and stepping outside your comfort zone to co-create your greatest life, what emotional and mental resistance do you experience?

Do you feel fear? Do you dread the challenges you might face? Are you most afraid of failing or of succeeding?

Rate how intensely you feel your resistance on a scale of 0 to 10.

Take a deep breath. We'll begin by tapping three times on the Karate Chop point.

KC *(repeat three times)*: Even though I'm scared about continuing to manifest my greatest self and co-create my greatest future, I love myself and accept how I feel.

Eyebrow: This fear

Side of Eye: There's just so much that's unknown

Under Eye: It's scary not knowing

Under Nose: This fear

Under Mouth: It's in me

Collarbone: I can feel it in my body

Under Arm: All this fear

Top of Head: All this anxiety

Eyebrow: What if I fail at being my greatest self?

Side of Eye: What if I fail at co-creating my greatest life?

Under Eye: This fear

Under Nose: I can feel it

Under Mouth: There's so much that's unknown

Collarbone: It's scary

Under Arm: What if I fail?

Top of Head: What if I succeed?

Eyebrow: I won't be able to hide anymore

Side of Eye: I'll have to shine

Under Eye: People will see the real me

Under Nose: And hear the real me

Under Mouth: How will they react?

Collarbone: It's a little exciting

Under Arm: But scary, too

Top of Head: It's all so unknown

Eyebrow: It makes me nervous

Side of Eye: I can let myself feel this discomfort now

Under Eye: And I can let it go

Under Nose: There's a lot of uncertainty

Under Mouth: And that's okay

Collarbone: I have Tapping now!

Under Arm: I can do this!

Top of Head: I can shine

Eyebrow: I can trust this process

Side of Eye: And keep moving forward

Under Eye: Even when setbacks come

Under Nose: Even when all the unknowns feel overwhelming

Under Mouth: I can do this!

Collarbone: I can trust this journey

Under Arm: And I can trust my greatest self

Top of Head: I can relax and enjoy this journey!

Eyebrow: I can let more joy in

Side of Eye: And spend more time celebrating victories!

Under Eye: It's safe to feel safe

Under Nose: It's safe to trust this journey

Under Mouth: And trust my greatest self

Collarbone: I can let it guide me

Under Arm: I can co-create my greatest life!

Top of Head: I can relax and enjoy this ride!

Take a deep breath. Rate your resistance again on a scale of 0 to 10.

Keep tapping until you feel the desired level of peace and joy.

DAY 21 TAPPING MEDITATION: LET'S CELEBRATE!

Some people feel the rain. Others just get wet.
– Roger Miller

Nothing to rate, nothing to notice. Just take a deep breath, and let's dive right in!

KC *(repeat three times)*: I've shed stress; I've shed some of my past. I'm not sure if I'm my greatest self yet, but I love myself and accept how I am.

Eyebrow: It's time to start celebrating!

Side of Eye: I made it to Day 21!

Under Eye: That's huge

Under Nose: I can celebrate that!

Under Mouth: I still don't know what the future holds

Collarbone: And that's okay

Under Arm: Everything's not perfect

Top of Head: And that's okay, too

Eyebrow: I can celebrate this

Side of Eye: I can hear any critical voices that come up

Under Eye: And then let them pass

Under Nose: I can let joy in

Under Mouth: I can feel true joy

Collarbone: I can feel this celebration

Under Arm: I can let this good feeling into my heart

Top of Head: And into my body

Eyebrow: I can let it in fully now

Side of Eye: I can feel safe feeling joy

Under Eye: I can celebrate now

Under Nose: Even though I can't yet see a finish line

Under Mouth: Even though I'm not always sure if I'm my greatest self yet

Collarbone: I can celebrate now!

Under Arm: I can let more joy in now

Top of Head: I can feel this joy

Eyebrow: And know that my greatest self is always inside me

Side of Eye: I don't ever have to search

Under Eye: I don't ever have to find

Under Nose: My greatest self is always within me

Under Mouth: And we can connect anytime I choose

Collarbone: I can shed my layers

Under Arm: Tap away my inner roadblocks

Top of Head: And get access to my greatest self

Eyebrow: I love my greatest self!

Side of Eye: My greatest self is awesome!

Under Eye: And powerful

Under Nose: My greatest self can step into my greatest life

Under Mouth: I can let myself feel the love and abundance around me

Collarbone: I don't have to limit those anymore

Under Arm: I can release those chains

Top of Head: And love my greatest self now

Eyebrow: I am my greatest self

Side of Eye: My greatest self is always available to me

Under Eye: I can relax and feel safe as my greatest self

Under Nose: I can let myself shine

Under Mouth: It feels great!

Collarbone: I love my greatest self

Under Arm: I accept my greatest self

Top of Head: Feeling the joy now

Take a deep breath and keep tapping until you're as filled with peace and joy as you choose.

BONUS: ALL IS WELL TAPPING MEDITATION

This is an extra meditation that's especially useful when you're feeling really over-whelmed, whether from looking at the past or tapping through other issues. This Tapping Meditation will help you return to your center by providing a peaceful and safe emotional landing pad. Use it anytime, as often as you like.

If you're here, it's because you're already aware of how overwhelmed you're feeling.

First rate how unsafe or overwhelmed you feel on a scale of 0 to 10.

Take three deep breaths. We'll begin by tapping on the Karate Chop point.

KC *(repeat three times)*: Even though I feel really unsafe looking at all of this, I actually am safe and I can let myself relax now.

Eyebrow: I'm safe

Side of Eye: Everything's okay

Under Eye: I can let go of this panic

Under Nose: I'm safe and can relax now

Under Mouth: All is well

Collarbone: And I'm really, really safe

Under Arm: I can relax now

Top of Head: I'm safe in every cell of my body

Eyebrow: Everything's okay

Side of Eye: I'm safe right where I am

Under Eye: Feeling safe and grounded

Under Nose: In every cell of my body

Under Mouth: I'm safe and my body is safe

Collarbone: I can let myself relax now

Under Arm: I can let my breathing slow down

Top of Head: And feel calmer in my body

Eyebrow: I'm safe now

Side of Eye: And all is well

Under Eye: I can feel safe to relax

Under Nose: And to let go

Under Mouth: Feeling safe and grounded

Collarbone: I can let my body relax now

Under Arm: Every cell of my body

Top of Head: Relaxes now

Eyebrow: I don't need to fix anything

Side of Eye: Everything will be handled in the right time

Under Eye: And all is well

Under Nose: Feeling safe and grounded

Under Mouth: Feeling present in space and time

Collarbone: I am here and safe now

Under Arm: And all is well

Top of Head: All is well

Eyebrow: Grounding

Side of Eye: Breathing

Under Eye: Rooting my body to the earth

Under Nose: Coming back in to my body

Under Mouth: And knowing I'm safe

Collarbone: And that it's safe to relax

Under Arm: My breathing slows down

Top of Head: My heart rate slows down

Eyebrow: And I can relax now

Side of Eye: And trust that I'm safe

Under Eye: I can relax more and more

Under Nose: And give my body the rest it needs

Under Mouth: Feeling safe

Collarbone: All is well

Under Arm: Feeling safe

Top of Head: I can relax and feel safe now

Again rate your overwhelm and sense of not being safe on a scale of 0 to 10. Keep tapping through this script as many times as needed.

RESOURCES

If you're looking to take your tapping experience to the next level, we have a variety of resources on virtually every subject covered in this book:

A Monumental Discovery: Get more information on the exciting new science and research behind tapping at www.thetappingsolution.com/research.

Quick Start—Experience Tapping Now: Watch a short video that takes you through the tapping process at www.thetappingsolution.com/tappingvideo.

Relieving Anxiety, Feelings of Being Overwhelmed, and Stress: Want to get a real grip on your daily stress? Get a free daily stress relief meditation (normally sold for $19.95 and free to all purchasers of this book) at www.thetappingsolution.com/stress.

Overcoming Your Resistance to Change: Learn more about overcoming specific barriers to change at www.thetappingsolution.com/change.

Tapping through Your Past: Do you feel like traumas from the past are holding you back and keeping you stuck? Finally break through at www.thetappingsolution.com/thepast.

Healing the Body: Tapping has proven incredibly effective at supporting the body's healing process. Learn more at www.thetappingsolution.com/heal.

Releasing Physical Pain: Our Pain Relief World Summit, an online event attended by more than 100,000 people, could be just what you need to overcome physical pain. Get a free preview at www.thetappingsolution.com/painrelief.

Losing Weight and Letting Go of Fear, Guilt, and Shame around Food: Download a free tapping meditation designed to help you lose weight (normally sold for $19.95 and free to all purchasers of this book) at www.thetappingsolution .com/weightloss.

Creating Love and Healthy Relationships: Manifest the love you desire or improve your existing relationship at www.thetappingsolution.com/love.

Making Money and Achieving Your Dreams: Download a free tapping meditation to relieve financial stress and anxiety and create a more abundant life (normally sold for $19.95 and free to all purchasers of this book) at www .thetappingsolution.com/money.

Eliminating Phobias and Fears: From fear of flying to fear of public speaking, eliminate your specific challenge at www.thetappingsolution .com/overcomingfears.

ENDNOTES

Introduction

1. Dawson Church, *EFT Insights Newsletter*. http://www.eftuniverse.com/index
   .php?option=com_acymailing&ctrl=archive&task=view&mailid=1014&key=Ci074lpL&t
   mpl=component.

Day 2

1. Rick Hanson, *Hardwiring Happiness* (New York: Harmony Books, 2013), 23–24.

2. Brené Brown, *Daring Greatly* (New York: Avery, 2012).

Day 3

1. Guy Winch, "Why We All Need to Practice Emotional First Aid," TEDx talk, November
   2014. https://www.ted.com/talks/guy_winch_the_case_for_emotional_hygiene.

2. Adam L. Penenberg, "Social Networking Affects Brains Like Falling in Love," *Fast Company*, July 1, 2010. http://www.fastcompany.com/1659062/social-networking-affects
   -brains-falling-love.

Day 6

1. Gabor Maté, *In the Realm of Hungry Ghosts* (Berkeley: North Atlantic Books, 2008), 249.

2. Ibid., 249–250.

Day 7

1.   Francesca Gino and Michael I. Norton, "Why Rituals Work," *Scientific American*, May 14, 2013. http://www.scientificamerican.com/article/why-rituals-work/.

Day 9

1.   Nick Ortner, *The Tapping Solution* (Carlsbad, CA: Hay House, 2013), xix.

Day 10

1.   Vincent Felitti, "How Childhood Trauma Can Make You a Sick Adult," *Big Think*. http://bigthink.com/videos/vincent-felitti-on-childhood-trauma.

2.   Daniel Honan, "Neuroplasticity: You Can Teach an Old Brain New Tricks," *Big Think*. http://bigthink.com/think-tank/brain-exercise.

3.   B. Sebastian and J. Nelms, "The effectiveness of Emotional Freedom Techniques in the treatment of posttraumatic stress disorder: A meta-analysis," *Explore: The Journal of Science and Healing*, 2016. http://www.eftuniverse.com/index.php?option=com_content&view=article&id=12007.

Day 11

1.   Bessel Van Der Kolk, *The Body Keeps the Score* (New York: Viking, 2014), chapter 4.

Day 12

1.   Elisa Davy Pearmain, ed., *Doorways to the Soul* (Cleveland: The Pilgrim Press, 1998).

Day 14

1.   James Clear, "How Long Does It Actually Take to Form a New Habit? (Backed by Science)," http://jamesclear.com/new-habit.

INDEX

NOTE: Page numbers in **bold** refer to Tapping exercises.

ACKNOWLEDGMENTS

The amazing people in my life are really the secret sauce that help me manifest my greatest self. It is their love, their guidance, and their wisdom that makes my incredible life possible. To my wonderful wife, Brenna, who is now also an amazing mother, best friend, and companion—I love you with all my heart. To June, you light up my life, you make me smile every single day, and I can't wait for the day when you find these words in the back of this book. I love you with every part of my heart.

Alex and Jess, you both inspire me and surprise me every day with your dedication, your wisdom, and your friendship. None of this would be possible without either of you and I'm grateful for both of you every single day.

Mom and Dad, I hope you know that this book is only possible because of the steady guidance, love, and support you've ALWAYS shown me. You should be so proud of the life you've given all of us. Karen, Malakai, Lucas (big and small—LOL), Olivia, Penny, the first reader of my first book, the Taylors, and especially Alison Taylor Patridge, whose life goal is to see her name printed in as many languages as possible (you're welcome ONCE again and now with the Patridge addition), and so much other amazing family. Nolan, I'll put your name in here so I don't get any grief from you. But now you have to read the book. Ryan, you're too new to the family, so you don't make it in yet. Better luck next time . . . but wait . . .

Much love to you all.

Erin Walrath, Pete Mariano, Nick Polizzi, and Kevin Gianni, I am grateful on a daily basis for our friendship, the great times we have, and the mutual support. Kris Carr—I love you and I won't put anything embarrassing in these acknowledgments (see my book on pain relief if you'd like some of that).

To Wyndham Wood—well, this was FUN! Truly, such an incredible pleasure. To say this wouldn't have been possible without you is an understatement! Thank you—thank you—thank you!

To the amazing family at Hay House, because it truly is a family. Reid Tracy, not many people can call their publisher a dear friend and mentor, and I can. Thank you. Patty, thank you for your friendship and incredible support. Anne, thanks for wisdom and faith in this book. And of course, Louise Hay, who made all of this possible and continues to be a bright light in the world.

To Wayne Dyer—I feel your influence SO strongly in this book and in my life on a daily basis. You are missed and you are with us.

To Cheryl Richardson—you have been such a steady presence and incredible support in my life for the 10-plus years of this particular journey and I am SO grateful for that.

To the Tapping Solution Team, thank you for all your support and hard work on getting this important message out to the world. To Kelly and Lori especially, thank you for your hard work, dedication, and love over the past year.

And lastly, to the person (hopefully not plural . . .) I inevitably forgot in these acknowledgments. My advance apologies and I'll make it up to you in the next book!

ABOUT THE AUTHOR

Nicolas Ortner is CEO of The Tapping Solution, LLC, a company with a mission to bring into the mainstream a simple, effective, natural healing method known as Emotional Freedom Techniques (EFT) or "Tapping." Tapping is a healing modality that combines ancient Chinese acupressure and modern psychology. Nick's goal is to empower people to create healthy, abundant, and stress-free lives through his books, films, CDs, online events, and speaking engagements attended by participants from all over the world.

He is the *New York Times* best-selling author of *The Tapping Solution: A Revolutionary System for Stress-Free Living* and *The Tapping Solution for Pain Relief: A Step-by-Step Guide to Reducing and Eliminating Chronic Pain* and creator of the breakthrough documentary film *The Tapping Solution*, which follows 10 people who used Tapping to overcome significant challenges, including chronic back pain, fibromyalgia, insomnia, devastating grief, and more. He has also produced first-of-their-kind online programs that teach easy, effective ways to apply Tapping to anything limiting a person's life or health. Nick lives in Newtown, Connecticut, with his wife, Brenna, and daughter, June. Follow Nick on Facebook at Facebook.com/Nortner and on Twitter@NickOrtner. Website: www.thetappingsolution.com, www.nickortner.com

Hay House Titles of Related Interest

Also by Nick Ortner

The Tapping Solution

The Tapping Solution for Pain Relief

The Big Book of Hugs: A Barkley the Bear Story

All of the above are available at your local bookstore,
or may be ordered by visiting:

Hay House USA: www.hayhouse.com®
Hay House Australia: www.hayhouse.com.au
Hay House UK: www.hayhouse.co.uk
Hay House South Africa: www.hayhouse.co.za
Hay House India: www.hayhouse.co.in

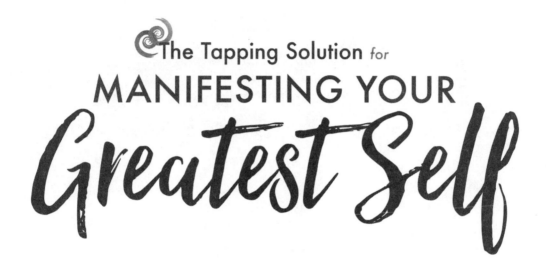

The Tapping Solution *for*

MANIFESTING YOUR
Greatest Self

Praise for *The Tapping Solution for Manifesting Your Greatest Self*

"The Tapping Solution for Manifesting Your Greatest Self *gets right down to the business of getting you out of your own way and on to the full realization of your dreams. It doesn't waste time and neither should you. Get your copy now because simply put, it works."*

— **Sonia Choquette**, *New York Times* best-selling author of *Your 3 Best Super Powers*

"Utilizing tapping exercises is a fascinating approach to working through personal life challenges."

— **Caroline Myss**, author of *Defy Gravity* and *Anatomy of the Spirit*

"I love this book for so many reasons. It's funny and entertaining. It's filled with science and inspiring stories. It introduces you to a wise and caring soul who understands the power of energy and its role in healing. And it tells you exactly how to use tapping therapies to dramatically change your life. When you read this book and do the exercises, you'll realize that big changes might just be easier than you think!"

— **Cheryl Richardson**, *New York Times* best-selling author of *Take Time for Your Life*

"This book will help you overcome your blocks so you can move from dreaming to doing—from self-doubt to self-empowerment. It's simple, accessible and deeply motivating. The life you're aching to live is well within reach, all you need to do is tap your way to it!"

— **Kris Carr**, *New York Times* best-selling author (and EFT lover)

"A gorgeous book about a powerful technique for anyone ready to live like they've never lived—in their full power, connected to the Divine, in a world where all things are indeed possible. Through years of application and experience, Nick has taken an ancient system and made it modern, fast, and efficient. Herein, you'll find a roadmap devised to help readers make the most of their lives while making their dreams come true."

— **Mike Dooley**, *New York Times* best-selling author of *Infinite Possibilities* and *Leveraging the Universe*

"I believe that a daily practice creates powerful change. In his new book, The Tapping Solution for Manifesting Your Greatest Self, *Nick Ortner offers 21 daily exercises for life-changing growth and profound transformation. Nick's unique Tapping Meditations will help you create quick shifts and feel immediate relief. I love this book and highly recommend it to anyone on a path of personal growth."*

— **Gabrielle Bernstein**, #1 *New York Times* best-selling author of *The Universe Has Your Back*

"You don't need a doctor. You don't need a coach. You don't need a pill or even a placebo. Tapping is a life-changing modality you can do for yourself. Many kudos to Nick and the whole Ortner family for bringing this powerful technique out into the light. It's easy. It's revolutionary. And it's available to all of us."

— **Pam Grout**, #1 *New York Times* best-selling author of *E-Squared* and 17 other books

"Nick Ortner is on to something that the world is in sore need of right now. The Tapping Solution for Manifesting Your Greatest Self *offers a refreshingly honest and easy-to-follow blueprint for anyone who wants to get to the root cause of what is holding them back. Rich with tools and guidance, this fourth installment from the man who put EFT tapping on the map is a worthwhile and captivating read."*

— **Nick Polizzi**, founder of The Sacred Science

WE ARE SO EXCITED TO

Welcome you

to the

TAPPING INSIDER'S Club

Tap! :)

Love,
Nick Ortner